MARRIAGE AS A SEARCH FOR HEALING

Theory, Assessment, and Therapy

Jerry M. Lewis, M.D.

Material cited on pages 47–48 from Larry L. King. "Redneck Blues" in *Warnin : Writer at Work*. Fort Worth, TX: Texas Christian University Press, 1985. Copyright © 1980, 1985 The Texhouse Corporation.

First published 1997 by Brunner/Mazel, Inc.

This edition published 2014 by Routledge
711 Third Avenue, New York, NY 10017, USA
27 Church Road, Hove, East Sussex, BN3 2FA

First issued in paperback 2015

Routledge is an imprint of the Taylor & Francis Group, an informa business

Library of Congress Cataloging-in-Publication Data
Lewis, Jerry M.
  Marriage as a search for healing: theory, assessment, and therapy / Jerry M. Lewis.
     p.   cm.
  Includes bibliographical references and index.
  ISBN 0-87630-831-0 (hardcover)
  1. Marital psychotherapy   2. Marital conflict   3. Communication in marriage.   I. Title
RC488.5.L47   1997
616.89'156—dc21
                                                                    96-54242
                                                                       CIP

Copyright ©1997 by Brunner/Mazel, Inc.

All rights reserved. No part of this book may be reproduced by any process whatsoever without the written permission of the copyright owner.

ISBN 13: 978-1-138-88377-2 (pbk)
ISBN 13: 978-0-87630-831-8 (hbk)

Contents

	Acknowledgments	v
	Introduction	vii
1.	At the Beginning	1
2.	Out of All the Millions of People...	17
3.	Enduring Interactions and Collective Illusions	46
4.	Competent Marriages and the Continuum of Marital Competence	67
5.	A Theory of Marital Systems	96
6.	Assessment: First Contacts	128
7.	Assessment: A Structured Approach	148
8.	Marital Therapy: Initial Considerations	184
9.	Marital Therapy: Therapeutic Effects of the Assessment and Stabilizing the System	198
10.	Marital Therapy: Teaching Relationship Skills	221
	Reading Notes	246
	References	259
	Name Index	269
	Subject Index	271

To Pat, for 47 years of loving

Acknowledgments

For many years, my interest in learning more about marital systems has received stimulation from three sources. One important source is the couples who come to me for assessment and treatment. For many reasons they are a remarkable group of men and women—bright, articulate, and excellent teachers. Their ability to describe, disclose, and challenge serves as a daily stimulus for my continued learning.

A second source is my friendship with two psychologists, John Gossett, Ph. D. and Margaret Tresch Owen, Ph.D. and our collaborative research activities at the Timberlawn Research Foundation. Our shared interest in interactional structures that facilitate individual growth and development is the background for thousands of discussions about power, intimacy, and other crucial system variables. More than that, however, both John and Margaret have the ability to engage in dialogues that so often lead to new understandings. I am in their debt for so very much, but, most of all, for encouraging my intellectual growth and clinical insights.

At a very different level, my wife, Pat, has been another teacher-facilitator. Our "end-of-the-day" reviews often lead to deeper explorations of each other's subjective reality and I am repeatedly impressed with how much I learn about her, about myself, and about human systems.

Once again, this book's gradual evolution has been nurtured by the interest and encouragement of my publisher, editor, and dear friend, Bernie Mazel. He knows how deeply appreciative I am.

Mary Anne Leistra has worked long and hard to transcribe my scrawl, find elusive references, and bring forth from the word processor a clear manuscript. For all of this I am truly grateful.

Introduction

There is, perhaps, an inevitable undercurrent of anxiety when one writes about his or her approach to treatment. Although some of that may spring from the conflict between the wish to be honest and the ever-present pull to embellish—to present only the better parts of one's self and work, much of the anxiety for me comes from a different source. I am concerned that readers may not understand that there are multiple ways of being a doctor, a healer, or a psychotherapist and, thus, may judge my way as suspect because it is outside of any one theoretical mainstream. Indeed, my pluralism—the use of multiple theories and perspectives—is at the heart of my approach to couples therapy.

The differences among professionals and their ways of approaching treatment are illustrated by my internists. Last year, I changed to a different internist in order to have all my personal doctors practicing at the same hospital and knowing each other well. That change—in itself a difficult event—gave me pause to recall the two internists who had cared for me over a 40-year period. There were two in that span because my first internist left me and his practice to become Dean of Students at our local medical school after 15 or so years of seeing me through both minor and serious illnesses. My second internist took care of and cared for me for over 20 years and faced with me several life-threatening surgical interventions that I confronted in recent years.

Both internists are superb doctors and clearly communicated their emotional investment in their patients and the practice of medicine. Both were trained in Boston during an era in which that training locale was generally considered tops. For Texas boys to be accepted at Brigham, Mass General, or one of several other Boston teaching hospitals was a clear mark of distinction only received by the best the Lone Star State's medical schools produced.

In addition, both internists had apparently stable marriages and children who appeared to turn out well. They were both well-known in the community and recognized as excellent doctors. Here, however, the broad similarities cease. Their ways of practicing medicine were very different.

Internist #1 was one of two or three doctors associated in practice. He had, however, his own waiting room and almost always I was the only patient in that room. Usually, some minutes before my appointment time, the patient before me came out of the labyrinth and left the office. A few minutes later, my internist opened the door, smiled at me, and quipped something like, "You really look bad," or "God, you're getting old." With that, he would pat my shoulder and lead me into the inner sanctum.

More about his waiting room is pertinent. It was small and somehow both tasteful and cozy. The furniture was of quality—in particular, the tables looked like fine antiques. The walls were covered with impressionist paintings and Mozart usually played softly in the background. The magazines included *The New Yorker* and several literary types. This internist's inner office was much the same—soft pastels, lighting by lamps rather than overheads, and the usual diplomas and artifacts nowhere in sight.

His approach seemed to combine the best traditions of small-town Texas warmth and Eastern intellectualism. You were always the center of his attention; no phone calls shattered the specialness. He was thorough and yet unhurried. If lab work was necessary, the blood was drawn there in his office—no going to the laboratory to be punctured by an anonymous phlebotomist. Overall, there was the sense of quiet efficiency and a smoothness that was comforting to me. It was as if my doctor had thought it all out very carefully and designed a system that both suited him and provided patients with dignity and a sense of their importance.

Internist #2 had a very different way of doctoring. He was the senior partner in a group practice of six or seven doctors located in a middle-class neighborhood close to a suburban hospital. The one large waiting room had 30 or 40 inexpensive plastic chairs arranged in rows of 10 or so. The floor was linoleum and the lighting overhead. Most of one side of this large room was a counter with sliding glass windows. Behind the receptionist, one could see a segment of the long hall from which examining rooms and doctors' offices were entered. At times, the doctors were seen hurrying back and forth in their white coats. The rapid pace of their activity reminded me of the old Charlie Chaplin movies.

You waited, and often for some time, to see your doctor. This seemed to reflect many factors, including the fact that patients who arrived clearly quite ill were taken immediately to an examining room. When the time came, a doctor's assistant called you, using only your last name. She took you to an alcove where she took your blood pres-

Introduction

sure, pulse, and temperature and then escorted you to a small examining room. She always told me to strip to my shorts and assured me that the doctor would be there soon.

Such was only rarely the case. It was wise to take a book for often the wait was 15 or 20 minutes. When internist #2 arrived, he was usually breathless. He would collapse onto a stool, smile, and often say something like, "Just saw a woman with syncope and complete heart block. Had to admit her to the hospital. Now, let's see"—here he would open my chart—"Where are we? Haven't seen you in a year. How are you doing?"

With those words, it was clear that I was the sole object of his attention. The MASH-like quality of his office, the woman with heart block, and all other concerns were suddenly gone. His questions probed the systems of my body that had previously been troubled. More than that, he asked about my wife and children, often adding brief comments about his family.

After his examination, we went to his office. Patients' charts, books, unopened mail, and whatnot seemed everywhere. His intercom buzzed often and a typical response might be, "Okay. Tell her to stop taking the antibiotic and come in tomorrow. Work her in between things or during the lunch hour. I need to see her. Tell her also if she feels worse to come to the emergency room between 6:00 and 7:00 this evening."

Although diverted by the interruptions, he seemed able to quickly shut them out and return to me.

It is this capacity to make the patient feel that he or she is momentarily at the center of intense and caring attention that my two internists shared. Their styles of doctoring, the contexts they had created, the profound differences in their approaches fade into the background in the light of their ability to make one feel cared about.

During what proved to be his terminal illness, Anatole Broyard wrote movingly about the importance of the doctor-patient relationship (Broyard, 1990). What patients want from their doctors is "not love but a spacious grasp of his situation" (p. 36). "A doctor," Broyard says, "must have a voice of his own, something that conveys the timbre, the rhythm, the diction and the music of his humanity..." (p. 36). "Whether he wants to be or not, the doctor is a storyteller, and he can turn our lives into good or bad stories, regardless of the diagnosis" (p. 30).

My two internists had very different rhythms—internist #1 played Mozart, while the "music" of internist #2 was Alexander's Ragtime

Band. Each in his own way, however, made me feel that for a brief interlude I was the sole object of attention, not a diagnosis but an important and interesting story. "All cures," Broyard wrote, "are partly 'talking cures'—for talk is the kiss of life" (p. 36).

For psychotherapists, the issue of cultivating a voice that expresses their own humanity is made more important because of the lack of a helpful technology. There are no machines between the therapists' theories and the patients' disturbances—only the treatment alliance and the thoughtful ways in which therapists use their knowledge to establish trust, to instill hope, to find relief.

Thus, in presenting my theory of dyadic relationships and the treatment processes that flow from that theory, I wish to emphasize that I know that my voice is but one of many. Further, it is important to acknowledge that many therapies can be helpful and, collectively, we do not yet know nearly enough about which treatments work best in which situations. Thus, we practitioners must continue to inform each other about our theories and treatment efforts, trusting that out of multiple dialogues, consensus will be found and later tested in controlled outcome studies.

This book's chapters follow a predictable pattern. Chapter 1 deals with the issue of how clinical problems get defined and, in particular, whether they are defined as primarily individual disturbances or disorders of human systems. Chapter 2 addresses some of the empirical literature that suggests that adult relationships can have healing impacts on the participants. In this chapter, the influence of marriage or other committed relationships on emotional health, physical health, overall life satisfaction, and life's meaning are also highlighted.

Chapter 3 presents my perspective on the current dialectic in marital-family theory and therapy brought about by constructivism. The challenge this perspective raises for the more traditional and empirical perspective is understood to be a positive phenomenon in the extent to which it facilitates the empiricists' reexamination of several fundamental premises about human systems.

Chapter 4 briefly reviews the three major studies of nonclinical families accomplished over the last 25 years at the Timberlawn Research Foundation. In particular, this chapter focuses on what has been learned about well-functioning marriages and the Continuum of Marital Competence. In the discussion of this continuum a small number of readily identifiable marital types are briefly described.

Chapter 5 presents my current theory of marital relationships in the form of 15 premises. It will be clear to readers that in this theory I have drawn upon multiple perspectives. At its core, however, the theory is a derivative of psychoanalytic object relations psychology, with a major focus on the balance of separateness-autonomy and connectedness-intimacy that each couple must either negotiate successfully or else see it become the basic source of their conflict.

Chapters 6 and 7 present my current approach to a systematic assessment of a relationship system. Beginning with the couple's definition(s) of the central problem, the assessment addresses the desired areas of change, a comprehensive history of the relationship, detailed family-of-origin histories, and special areas such as rituals, money, religion, sexuality, and life dreams. In Chapter 7 I also present my current thinking about dyadic formulations.

Chapters 8, 9, and 10 discuss my approach to couples therapy. A three-stage process is described: the therapeutic effects of the assessment procedure; the methods of moderating the couple's angry blaming; and the attempts to teach the processes of intimate communication through structured exercises that focus initially on experiences of vulnerability.

In addition to the many references presented, I have also included a section briefly describing the published work of others that has had particular impact in shaping my thinking and clinical work. This section of reading notes can also be used as a suggested reading list for those who wish to pursue some of my ideas to their roots in the thoughts and experiences of distinguished colleagues.

It is my hope that the pages to follow will increase the interest of those whose clinical attention has been entirely elsewhere and, at the same time, provide more experienced colleagues with the stimulus to reexamine their own theories and therapies.

At a different level, each writer writes for his or her own purposes, which can range from the attempt at working through personal conflicts to the intellectual challenge to reexamine what one really thinks and how one actually behaves. For others, writing is a form of nurturing or soothing one's self. To these and other forces I am far from immune.

1

At the Beginning

"We came," she said, "because after all these years he has begun to chew me up. He's so hostile, irritable with everyone, but with me it has been murder ever since he retired." She reported all of this with obvious rage, her face contorted with contempt.

He sat glaring at me, and I guessed it was humiliating for him to be a patient or, at the minimum, a candidate for patienthood. I knew him only by reputation—good doctor, a general internist with a large practice and more than usual participation in hospital affairs.

"I may be depressed," he said, "but, if so, it's not all that far from what I've always been. Retirement has not been easy—maybe it never is—but a big part of it for me is her unavailability. She leaves after breakfast most days—all sorts of meetings, luncheons, charities, art lessons, whatever—she's back home by five, we have a couple of drinks, eat, and most nights we're in bed by 8—reading, lights out by 9:30 or 10. Not much of a life."

"And during the day . . . ," I reflected.

"Oh, I walk 3–4 miles in the mornings, read, fix a bite for lunch, nap, read some more. Watch any sports but bowling and soccer on cable."

"Alone most of the time. . . ."

"Yeah. I've never been very social. You know what medical practice is like. It's draining and I've gotten in the habit of not wanting much to relate socially, except, of course, with Nan—who's never there."

I nodded, turned to her and said, "Sounds like he wants more of you, but, for you, more of him means catching more hostility."

"I am busy," she responded, "but it's no fun being with him. Perhaps I do stay away more than usual because of his anger. Most afternoons I know what it will be like when I get home." She paused, glanced quickly at him and then, with some urgency, went on, "I need to be honest—*we* need to be honest—if you're going to be able to help us. Jack *is* depressed—and different than ever before. He's never been this hostile—and I believe that's where all of this starts. *My retreating is real, but it's secondary to the anger in him.*"

Here, I thought, is something of the fascination of this work. In the first several minutes, Nan and Jack have each presented a narrative and, although they share common features, each has a different point of origin. Nan believes that Jack has responded to retirement with an angry depression and that their marital difficulty springs out of that depression. First things first. She lets me know she wants me to focus on his depression.

Jack's narrative acknowledges some degree of depression and, although retirement is a factor, it is more a relational issue—Nan's unavailability and their shared inability to make the necessary changes in their relationship—that he sees as primary. He seems as interested in establishing with me the validity of his view as she is in documenting her perspective.

The issues of how the problem is to be defined and what the process of definition is to be are crucial to any helping process. Years ago, I was introduced to this subject through the writings of Michael Balint (1972). Balint was interested in how medical diagnoses were arrived at by family physicians. In some cases, Balint suggested, the doctor makes the diagnosis mostly by himself or herself. Acute infections, broken bones, bowel obstruction, cerebrovascular accidents, and other, mostly episodic, disturbances are examples.

Balint proposed, however, that such episodes of sharp deviation from health are the exception rather than the rule in general medical practice. More often, patients come to their doctors with diffuse complaints for which there are few, if any, objective findings. Balint suggested that under these more usual circumstances diagnoses are subtly negotiated by patient and physician. Most often, patients negotiated out of fear and were willing to accept diagnoses that had few serious and no fatal implications.

Family physicians often negotiated from a base of those illnesses for which they had confidence about their treatment plans. Doctors would be drawn to diagnoses for which they believed they could be most helpful. If nowadays, for example, a patient presented with loss of general zest, easy fatiguability, and diminished interest in sex, a doctor with recent success with thyroid hormones might try to negotiate a preliminary diagnosis of subclinical hypothyroidism; this could lead to the prescription of thyroid hormones. Another doctor with recent success with antidepressants, however, would be more likely to negotiate a diagnosis of atypical depression, thus justifying the prescribing of an antidepressant. As Balint suggested, diagnoses in many situations reflect the physician's need to be helpful—the need to establish the presence of a condition that can be treated effectively.

Thus, Balint saw the diagnostic process in many clinical situations as a negotiated effort. Patients entered this process motivated to minimize anxiety about death, dying, and disability. Doctors negotiated diagnoses around their wish to be helpful and their fear of being unable to help. A successful collaborative process involved establishing a diagnosis that minimized the patient's fears of death or disability and facilitated the physician's ability to be helpful.

This orientation about diagnosis and the diagnostic process has shaped much of my thinking about clinical interventions. When is it most useful to the patient for the clinician to assign, more or less as the detached expert, a particular diagnosis and when is it most useful for the clinician to involve the patient in a negotiated diagnosis? As thus framed, the central issue is not the validity of the diagnosis; rather, it is its utility. Here, of course, another issue lurks in the background. A diagnosis is more apt to be useful if it increases the probability that both patient and clinician share a sense of agency. In other words, a diagnosis is considered useful to the extent that both patient and clinician believe there is something that each can do to effect the outcome.

Although Balint wrote about family physicians, general medical patients, and the subtle negotiation of many medical diagnoses, it seems that his ideas can be particularly helpful to mental health clinicians. Psychopathology is, with rare exception, the result of multiple causative variables, and the same syndrome in different persons can result from the interaction of different variables. The clinician's theoretical orientation about psychopathology determines which factors he or she attends and around which he or she plans treatment. In a previous publication, I used Beahrs' (1986) schematic representation of multiple variable etiology to illustrate how clinicians with descriptive, psychodynamic, and marital-family systems orientations would select those aspects of the case material that their theories emphasized (Lewis, 1991a). Again, the issue is not the validity of a particular perspective, but rather how best to help.

Most often, the best approach involves multiple perspectives and several different treatment modalities. As this is written, however, third party intrusions under the guise of efficient case management often proscribe any treatment modality that is not simple, brief, and deliverable by lesser trained clinicians. It is my belief that this unfortunate period of economically driven clinical reductionism will pass, and that our gravest danger is that we will not pass on to subsequent generations of clinicians the principles of high-quality treatment based on the use of complex multivariable models of psychopathology and multiple treatment modalities.

In Jack and Nan's clinical situation the issue of definition (diagnosis) is initially important because it involves the tension between an individualistic definition (Nan's focus on Jack's angry depression) and a relationship definition (Jack's focus on what is going on between him and Nan). Although there is tension between the two of them about the definition of the problem, there is no intrinsic reason these perspectives cannot be considered complementary. Indeed, if they cannot agree that both viewpoints are important, and if each pushes to have me validate only his or her perspective, that conflict may turn out to be an important part of understanding their situation. The clinician needs to acknowledge the differing perspectives and to avoid taking sides; rather, if possible, he or she would give something to each.

> "I can tell," I said, "that arriving at a proper understanding of this situation is very important to each of you—as well it should be. There is much more that I need to know, however, before we decide what is the best approach."
>
> They both stared at me and, although it may have been my imagination, I thought I could detect a slight softening in Jack and, perhaps, subtle disappointment in Nan.
>
> "Well, let's see," I reflected . . . "where to start?"

At this point, I decided to move towards a period of more structured inquiry. I would ask a series of "easy-to-answer" questions, all the

At the Beginning

while making a few notes. I decided to do so for several reasons. First, I wished to move away from their tension and conflict until I had a chance to better sort out some of my initial impressions. Second, I wished to see how each would respond to my taking charge of the direction of the interview. Would either or both resist this change of focus and insist on continuing his or her own agenda? Third, I needed a period of less compelling attention to bring together my initial thoughts and feelings about them. For example, Jack might invite from me, as a physician, an early positive identification. On the other hand, because he was depressed and more uncomfortable than Nan and hinted that he was victimized by her distancing of him, I had to guard against prematurely deciding that he was the patient.

Nan seemed more assured and, in some ways, more definite about the validity of her way of seeing things. She had seemed a bit disappointed when I didn't endorse her perspective. Could this represent my introduction to her sense of entitlement . . . her need to be right about most things? Would I need to recognize in myself early signs of negative feelings about individuals who are certain that their way is right?

These early impressions of my feelings are more like the tuning-up sounds of an orchestra before the symphony begins. More than anything else, I am tuning my instrument with the awareness that what I am experiencing may turn out to be more noise than music. Despite this tentativeness, it is important from the beginning for the therapist to closely monitor his or her feelings. They often provide important understandings and, if not monitored, can impede or destroy effective treatment.

Finally, the "facts" themselves are always interesting and frequently important. They place patients in certain cohorts, at certain stages of adult development, and provide clues about repetitive patterns, stressful ongoing life events, important losses, and a host of other issues important for understanding clinical situations. Clinicians who treat marital and family systems also want to know about the relationship as an entity: where it is now, where it has been, and where the participants hope it will go. Thus, I began to collect facts about Jack, Nan, and their marital relationship.

"Jack, you are how old?"
"Sixty-seven."
"And you've been retired how long?"
"A little more than a year."
"Nan, how old are you?"

"Sixty."

Jack quickly corrected her. "You were 61 two months ago."

"Easy to forget when you want to," Nan responded in a matter-of-fact way.

"How long have you been married?"

Nan responded, "We got married during his last year of residency. I was a senior in college. It was 1953—that makes it 41 years."

"Children?" I asked.

"Well," Jack said, "we have two sons. Judd is 36, a plastic surgeon, married with two daughters. Stuart is 33, a lawyer, still single."

I sensed from a hint of sadness in Jack's voice that there was more to the story of their children. "Something else?" I asked.

Nan responded, "We lost our daughter—she was 17, our third child—she overdosed—it was 15 years ago but we've never gotten over it." She seemed on the verge of tears and the need for comfort was palpable. I waited, but Jack stared straight ahead, and each seemed entirely alone with the awful sadness.

Finally, I said softly, "I don't think you ever get over it. Maybe the pain becomes somewhat more tolerable, but get over it, no."

Jack sighed and said, "We were so-so until then. I'm kind of a loner and Nan's really outgoing and friendly so there has always been disagreement—but, it was manageable by each of us doing a lot of our own things. I read a lot, gardened, and Nan was always with people. But, after Diane's suicide—well, somehow we couldn't be together in our pain—probably more correct to say I couldn't share my pain. I felt so responsible. So, since that time, we've been even more distant, had more separate lives."

There may be nothing like the pain of the loss of a child. There are survey data to suggest that such a loss is considered one of the most severe life stresses (Holmes & Rahe, 1967). There is much to suggest that the circumstances of the death may make the loss more unbearable or less so. A child's suicide may be the most grievous loss of all.

At the Beginning

When a clinician is with a person or couple who disclose such a loss, he or she can experience an emotional jolt. The immediate issue is whether to get caught up in that pain or to fight against experiencing it by keeping it "out there" as something that has no possible personal relevance.

The dilemma of how close to the experience of the patient one wishes to be is present in every clinical interview. How much does the clinician enter into the other's experience, feeling what the other feels, and how much does he or she seek only to understand the experience? The clinician should be able to do both—to move into the experience and then retreat from it in order to digest and understand it. Both experiencing and understanding are elements crucial to the psychotherapeutic process.

There are, however, some experiences that are so charged with deep emotion for all of us that avoidance of them is tempting. The suicide of a loved one is one such experience. There are also experiences of others that have emotional implications for some but not for all individuals. A clinician whose father deserted the family when the clinician was very young, for example, may respond to patient material involving the theme of desertion with heightened emotionality and, perhaps, increased need to avoid experiencing the patient's pain.

Thus, at this point in my initial interview with Jack and Nan I had another decision to make about the direction of the interview. As earlier in the interview, when I deliberately moved away from the tension between their conflicting narratives, I now must respond to the issue of Diane's suicide and what sounds like the divisive role it played in their marriage. To not respond and to move on with my "factual" format could suggest that I am uninterested or afraid, but actively pursuing it at this point may involve moving into an area that Jack and Nan are not ready to face with me or with each other.

In such situations, the safest position to take is to share that decision with the patient or couple. One technique for doing so is to present a brief summary and see in which direction Jack and Nan move. I decided on such a course and said,

> "Let me see if I'm beginning to understand. The two of you have always been very different—Jack, you're more the loner and Nan, you're more outgoing. It sounds like your marriage has always been one in which there was considerable emphasis on separateness, autonomy, doing your own

thing. And then Diane's suicide—the worst kind of tragedy—and somehow you couldn't share much or any of that terrible pain. Rather, each of you has had to try and deal with it alone. So—it's been that way the past 15 years. Now, Jack, your retirement, maybe depression, and more tension between the two of you. . . ."

The silence that followed was painful and it seemed to last longer than the 8 or 10 seconds that actually elapsed before Nan spoke. "I don't know that we *can* talk about it. There's so much water gone under the bridge—so much not being there for each other. Pain, disappointment, resentment—I always felt cheated by Jack. Everyone talked about what a good doctor he was, a wonderful listener, very empathic—really cared about his patients. Hell, I got none of that. I've *had* to find all of that with friends. For all these years I've felt shut out . . . ."

Tears began to roll down Nan's cheeks, and Jack kept his eyes riveted on me. After a short silence, Nan continued. "Now that he's retired and doesn't have his patients to relate to, he suddenly wants to change everything—spend time with me and try to put something together that we've never had. I know he's depressed and angry, but I'm not sure I have it in me to try to help. Maybe I don't even want to—maybe I think his depression is deserved."

Nan's statement contained many messages. At the level of her feelings, she described feeling shut out, deprived, hurt, angry, and, perhaps, vengeful. At another level, she was describing a particular kind of marriage, something about what her expectations had been, her disappointments, and, more importantly, the fact that she might not be emotionally available for any attempts to rework the relationship after all the painful years. For my immediate purposes, however, her statement moved the focus away from Diane's suicide. In a sense, Nan was saying that she wished not to get into that pain, but rather to focus on the chronically disappointing marriage and, perhaps, Jack's depression.

"You've been hurting for a long time, Nan, and, although you're here today, it sounds like you've got lots of doubts about what can be accomplished, maybe even what you want from the marriage. Jack, how is it for you listening to that?"

At the Beginning

> Jack glanced briefly at Nan and then said, "Nan is mostly right, though it may not be as one-sided as she makes it sound—that is, I think I've tried at various times to be more available to her, but never felt she responded. But I didn't try very hard or very long. My practice provided me with easier gratifications. But it is painful to hear her lay it all out. It does help me to understand better her unavailability...." Then, turning to Nan, "You're too angry with me to be available. You're punishing me by shutting me out just as you've felt shut out all these years."

Jack accepted Nan's focus; together, they were saying that they were not ready or did not wish to deal with their daughter's suicide. Further, they appeared to be coming closer in their individual definitions of the problem. Nan was now taking a leading role in defining the problem as their relationship, the chronically unsatisfactory level of closeness, and her angry feelings of being shut out by Jack. Generally, Jack appeared to agree with Nan's description, although suggesting that Nan may not have been as available for a closer relationship as she proclaims.

> I glanced at my watch and noted that there were only a few minutes left in the time allotted for this initial interview. "Before long," I said, "we're going to run out of time. Let me share a perspective with you. In the earlier part of the interview, I thought I heard you, Nan, say the problem was Jack's depression . . . he was what needed fixing. You, Jack, were defining the problem more in terms of Nan's unavailability . . . as a relationship problem. As the interview moved on, it seems that what you may agree on is that you both have experienced chronic problems in your relationship—worse since Diane's death, but present pretty much from the start. If one of the issues is how I am to try to help, it is important for us to be clear on what the problems are and how that gets decided."
>
> They both nodded, and I went on. "As you may know, my approach is to offer to you an evaluation—a series of exploratory interviews, some together, others with each of you alone. I have a particular format—there are some specific things I need to know about each of you and your relation-

ship—how it came to be, for example—and also about your early experiences in your families of origin. Generally, it will take three or so double sessions together and one or two regular individual sessions. I will ask you each to fill out certain questionnaires and may want you to do a videotaped session that we will look at together. All of this will help me to develop some ideas of how I might be helpful—although the final decision will be up to the two of you."

Nan asked, "Will you tell us what you think?"

"Yes—in the sense that I come to understand the two of you and your relationship. Often, I find myself spelling out options as I see them. Options for you both to decide about. For example, I don't know whether I might come to believe you should try an antidepressant, Jack, or whether either or both of you might profit from individual therapy, or whether an important approach would be marital therapy—these are some of the big questions."

"It seems reasonable to me," Jack said. "How about you, Nan?" She nodded and said, "I like the idea of evaluation—and then maybe recommendations for us to consider."

"Good," I said, "but first are there some things you'd like to know about me?"

"We know some things," Nan responded, "like your research in healthy families—and I've heard you talk several times. You've got a good reputation."

"That's really why we're here," Jack added. "I've read several of your books and a number of your papers. Always thought you seemed solid."

"Shall we make an appointment?" Nan asked.

"Let me suggest something," I responded. "Let's not make an appointment until each of you has had a chance to sleep on it—and, more specifically, I'd like the two of you to talk about it. I've no doubt that something needs help—but fit is so important. Why don't each of you think about how you felt about this session—and me—and talk about it. Try to make the decision together. If you have some reservations, I'll suggest some other names."

"But you're willing to work with us—at least for an evaluation?" Jack asked.

At the Beginning

"Oh, yes—I'd be pleased to do so. It's just that who you work with is important, and your deciding together has a real advantage."

"Want one of us to call you, then?" Nan asked.

"Please do—I'll be back in the office on Monday."

They left and I took a 15-minute break before my next appointment. During that time I began to put my thoughts together—to begin making what is called a clinical formulation. In actual practice that usually involves making some additional short notes—often, questions that need answering. For these purposes, however, let me more formally write my initial impressions.

> Jack could have an atypical depression and may need an antidepressant. I need to explore this possibility with him and get a clearer idea of his symptoms, particularly the presence of vegetative symptoms such as sleep disturbances, appetite changes, and the like. I need also to know his family history and whether there is depression in his family.
>
> I also need to know more about his definition of himself as a loner. How pervasive has this characteristic been; when and how did it start? I will be particularly interested in whether his emotional distancing began in the context of a disturbed relationship with one or both parents during childhood. If so, I need to understand what adaptive function emotional distancing played in his childhood relationships.
>
> I am also interested in the circumstances leading to his retirement. How did it come to be that a physician who found his only experiences of psychological intimacy in his work gave up that work? There is, I suspect, a great deal more to his decision to retire than what came out in this initial joint interview.
>
> It will also be important to develop some understanding of the unconscious factors that influenced his marrying Nan. What was it about her that he needed? Did he unconsciously hope that their relationship would heal him? If so, of what? Did he secretly wish that she would break through the emotional wall around him, that she would teach him something

about how to have a relationship that included emotional intimacy? Or—and from an opposite direction—did he unconsciously "know" that Nan was safe—safe in the sense that, despite her complaints, she would neither press too hard for intimacy nor leave him when it was not forthcoming?

Although on the surface Nan seemed matter-of-fact, controlled, and interpersonally more skilled than Jack, it was clear that beneath the surface she was sad and angry. Her marriage had been less than what she wanted, she felt emotionally deprived by Jack, and felt that his depression served him right. Yet, I heard nothing from her about thoughts of leaving Jack or of earlier separations. How can I understand why she stayed in a marriage that she describes as involving so much emotional deprivation?

Although there may be economic or religious reasons that help to make her staying more understandable, I must also try to comprehend both the psychological reasons that explain why she was drawn to a relatively unavailable man and why she has stayed for 41 years in an unsatisfactory relationship. Were the psychological roots of wanting and not finding closeness and intimacy to be found in an important early childhood relationship? Did Jack represent an emotionally unavailable parent with whom her early deprivation was to be healed? Or, despite her complaints, is she, too, afraid of closeness and intimacy? If somehow Jack becomes more emotionally available to her would she become the distancer? Is this a pattern of mutually sustained distance, with Nan hiding her fears of closeness and intimacy behind her complaints of Jack's more openly acknowledged distancing?

There is also the possibility that Nan is depressed and has been so since Diane's death. Her initial focus in this interview on defining the problem as Jack's depression can, at a deeper level, be an attempt to alert me to a more "hidden" depression of her own. I need to explore that possibility with her in order to understand this complex situation as well as possible and to avoid missing an important element that could be crucial for successful treatment of both of them.

As I thought about their marriage as an interpersonal system, it seemed clear that the marriage was unhappy and dys-

At the Beginning

functional. Neither of them discussed their strengths as a couple and, yet, there were bound to be some. I wondered about the shared satisfactions that likely played some role in keeping them together. It appeared that for many years, perhaps from the very start of their relationship, they had not been able to negotiate a mutually satisfactory definition of what their relationship was to be.

On the surface, the disagreement appeared to center on the level of closeness and intimacy, but other aspects of the relationship were likely also involved. Who, for example, gets to decide about closeness and intimacy? This is the issue of power in a relationship and, if the initial impression holds up, Jack's unavailability is in a very powerful position. Nan is unable to "make" him be more available to her emotionally.

What about the many other areas in which decisions must be made and conflicts resolved? Is Jack's apparently more powerful position about the level of closeness and intimacy characteristic of other areas—sex, money, and all the rest—or is his position of emotional unavailability the exception? Does Nan have more power in other areas and is her discomfort about Jack's unavailability mostly because it is an exception to the rule?

There is also the issue of Diane's suicide and what appears to be their inability to deal with this together. There is much in the professional literature to suggest that it can be helpful to assist individuals, couples, and families in an attempt to face together such a loss and do what is called delayed grief work. Jack said he felt so responsible, and it is necesary to understand exactly how he feels responsible. It could be as simple as his being a physician and believing that he should have somehow prevented Diane's death, but other scenarios are possible.

The fact that they have not been able to be together for even brief periods of shared grief for 15 years suggests something of the degree of their alienation from each other. The evidence from this initial interview seems clear: They are not ready to explore their loss. Perhaps it will be possible to establish an alliance with them that will allow them to hazard what will almost certainly be a painful exploration.

An initial interview with a couple involves, at the minimum, the effort to accomplish two initial goals. The first goal for the therapist is to effect a beginning positive relationship with both individuals. This often involves a number of factors. First, I try to offer them some much needed hope. I do so by presenting myself as something of an expert—hopefully, not an omnipotent one, but a professional who has experience and knowledge. I like Minuchin's definition of expertise as "informed uncertainty" (Minuchin, 1992) and I try to emphasize from the start that my work with them will be collaborative. They will make the important choices about whether they choose to work with me and how much of themselves they will invest in the process of therapy.

I also let them know that there is an initial structure to my work, that there is a lot I need to know about them, and that I have a particular way of obtaining that information. Once again, I do not impose a rigid "my way only" attitude; they are free to introduce their own concerns at all times. But ultimately there are certain topics that I have found to be important and will need to explore with them. The issue of structure during the early interviews is important—imposing some structure often leads to the impression that I am knowledgeable, data-based, and, perhaps, not too quick to reach conclusions. It also slows things down and serves as a temporary holding process. However, if the structure is too encompassing, too strongly imposed, or if it does not accommodate their immediate concerns, it reflects an autocratic, inflexible system and invites rejection.

I am much interested in seeing how each of them responds to this initial structure, and in seeking evidence that one or both struggle against it. Despite my efforts to make it a flexible structure, is it experienced as rigid, unpleasant, or undesirable?

Thus, I hope to begin establishing a working alliance with them, a relationship based on hope, an initial clear but flexible structure, and an emotional ambiance that involves respect for their concerns, concern about their pain, and awareness of their strengths. The details of the assessment process will be presented in later chapters.

The several stages of my approach to couples therapy include: (1) the therapeutic effects of the assessment procedure, and, in particular, introducing a couple to the idea that marital problems often stem from a failed search for healing from a childhood relationship; (2) interventions designed to neutralize or control the presenting conflict and relate it to the struggle to define or redefine the relationship; and (3) structured exercises designed to facilitate the development of greater closeness and intimacy within the relationship.

The specific details of this approach to couples therapy will be described in subsequent chapters. For present purposes, however, it is well to note at the onset both that I have borrowed much from the writings of other therapists and that the interventions I use are derived from psychoanalytic, cognitive, behavioral, psychoeducational, and systems frameworks.

In the next several chapters, I will deal with my attempt to be guided by empirical findings whenever possible. Marital-family systems research has been remarkably productive in the past several decades and I borrow broadly from the research of outstanding colleagues. The challenge to this empirical stance by constructivism and the intellectual excitement this challenge has brought to marital-family research and therapy is also the subject of another chapter.

The reader will find that I draw heavily on two professional endeavors that have occupied center stage throughout my career. The first involves my efforts to teach, systematically, crucial psychotherapeutic processes to residents and graduate students (Lewis, 1974, 1978b, 1991a, 1991b). For over 25 years, I have sought to develop or borrow experiential exercises that facilitate learning for these beginning therapists. I have adopted a number of these teaching techniques for use in couples therapy; thus, it seems appropriate to review briefly that teaching endeavor.

The second endeavor involves the study of well-functioning marriages and families conducted for over 25 years at the Timberlawn Research Foundation (Lewis, Beavers, Gossett, & Phillips, 1976; Lewis, 1986, 1988a, 1988b; Lewis, Owen, & Cox, 1988; Lewis, 1989, 1991a, 1991b). This research has taught me much about relationships that facilitate growth—marriages that heal. I have reviewed this work in Chapter 4.

There has been no more rapidly expanding empirical field than that of attachment research. The remarkable predictive powers of infant-parent attachment behaviors, measured early in life, for the subsequent development of the child, have generated new optimism about the possibility of a science of interpersonal relationships. Such a science would search, for example, for similar interpersonal processes that may be present in all emotionally important, long-term relationships. I have briefly outlined my thoughts about the implications of attachment theory and research for couples therapy in Chapter 5.

With these chapters as background and context, I describe the theory that directs my work and then the assessment and treatment processes themselves.

Throughout these chapters, a large number of clinical vignettes are used to illustrate various points. These vignettes draw heavily upon my clinical work, but also rely on experiences with research volunteer families, as well as on observations of friends. Personal experiences with my wife and within our family have also been a rich source of data. In all of this, I have taken pains to disguise the identities of particular couples and families. Despite these precautions, patients, friends, and family will doubtlessly recognize pieces of themselves in what I have written. Partly, I believe, this grows out of the ubiquitousness of crucial relationship processes, but it also represents the inevitable limitations to how many people or human systems one can really know well. For those who see something of themselves in these pages, I can say there is also a great deal of me and the life I have lived as husband, father, friend, researcher, teacher, and therapist.

2

Out of All the Millions of People . . .

Over 30 years ago, I spent several days with Don Jackson, one of the early leaders in Family Systems. At one point, I asked him how he would approach measuring family variables in an effort to assess their role in the outcome of treatment with severely disturbed, hospitalized adolescents. Jackson introduced me to the idea of measuring *how* family members talk with each other rather than relying solely on *what* they say about their families. Thus, I entered the world of 'who-speaks-after-whom,' 'who does the interrupting,' 'which feelings can and cannot be expressed,' and all those variables that have occupied family clinicians and researchers for the past three or four decades.

At the end of this exciting conversation, Jackson said, with a twinkle in his eyes, "There is, however, a shortcut to distinguishing relationships that work and those that don't. Ask each spouse privately, 'Out of all the millions of people in the world, how did you come to marry your wife (or husband)?' If the response contains any of the spouse's personal characteristics, there is a good chance the relationship works. If it does not, chances are the relationship is troubled." Later this idea was formally tested and found valid (McGlynn, 1979).

A day or so later, I asked this question of a mostly silent West Texas rancher as part of a study exploring personality and coronary artery disease. He looked at me with thinly disguised disdain and responded, "That's easy, same county." This rancher's laconic reply is a funny but tragic example of those whose recall of one of life's most important decisions emphasizes the role of depersonalized circumstances rather than any personal characteristics of the persons with whom they hope to spend their lives.

Although I would guess that the relationship between marital quality and the presence or absence of personal characteristics in the response to the shortcut question is complex and involves both the impact of current marital quality on how the past is reconstructed and how past decisions were actually made, I believe Jackson's semiserious question addresses a profoundly important determinant of the quality of life. Whom one marries and the type of relationship jointly constructed are clearly factors that may shape the individual's overall happiness, the meaning one finds in life, one's level of psychological health, and the status of one's physical health.

Let me quickly qualify that powerful statement. First, it need not be a marriage. Despite its awkwardness, the phrase "central dyadic relationship"* is closer to what I mean. All but a few individuals search for a central relationship that provides the crucial interpersonal context in which life is lived. The relationship may be a deep friendship, a long-lasting heterosexual or homosexual love relationship, a sibling relationship, or other two-person relationships that stand at the center of life. Whatever its form, the relationship is experienced as the single most important emotional bond for both participants.

A second qualification is that the impact of the central relationship on the lives of the participants is not simple or linear; rather, it acts in conjunction with other important influences. Freud is said to have noted that the two most important indices of psychological health are the capacities to work and to love (Vaillant, 1977). Tolstoy suggested something more complex when he wrote:

> One can live magnificently in this world if one knows how to work and how to love, and how to work for the person one loves and to love one's work. (Tolstoy, quoted in Vaillant, 1977)**

More recently, my colleagues and I explored the lives of physicians, dentists, and their spouses in a large mail survey (Lewis, Barnhart, Howard, Carson & Nace, 1993a, 1993b; Lewis, Barnhart, Nace, Carson & Howard, 1993; Lewis, Nace, Barnhart, Carson & Howard, 1994). We

---

* In that which follows I will use the word "marriage" and ask the reader to keep in mind that "central dyadic relationship" is the better descriptor of my intent.

** See my review of Vaillant (1977), *Adaptation to Life,* in the Reading Notes on pp. 256–257.

used standard paper and pencil instruments to measure marital satisfaction, work satisfaction, work stress, and anxiety, depression, and other psychiatric symptoms. We found significant correlations between these life domains. Those individuals who reported higher levels of marital satisfaction also reported higher levels of work satisfaction, lower levels of work stress, and lower prevalence of psychiatric symptoms. Their spouses' levels of marital satisfaction correlated in similar ways with the levels of work satisfaction, work stress, and psychiatric symptomatology reported by the physicians and dentists. We did not interpret these findings, however, to mean that greater marital satisfaction causes increased work satisfaction, lower work stress, and fewer psychiatric symptoms; rather, we posit that satisfaction with love, work, and self are related to each other, doubtlessly in complex ways.

Having stated this qualification, let me qualify it. The influence of marital quality on the lives of individuals must surely be one of the most powerful. The results of qualitative research on work satisfaction, for example, Terkel's (1972) interview study, suggests that those who find satisfaction, let alone meaning, in their work are the distinct minority. Thus, for many, the role of marriage and the family becomes an even more important factor in determining how satisfied one is with one's life.

Another example of the particular significance of marital quality on overall life satisfaction is reported by Vaillant (1978). In summarizing the predictors of successful life outcome in a group of Harvard students followed systematically into late life, he noted that there is no stronger predictor of good outcome than the nature of these men's marriages.

Thus, I wish to avoid suggesting either that marital quality acts as the sole determinant of the quality of the individual's life or that it is but one of many and, hence, of no special significance.

A third qualification involves the impossibility of separating the influence of an individual's psychological health from the quality of his or her central relationship. For those who would argue that a marriage of good quality is no more than an indirect measure of the high levels of psychological health of both participants, I would point out that, although two healthy individuals may have a somewhat greater probability of constructing a marriage of high quality, there is little empirical evidence to support this conjecture. Years ago, for example, in a study of McGill freshmen, Canadian researchers found evidence that suggested that having one neurotic parent did not predict the psychological health of the children; rather, if a healthy parent and a neurotic parent had a warm, supportive relationship, there was a good probability that the children would turn out well (Westley & Epstein, 1969). The emphasis for our purposes, however, is that one healthy spouse and one neurotic spouse may have a warm, supportive relationship. Indeed, our study at Timberlawn Research Foundation suggests that two psychologically healthy individuals may be no more likely to construct a high quality marriage than one healthy and one not so healthy person (Lewis, 1989). It is when two less than healthy individuals marry that the chances for a high-quality relationship are clearly reduced. Although it appears that what is necessary for a high-quality marriage is the presence of at least one healthy spouse, the currently available data suggest that marital quality is more than simply a direct reflection of the health of both spouses.

Another qualification involves the need to distinguish two different approaches to the measurement of marital quality. One method involves measuring each spouse's level of satisfaction with the relationship. A relationship of high quality would be defined as one in which both participants report high levels of satisfaction. The second method involves having experts rate the level of relationship quality, usually from conjoint interviews or videotaped couple interactions.

These two approaches—the insider and the outsider perspectives—do not always agree. When they do agree, it is more likely to involve relationships rated as being of high quality by outside experts. In such relationships, the participants have a high likelihood of being very satisfied. The same is not true for relationships rated by outside experts as dysfunctional. In these instances, the participants may also rate the relationship as unsatisfactory, but a considerable number of couples express high levels of satisfaction with what are seen by experts as dysfunctional relationships. Thus, the correlations between the insider and the outsider perspectives on relationship quality are stronger at higher levels of perceived quality than they are at lower levels.

Most of the studies relating marital quality to life satisfaction and health have used the simpler paper and pencil measures of marital satisfaction. Our research at Timberlawn Research Foundation has used both insider and outsider approaches in an attempt to understand better the construct of marital quality (Lewis, 1989).

Despite these and other qualifications, there is much that suggests that whom one marries and the type of relationship that is constructed have major effects on the lives of the spouses and on the children raised by them. Before discussing the data supporting this statement, it seems prudent to address the widespread opinion that marriage and the family are in decline, that this is the age of narcissistic self-preoccupation, and that there is no longer a primary concern with enduring connections with others.

I am of the opinion that such a perspective on marriage and the family is unduly pessimistic. To be sure, there are serious problems that deserve the highest priority. Too many children are born to young mothers who are single and poor, and who, without external support, parent in incompetent ways that increase the likelihood that their children will repeat the pattern. Child abuse is clearly much more common than we ever allowed ourselves to know, and methods of successful intervention are unproven, intuitive at best. Child abuse is also clearly transmitted across generations. The best available information is that 30 percent of women abused as children will abuse their children (Egeland, Jacobvitz & Sroufe, 1988). Family violence of all forms is more common than ever imagined. These and other disturbances of marital and family life leave terrible scars.

At another level, however, there are also scars inflicted by living in constant conflict with one's spouse, even when physical violence does not occur. The children also suffer. As Gottman has demonstrated, children exposed to parental dissatisfaction and strife show physiologic evidence of its toll by age three or four (Gottman & Katz, 1989). At yet a different level, there is the scarring of the spirit that grows out of being locked into a marriage or family in which there is little emotional bonding, no shared celebration of that which is possible in life together, no encouragement to grow, no love.

The tabloids focus disproportionately on the blatant infidelities of political leaders, European royalty, and those who occupy center stage in the entertainment fields. Too often, the implication is that everyone is unfaithful, and that a lasting commitment to a spouse is the rare exception. "Everyone plays around" is the media's message.

Thus, when I say we are unduly pessimistic about marriage and the family, it is not, I trust, because I wish to avoid the problems. Indeed, a considerable portion of my time is spent trying to help individuals, couples, and families find ways to change their lives. Rather, the reasons for my doubts about the level of pessimism are to be found in other, less sensational data collected from persons selected in order to be more representative of the whole population. Let me illustrate with several examples.

Surveying representative samples of Americans regarding their value priorities consistently reveals that family security, defined as "taking care of loved ones," is the highest ranked value. It surpasses "happiness," "a sense of accomplishment," "inner harmony," and other individual-based values (Rokeach & Ball-Rokeach, 1989).

Despite some popular estimates that 50 to 75 percent of married women have extramarital affairs, the National Opinion Research Center at the University of Chicago reported in 1993 that only 13 percent of married women reported ever having cheated on their spouses (Smith, 1993). The comparable figure for men was 21 percent. These figure were the same as those reported in 1988.

A 1993 national survey of sexual attitudes and lifestyles reported by the London School of Hygiene and Tropical Medicine reported that less than five percent of men and two percent of women acknowledge an extramarital affair during the past year (Wellings, 1994).

There is a widespread belief that half of all marriages end in divorce. This is simply not true and represents a misunderstanding of statistics. The facts are that each year there are approximately 2.5 million new marriages and 1.25 million divorces. Thus, in any one year, half as many people get divorced as get married. If, however, consideration is given to the fact that there are over 50 million existing marriages, the percentages are very different. If to the 50 million existing marriages are added the 2.5 million new marriages, the number of divorces (1.25 million) represents less than two percent of all marriages ending in divorce each year. When the data are looked at over 20 or 25 years, it is clear that less than 50 percent of marriages end in divorce (Weems, 1994; Dyer, 1995).

Happiness in marriage appears to be the strongest predictor of overall life satisfaction. I shall cite only one of several studies that confirm this observation. Glenn and Weaver (1981) use data from a National Opinion Research Center survey involving face-to-face interviews with about 1,500 representative American adults and report the following findings. On a three-point scale (very happy, pretty happy, or not too happy), 67 percent of the subjects reported they were very happy with their marriages. Further, the level of marital happiness uniquely explains more of the variance in overall life happiness than do the other seven satisfaction variables combined (work, financial situation, community, nonworking activities, family life, friendships, and health). The authors suggest that the "fragility and vulnerability" (p. 162) of marriage relationships and the high divorce rate may be directly related to the central importance of marital happiness in relation to overall life satisfaction. From this view, divorce rates reflect more the importance of marriage than they do its unimportance.

In the previously noted survey research from Timberlawn Research Foundation involving physicians, dentists, and their spouses, 70 percent of the respondents reported average or high levels of marital satisfaction (Lewis et al., 1993). Further, there were strong positive correlations between spouses' ratings of marital satisfaction. In other words, if one spouse reported a high level of marital satisfaction there was a high probability that the other spouse would independently report a similar level of marital satisfaction.

These and other studies suggest that, although the institutions of marriage and the family are under stress, they are not in extremis. Rather, many persons are firmly involved with their spouses and families, value them highly as major sources of life meaning, and remain faithful to each other.

Despite the lessons from these studies, why is there such widespread acceptance of a doom and gloom perspective? Why are so many so willing to accept the most pessimistic perspective? There are undoubtedly many factors involved, including the disproportionate attention given by the media to the pathology of human relationships, particularly when it involves public personages. Yet, I believe the pessimism has deep roots and wish to emphasize one of those roots.

MARRIAGE AS A SEARCH FOR HEALING

My thesis is that marriage is an unconscious attempt at self-healing. Many persons come to adulthood with scars left over from childhood experiences. Through marriage or other long-term committed relationships, an individual may learn to trust, to share vulnerabilities, to be more self-reliant, to be softer, to be clear about beliefs and feelings, indeed, to be more certain about his or her boundaries, limitations, and strengths. For others, participation in a dysfunctional central relationship may be the beginning of a downward trajectory, a life filled with disappointment, bitterness, diminished self-esteem, and psychiatric symptomatology.

Perhaps for many, an "on balance it works" is the best description. The relationship neither facilitates healing and growth nor leads to diminished capacity; rather it more or less maintains the psychological status quo of both individuals. Thus, the possibilities are multiple, ranging from a remarkable healing to maintenance of the status quo to madness itself.

It is possible in clinical samples to almost always identify a central problematic relationship from childhood that stands out, often as a template for adult life. Although I have not seen systematic data from nonclinical samples, our experiences in assessing the family-of-origin histories of research volunteers demonstrate that, in these samples, a history of parents with a strong, caring marital bond and only relatively minor parent-child difficulties is less common than one might believe. What one would find in truly representative samples, however, is simply not known.

If marriage offers to many the opportunity to rework the problems, fears, and feelings carried within the individual from the central problematic relationship(s) of childhood, how often is the result a healing process? How often is the relationship a healing process for both partners? The answers are unknown. In some research volunteer couples, with relationships rated both by them and experts as of high quality, the scars from childhood appear to have been worked through in the marriage. In distressed couples seen in my couples therapy practice, it is rare for me not to find evidence for the process of failed healing.

I introduce the idea of marriage as a search for healing at this point, not to deal with it in great detail (that will come in a later chapter), but for two reasons. The first is to suggest that the underlying wish to find a source of healing in a spouse may play a role in the high hopes most persons have about marriage. Pessimism about marriage may spring from the disappointment experienced when those hopes are dashed—when marriages fail to heal.

An example of this theme from fiction is the 1975 novel, *Ecotopia*, by Ernest Callenback. He describes the secession of the Pacific Northwest states and the formation of an independent nation based on sound environmental principles. Associated with the profound ecological emphasis are changes in basic values, education, health care, and, most of all, interpersonal relationships. Ecotopians' marriages, for example, shade off more gradually into extended family connections and friendships. There are always good, solid alternatives to any relationship, however intense, and concerns about being alone are greatly reduced. Because a marriage is a less central fact of the individual's life, it is less crucial that it be altogether satisfying and, perhaps, as a consequence of the reduced expectations, there is a greater likelihood of basic satisfaction. Although the reduced centrality of the marital relationship may "dilute something intense and precious in life" (p. 139), it can be seen as individuals taking better care of themselves.

A second reason to introduce the search for healing here is to set the stage for a selective review of studies that suggest the possible healing impact of some marriages. There are several types of relevant studies. The first involves research studying marriages, some of which appear to have had a healing effect on one or both participants. The second is to search out the literature on developmental discontinuities in the lives of individuals at risk for some form of psychopathology. In the latter instance, marital healing may be suggested if the developmental discontinuity appears to be associated with a stable marriage. The following abbreviated case description is presented to illustrate the observations from a research setting that suggest that marital healing has occurred.

> John and Cindy volunteered to participate in a study of young families when Cindy was pregnant with their first child. John was a graduate student in computer science and Cindy was a legal assistant. He was 26 and she 24, and they had been married four years when the initial studies were done.
>
> For present purposes, it is important to note that John and Cindy both rated their marriage as highly satisfactory on a

standard marital satisfaction inventory. Two members of the research team rated the couple's videotaped marital discussion tasks and read the transcripts of several exploratory conjoint interviews. The research team members used the evaluation format developed over the past 25 years at the Timberlawn Research Foundation. The research team members independently rated the couple in very similar ways and here I shall present the concluding overview of one of the research team members:

"This couple appears to have constructed a highly competent relationship system. Their interactions contain much warmth and caring. They laugh and touch a lot. The spouses appear to have relatively equal power and each appears to be very respectful of the other's subjective experiences. When confronted with differences, they explore the differences carefully, search for compromises, and on several occasions agree to differ. There is no observed tendency for their disagreements to become rancorous and to escalate. Their relationship appears to be open to the sharing of a wide range of feelings; empathic responses to each other are occasionally noted. Their responses to experimental problems demonstrate the use of negotiation and high levels of effective problem-solving.

The interview transcripts also suggest a very functional relationship. It seems clear that they are able to be very open with each other and each discusses how fortunate it is that they can talk with the other about very private matters. Their sexual relationship is highly satisfactory to both. They enjoy a wide variety of sexual activities with each other, and each believes the other to be an excellent lover.

At the same time, it seems clear that it is acceptable that each has an important private life. He is an avid sports fan and she is not, so he attends sporting events with male friends. She is much inclined to classical music and contemporary art and he is not; she pursues these interests with her younger sister, who lives nearby.

In sum, I see this couple as having a relationship that involves high levels of closeness and occasional periods of psychological intimacy, as well as high levels of individuality and autonomy. It is, I believe, an example of a very well functioning marriage."

John and Cindy's relationship is fairly typical of those marriages experienced as highly satisfactory by the participants and also evaluated by experts as healthy or highly functional. It is, therefore, instructive to summarize the family of origin data.

> John's family of origin is described by him as clearly dysfunctional. His father, a mechanic, was a binge alcoholic who, when drunk, was verbally and occasionally physically abusive to John's mother. John's mother was long-suffering and seemed to accept without complaint or retaliation her husband's abuse. John became his mother's protector when he grew large enough to physically confront his father. As an only child, John described the torment he experienced being caught in the middle of his parents' chronically conflicted relationship. Although he believed he had problematic relationships with both parents, he described his relationship with his mother as more troubling for him. He described being caught between his need to protect her from his father and his disapproval and anger at her passive, dependent, and long-suffering ways.
>
> Cindy's family of origin was described as moderately dysfunctional. Her father was a rags-to-riches country boy who had transformed a small family hardware store into a chain of home repair stores. He was clearly the dominant parent, but Cindy's mother was no pushover. She was a bright, energetic woman who was warm and supportive to her three daughters. Cindy was the oldest and perhaps the brightest of the three. Her most problematic relationship was with her father, who pushed her to excel. She felt she never really pleased him, and pointed out how clearly disappointed he was and is about her working as a legal assistant rather than going to law school. Her conflict with her father involved her wish to please him and her anger at him both for his failure to accept her as she is and his insistence on defining who she should be.

Neither Cindy nor John has significant problems with separateness and autonomy. Both have clearly demonstrated the ability to be separate, to take care of themselves, and to define their own boundaries. Both Cindy and John emerged from their early experiences with parents, however, with clear deficits in the capacity for closeness. Cindy feared that being too close—particularly to a man—would run the risk of her either being dominated or allowing the man to define her basic identity. As a consequence, she dated very little; when she did, she tended to select passive men with whom she felt no risk of domination.

John also feared closeness, but for different reasons. To be close—particularly to a woman—ran the risk of his becoming enmeshed in her problems and suffering. As a consequence, he was wary about closeness and dated girls who were outspoken, even argumentative, and seemed to have their own misgivings about closeness.

Cindy and John had a three-year courtship with many ups and downs. There were particular problems around closeness—both emotional closeness and sexual closeness. In retrospect, each acknowledged not only how drawn he or she was to the other, but also how threatening the relationship felt, particularly after a period of closeness, when one or both would provoke a disagreement that produced a period of distance.

Gradually, Cindy came to understand how important it was to John that she be in charge of her own self-definition, and how pleased and approving he was about her accomplishments. John came to understand that what Cindy wanted from him was a respectful, equal relationship that did not demand that he be responsible for her feelings. After several years of trial and error, both Cindy and John felt increasingly comfortable with their evolving closeness, and their commitment to each other deepened.

Cindy and John each had a healing experience in the sense that each overcame significant fears of closeness. It might have been easier for each to have made the more defensive choice of a more distancing partner and to have constructed a relationship strong on separateness-autonomy, but with little closeness or intimacy. They did not, and the result of their choices was a relationship that involved both high levels of separateness-autonomy and high levels of connectedness-intimacy. It was because their relationship provided each with the wished-for but feared closeness and intimacy that it can be considered a healing relationship.

As I turn to the literature on developmental discontinuities and their implications for the concept of healing relationships, I start with a personal experience that emphasized for me the possibility of relationships that heal.

About 25 years ago I met a young man who had been for many years an intravenous drug user and had stopped all drug use without benefit of any formal treatment. He had not seen a mental health professional, had not been hospitalized, and had not participated in a 12-step treatment program. He had simply quit using drugs and, when I met him, had been free of drugs for several years. He and I talked and it occurred to me that he and others like him were a remarkable source of useful information. If drug abuse is so difficult to treat successfully, how do some persons stop on their own? Don't they have something to tell us about addiction and recovery?

Growing out of that initial contact, I designed an exploratory study of the processes involved in self-cure of intravenous drug use.* Through advertisements in alternative newspapers and by word of mouth, I ultimately came to know 35 men and women who had been intravenous drug users and had stopped without involvement in formal treatment. I spent 6–8 hours with each subject and they were paid a modest honorarium for their participation.

Each of the subjects claimed to have been drug-free for at least six months. Supporting evidence included stable employment histories, absence of arrests or other legal problems, and the availability of a confirming informant. I quickly learned that relying only on a structured, question-and-answer interview format was not productive. I simply did not know which questions were relevant. If, however, I asked each subject to tell me everything he or she could recall about what was going on in his or her life in the months prior to and following giving up drug use, two patterns emerged from their narratives.

Both patterns involved new connections. About half the subjects described adopting a new belief system—almost always religious in nature—in conjunction with the giving up of intravenous drugs. The new belief system was not a part of a treatment program; rather, it was most often a fundamentalist, rule-oriented religious belief system that seemed to provide both a compelling life structure and a new sense of personal meaning. The subjects did not describe this new connection as the cause of their abstinence, but described their giving up drugs as occurring in the context of a connection with a new belief system.

The other half of the subjects described giving up drugs in the context of a new and emotionally charged relationship. Most often the relationship was heterosexual, but some were nonsexual and a few were homosexual. What seemed important was the intensity of the

---

*This explanatory study was supported by a grant from the Hogg Foundation, Austin, Texas.

new emotional bond. Some of the relationships seemed to be less than healthy, involving, for example, clear implications of excess dependency. Whether such relationships were healthy in a traditional sense, however, seemed less important than their emotional intensity.

The experiences with intravenous drug users who claimed (and appeared) to have given up drug use in the context of an emotionally charged connection to either a new belief system or a new relationship led me to wonder about turning points in people's lives, about so-called "spontaneous remissions" from serious psychopathology, and about the capacity of some new connections to heal.

The studies suggesting marital healing are often inadvertent findings from research projects designed to illuminate other areas. Parker and Hadzi-Pavolvic (1984), for example, were interested in exploring the recollections of fathers and stepmothers of young women who had lost their natural mothers during childhood, as those recollections predict state and trait depression. The unanticipated finding was that those young women who were currently married and had higher levels of affection from their spouses were protected against depression. The authors emphasize that the ability of close, affectional ties in adult life to modify childhood deprivations needs to be better understood.

Quinton, Rutter, and Liddle (1984) report on 94 institution-raised girls and a control group of 51 parent-raised girls. The institution-raised girls were given up by their parents because of the parents' inability to manage the girls' behavioral difficulties. These girls had a greater prevalence of both poor psychosocial functioning and parenting difficulties in young adult life, as compared with the control group. About one-fourth of the institutionalized girls had much better outcomes, which were associated with entering stable marriages with nondeviant, supportive men. The authors point out that entering a stable marriage is not explained by lesser levels of preexisting problems, and that the mechanisms underlying healing marriages are not known.

From a very different perspective, Malan and his colleagues (Malan, Heath, Bacal & Balfour, 1975) studied a small group of individuals who appear to have undergone major changes in psychiatric symptoms and psychodynamics following a single psychotherapy interview years earlier. Although finding some support for the efficacy of the single interview, the authors noted also the important role of new and therapeutic relationships. They comment that the neurotic consequences of an adverse childhood relationship can be worked through in an adult relationship.

An emotionally supportive relationship with a husband or boyfriend appears to be a factor that interferes with the intergenerational transmission of child abuse (Kaufman & Zigler, 1987; Egeland, Jacobvitz & Sroufe, 1988). The authors found that those women who were abused as children and did not go on to abuse their own children were more likely to have entered such an emotionally supportive relationship.

Brown and Harris (1978) describe the buffering effect of a confidential relationship with a man on the prevalence of major depression in women at high risk for such a syndrome. A similar protective effect of a confiding relationship with a woman for men has been reported (Roy, 1981) and is important because most of the reports suggesting marital healing have involved women and their relationships.

Another report involving men is the well-known 1940s study of delinquent boys by Sheldon and Eleanor Glueck, the followup of which was reported by Laub and Sampson (1994). The boys were followed for many years and it was found that two adult events reversed their delinquent life trajectories. The first involved obtaining a stable job with an employer who valued him. The second was marrying a woman with whom he felt a strong tie. In the latter instance, the percentage of those engaged in adult crime fell from 76 percent to 34 percent.

Caspi and Elder (1988) report on four-generational data from the Berkley Guidance Study that emphasize the interplay of individual problems, marital dynamics, and parenting skills as factors involved in the crossgenerational production of psychopathology. The implications for the concept of marital healing in this study involve women who demonstrated ill-tempered, problematic behaviors as children. These women were more likely to marry nonassertive men and to be undercontrolled in midlife, and were described by their children as ill-tempered mothers. If women with such childhood problems married more assertive men, they were not undercontrolled in midlife nor described by their children as ill-tempered. Once again, the authors note that the factors that account for the corrective marital experience are not clear.

A direct approach to the issue of marital healing is presented in the qualitative research of Paris and Braverman (1995). They investigated the types of marriages that appear to successfully interrupt the course of borderline pathology in young women. Their case reports suggest that selecting older spouses who accept the caretaking role and provide an accepting environment may reverse the course of the borderline syndrome, particularly in those borderline patients with more mature defenses. Interestingly, they suggest a parallel between such marriages and essential psychotherapeutic processes.

Another body of work that suggests the process of marital healing is based on attachment research and, in particular, the Adult Attachment Interview (AAI) (Main, Kaplan & Cassidy, 1985; Main and Goldwyn, 1988). Pearson and associates, for example, present data regarding men and women who describe destructive family of origin experiences, and data suggesting insecure attachments during early childhood (Pearson, Cohn, Cowan & Cowan, 1994). Some of these men and women are able to facilitate secure attachment behaviors in their young children, in contrast to the majority who did not facilitate secure attachments in their own children. Pearson and her co-workers believe that such discontinuities may come about through a "corrective attachment experience" in psychotherapy or marriage (Cohn, Silver, Cowan, Cowan and Pearson, 1992). What they believe is required is the revision of the subjects' internal working model of insecure childhood attachment through an intensive experience with an emotionally important and securely attached adult (Lieberman, 1991; Cicchetti & Greenberg, 1991; Egeland et al., 1988; Lynch, 1991; Paterson, 1988; Belsky, 1989; Cohn et al., 1992; Weiss, 1982). Further, the authors note the work of Cohn and collaborators who, in observing the interactions of insecurely attached wives and securely attached husbands, noted that with such husbands the wives behaved like securely attached women (Cohn et al., 1992).

In 1988, Belsky, Youngblade, and Pensky reviewed the data regarding the continuity of marital and parent-child relationships across the generations in both pathological and normal families. They also examined the evidence for discontinuity across the generations, concluding that it is as lawful as continuity and most likely results from relationship experiences ("corrective emotional experiences," p. 209) with spouses, teachers, and therapists that alter the internal working models formed as a result of destructive childhood experiences.

Although these studies increase interest in the idea of marital healing, they raise as many questions as they answer. The first question is how some persons enter into adult relationships that appear to be healing. Whether part of the answer is good fortune, and part, particular features of the young person's personality, is yet to be understood. Rutter (1988) has emphasized the capacity for planfulness, particularly as it applies to the selection of an important other.

Marriage as a Search for Healing

The second question involves the characteristics of the spouse, lover, or confidant. Does part of the answer involve certain healing characteristics in the other? The positive descriptors used by the various authors range from assertive, emotionally supportive, confiding, and affectionate to securely attached. It may be that these different descriptors are all used to identify one or several characteristics shared by the important others, but it is at least equally likely that there is no single healing personality; rather, different persons may need different characteristics from an important other in order to reverse the impact of harmful childhood experiences.

The third question involves the issue of whether that which heals is best understood not as a personality characteristic of either the subject or the important other, but as a healing process residing within the relationship. The work of Brown and Harris (1978) on depression suggests that the healing process may have to do with the exchange of confidences and the presence of psychological intimacy within the relationship. Whether it is this specific feature of the relationship is difficult to know without studies that explore directly the interactions in couples in which healing appears to have occurred.

The issue of where to look for the healing element or process—in the subject, the object, or the subject-object relationship—brings to mind parallel concerns in the history of psychotherapy research. Although it has been clear for at least several decades that psychotherapy is effective, the issue of *how* psychotherapy works (how healing occurs) is still up in the air. Initial psychotherapy research efforts focused on the question of which patient characteristics made for successful psychotherapy. When that search was only partially successful, the focus turned to therapists' characteristics associated with successful psychotherapy. Although the emphasis placed by Rogers and his followers on therapist empathy, warmth, and genuineness proved helpful, it seemed apparent that these general characteristics of therapists could be considered as perhaps necessary but, by themselves, insufficient to explain psychotherapeutive healing (Rogers, 1942).

More recently, the research emphasis has been on the nature of the treatment relationship in successful psychotherapy. Luborsky, for example, has demonstrated that certain characteristics of the psychotherapeutic alliance are positively correlated with successful psychotherapy (Luborsky, McLellan, Woody, O'Brien & Auerbach, 1985; Luborsky, Crits-Christoph, Mintz & Auerbach, 1989).

Another way of framing the issue of marital healing is to look at it as a delayed developmental thrust, a maturation of the ego, a change from reliance on immature defenses to the adoption of mature defenses. Vaillant (1993) has written from this perspective and here I summarize briefly his insights.*

Those most needful of an adult healing relationship are men and women who rely extensively on immature defenses. Vaillant considers these defenses to be projection, fantasy, hypochondriasis, passive-aggressiveness, acting out, and dissociation (neurotic denial). Vaillant notes that a different approach to the definition of immature defenses is based on the work of Melanie Klein and, more recently, Otto Kernberg, and is at the core of object relations theory. Splitting, devaluation, idealization, and projective identification are most commonly cited from this perspective. Vaillant considers these defenses as more complex than the immature defenses he describes in that they are interactional, thus requiring the participation of the object. They are thought to be used exclusively in relationships with others, whereas Vaillant's immature defenses are used in conflicts involving desire, conscience, and reality, as well as in conflicts with others. Most of all, however, these immature defenses can be understood as primarily concerned with anxiety and conflict stemming from interpersonal relationships. Immature defenses "share a peculiar capacity to bind user and object" (p. 57) and "help the user maintain an illusion of interpersonal constancy and attachment" (p. 58).

From the perspective of my emphasis on distance regulation as a central goal of relationship definition, it is instructive to quote Vaillant (1993):

> In their different ways the suspicious bigot, the schizoid dreamer, the passive-aggressive adolescent, and the reproachful hypochondriac all hug their love/hate even as they hold them at arms length. (p. 58)

Maturation of the ego can be thought of as the replacement of these immature defenses by more mature defenses of either the neurotic level (displacement, isolation of affect, repression, and reaction formation) or the mature level (altruism, sublimation, suppression, anticipation,

---
* See my review of Vaillant (1993), *The Wisdom of The Ego*, in the Reading Notes on pp. 256–257.

and humor). These more mature ways of dealing with desire, conscience, reality, and relationships then lead to the successful meeting of the adaptive challenges of adult life. Although theoretically this could extend back to even the childhood challenges of basic trust, autonomy, initiative, industry, and identity, most often it can be seen as involving the later adult developmental challenges of intimacy, career consolidation, generativity, keeper of the meaning, and integrity.

Vaillant reviews three models of ego maturation. The neurobiological model posits that continued ego maturation occurs as a result of "an inexorably maturing central nervous system" (p. 327). The environmental model emphasizes the facilitating qualities of the psychological environment. Being loved, valued, and responded to empathically are examples of the qualities of human systems that may heal.

Vaillant emphasizes the third model, which most broadly can be termed an assimilation model. At its core are the processes of internalizing loved others, their virtues and prohibitions. These adult introjects are then "metabolized" more or less completely and the more complete the metabolizing the more a part of the object's basic identity the subject becomes. Assimilation can be considered to involve a continuum of processes through which the subject takes in the object or part of the object. The processes are (from least to most effective assimilation) incorporation, introjection, imitation, internalization, idealization, and identification.

Vaillant's work answers some questions and not others. He gives us a way of thinking about healing marriages in which the capacity for intimacy, for example, is learned through identification with an empathic other. At the same time, however, we are left with uncertainty as to why some immature and neurotic persons select empathic others and participate in the construction of a relationship that facilitates ego maturation and others do not. Also left unknown is how a relationship may come to be healing for both participants. Although one can say that it is through the process of mutual identifications, we are still in the dark about how and why such occurs in some and not other relationships.

My speculation is that individuals whose ego defenses are primarily neurotic (displacement, isolation of affect, repression, or reaction formation) may have a healing experience with a broad range of others who deal more directly and openly with their feelings and are empathic with others. For those with immature defenses, however, the healing process must be more complicated in that it has to deal with more than intrapsychic conflicts and their affects. All sorts of boundary issues must often be negotiated—projection and projective identification are but examples of the more complex issues that are brought to the relationship. Although empathy with self and others may be necessary, I doubt that it is sufficient in these instances.

Rutter presents an informative analysis of the mechanisms of marital healing in which the spouses' individual characteristics are statistically separated from the marital relationship properties (Rutter, 1988; Quinton, Rutter & Liddle, 1984). In his research, there were contributions to marital healing both from spousal characteristics (absence of criminality, psychiatric disorders, substance abuse, or longstanding relationship difficulties) and from relationship properties, such as a warm, confiding marriage. Thus, it may be that understanding marital healing will involve studying relationship processes as well as individual characteristics.

HARMFUL RATHER THAN HEALING MARRIAGES

Another way of obtaining information on healing relationships is to look at the opposite process—relationships that harm one or both participants. One approach to this perspective is to consider the role of marital variables in the development and course of psychopathology.

At a clinical level, therapists who work with couples are often impressed by the ways in which psychiatric symptoms are involved in marital dynamics. There are several marital situations commonly seen that involve psychiatric symptoms. Most common, in my experience, is the development of depressive symptomatology by a spouse who is in the submissive role in a dominant-submissive marriage. Often, the symptomatic spouse complains primarily of the lack of closeness and intimacy in the marriage. The development of depressive symptoms signals her or his growing distress, but it is also an attempt to encourage the dominant spouse to pay more attention and be more concerned, and may also express underlying anger at the emotionally distant spouse.

Hafner (1986) has written about dominant-submissive relationships from the perspective of sex-role stereotyping, and emphasizes how such role assignments are detrimental to the mental health of women. My experience suggests that it is the submissive or powerless position in a dominant-submissive relationship (independent of gender) that is crucial. In clinical practice, this vulnerable position is more likely to be occupied by women, but marriages involving dominant women and more passive, submissive men who become symptomatic are not rare. As an example, I came to know three generations of strong, capable women, each of whom married a charming and handsome man who was less effective than his successful wife. After some years of marriage, each of the men developed depressive symptoms and alcoholism, partly, I believe, in response to the dynamics of their marriages—marriages in which they were clearly less powerful than their wives.

Another common clinical situation in which psychiatric symptomatology may develop is the chronically conflicted marriage. Here there is no clear pattern of dominance and submission, but rather a never-ending struggle for control of the relationship. In this struggle, psychiatric symptoms may develop in one or both participants and be used as tactics in the power struggle. Although any symptoms may be used, both psychosomatic and phobic symptoms are common.

In my practice, I am referred couples by other therapists who report that one spouse is being seen for depression or another syndrome and is refractory to treatment. The referring therapist suspects that some of the resistance to treatment involves the role of the patient's symptoms in the marital dynamics. Some years ago, I wrote about this topic (Lewis, 1984) and, perhaps as a consequence, am asked to consult in situations where the resistance to improvement may usefully be understood as existing in the marital relationship.

At the level of systematic research, the literature is most comprehensive regarding the role of marital variables in depression. But before turning to several representative studies, I wish to emphasize first several studies, including Vaillant's empirical findings from the Grant Study, regarding the association of marital quality and all psychiatric illness. Vaillant (1978) writes:

> Psychiatric illness (whether measured by immature, maladaptive defenses, psychiatric diagnosis or poor adult adjustment) seems incompatible with successful marriage. Indeed, as indices of psychopathology, the variables of poor marriage and diagnosed psychiatric illness were almost interchangeable. (p. 656)

There are also data from the study of marital Expressed Emotion (E.E.), defined as hostile, critical comments of the spouse, that suggest that high levels of E.E. are associated with a negative course in depression, bipolar disease, and some eating disorders (Hooley, Orley & Teasdale, 1986; Miklowitz, Goldstein, Nuechterlein, Snyder & Mintz, 1988; Fischmann-Havstad & Marston, 1984). Indeed, I am not aware of studies demonstrating the lack of effect of high spousal E.E. on any psychiatric syndrome.

It is important to keep in mind that the relationship between marital quality and individual psychopathology is not linear, but clearly more complex. At the simplest level, the relationship is circular—that is, poor marital quality leads to increased probability of individual psychopathology, and individual psychopathology leads to an increased probability of poor marital quality. I emphasize the issue of probability because, as noted in an earlier section, some couples in which one participant has a less than average level of psychological health construct warm, supportive, high-quality relationships.

In regard to the systematic study of marital quality and depression, the studies indicating that a close, confiding relationship protects both high-risk women and men have been noted in an earlier section (Brown & Harris, 1978; Roy, 1981).

Weissman (1987) has presented convincing data from a major epidemiologic study that demonstrates that there is a 25-fold increased risk for depression in both men and women who report unhappy marriages. Since the relationship between unhappy marriages and depression at the minimum is circular, studies are needed that help to distinguish antecedents and consequences. Barnett and Gotlib (1988) published an extensive review of psychosocial functioning and depression with a particular emphasis on distinguishing among antecedents, concomitants, and consequences. Their review resulted in a focus on four variables: social integration, marital distress, extraversion-introversion, and interpersonal dependence. They conclude, "There is consistent evidence that some disturbance in each of these four domains characterizes depressives' post-morbid or inter-morbid functioning, and, further that marital distress and low social integration may influence the onset of depressive symptoms" (p. 120).

Thase and Howland (1994) reviewed the literature on treatment refractory depression. They found that about 20 percent of depressed patients are refractory to both antidepressants and psychotherapy. Long-term marital discord was one of a small group of variables associated with failure to respond to treatment.

In a rare prospective study, Goering and colleagues studied the support that 47 women with major depressive disorder received from their husbands following hospitalization (Goering, Lancee & Freeman, 1992). Six months after discharge, only half the women were recovered and the strongest predictor of recovery was the women's report of high levels of support received from their husbands. These reports were given shortly after admission and well before any response to treatment occurred. Also of interest is that higher levels of the depressed women's criticism of their husbands (measured shortly after admission) predicted failure to recover six months after hospitalization.

Waring and his colleagues reviewed the evidence that implicates marital discord as a risk factor for depression, and suggest that deficiencies in the quality and quantity of marital intimacy are associated with the severity of depressive symptoms (Waring, Chamberlaine, Carver, Stalker & Schaefer, 1995). They suggest that depression comes about when all hope of obtaining a close, confiding relationship is lost. The use of Enhancing Marital Intimacy Therapy (EMIT), which involves structured approaches to the disclosure of personal constructs, resulted in a reduction of depressive symptoms in a small group of depressed women.

Finally, a large study exploring the intergenerational continuity of depressed affect demonstrated that depressed affect is associated with disturbances in parenting (Whitbeck, Hoyt, Simons, Conger, Elder, Lorenz & Huck, 1992). These parenting disturbances are experienced by children as rejection, and lead to depressive affect in the children, which, in turn, influenced negatively their adult ability to parent effectively.

These representative studies and extensive reviews appear to validate the clinical observations of marital therapists about the association of marital variables and depression. Although more research is needed to untangle the complex relationship of depressive symptoms, personality variables, and marital interactions, the empirical evidence at this point in time is such that the burden of proof is on those who minimize or deny the importance of relationship factors in depression.

MARRIAGE AND PHYSICAL HEALTH

When it comes to the relationship between physical health and central relationships, we are faced with intriguing findings from recent investigations. Twenty years ago, I summarized the then level of knowledge, suggesting that the available data favored the idea that interpersonal relationships can influence the general susceptibility to all diseases rather than the idea that certain aspects of relationships influence the onset and course of specific diseases (Lewis, Beavers, Gossett & Phillips, 1976). Individuals were more likely to become ill under the following circumstances:

1. When their social and interpersonal environments were experienced as stressful

2. When many life changes occurred

3. When severe separation or object loss was experienced; and/or

4. When a prolonged affective state of hopelessness or helplessness developed

All or most of these empirically supported processes either directly or indirectly involved the individual's interactions with important others. Although the studies varied widely in focus, taken as a whole they can be understood as leading to a series of questions about the qualities of the relationships that may influence the onset and course of illness. One such question involves whether certain basic patterns of relating, that is, certain system qualities, predispose members of the system to illness. The second question involves whether certain members of the system are more vulnerable than others in the system. A third question is whether certain processes within the system increase the likelihood of the illness becoming chronic. A fourth question is whether certain system structures and processes afford system members increased protection from illness.

Although much has been written about the system qualities that may predispose family members to illness, I will focus only on several contributors. Minuchin (1974) studied children with one of a small number of severe illnesses (diabetes, anorexia, and asthma) and found evidence to support the roles of family enmeshment, rigidity, and underlying parental conflict as important contributing characteristics. Family therapy was remarkably effective in altering dramatically the courses of these illnesses.

Although he wrote about the family and cancer, Meissner's (1993) observations can be usefully applied to all illnesses. He suggests that enmeshment, rigidity, overprotectiveness, and lack of conflict resolution are essential features. Meissner believes that the family affective system is at the heart of the matter in that members in vulnerable families demonstrate both high degrees of emotional responsiveness to each other and overinvolvement with each other. The self-esteem and basic identity of each member appear unduly caught up in the emotional responses of other family members.

According to Meissner, the family member most apt to become ill is that person whose immaturity renders him or her unusually dependent on the family. He or she is apt to become ill when there occurs a period of emotional disruption in the family, often coming as the result of the loss of a family member. The enmeshed family is unable to mourn the loss successfully and this phase of "morbid grief" (p. 517) is the antecedent to the development of the physical illness in the vulnerable family member.

The similarities in Minuchin's empirical findings and Meissner's clinical observations and theory are supplemented by early findings from the Timberlawn Research Foundation suggesting that families who are unable to respond to a death and dying experimental stimulus by discussing personal experiences involving these themes are more likely to experience a variety of illnesses in the ensuing six months (Lewis et al., 1976). Thus, the characteristics of human systems that may predispose one to physical illness include enmeshment, rigidity, underlying and unresolved conflict, and difficulty dealing with losses.

The issue of why certain family members are particularly vulnerable has been addressed by Meissner, as noted above. Most writers focus on such individual characteristics as immaturity, overdependence, or some other personality characteristic. It is, however, equally likely that the vulnerability involves either certain family roles (e.g., scapegoat) or a biological vulnerability (e.g., an inherited tendency to develop a particular illness).

Another question involves the issue of family factors that may facilitate the development of chronicity. In an early and seminal paper, Weakland (1974) proposed that *how* a system problem got started was often less important than what caused the problem to persist and develop. In suggesting that this concept may apply to physical illnesses in family members, Weakland points to areas that may produce clinically relevant data. These include the family's understanding of the illness, the ways in which the illness poses a problem for the family, and the family's methods of dealing with the illness.

Although the factors that influence chronicity are likely multiple, Reiss and his colleagues take a different perspective on chronicity by exploring the family characteristics that interfere with successful coping with chronic illnesses (Reiss, Gonzalez & Kramer, 1986). If an illness has become chronic, what are the family variables that make for inadequate coping with a now chronic process? Studying families in which one parent (usually the father) had end-stage renal disease and was undergoing dialysis, the investigators discovered a paradoxical vulnerability of "strong" families. Families in which members are highly involved with each other and experience stressful situations as a group may deal effectively with acute stresses, but do not do well with chronic illness in a family member. The authors suggest that the level of involvement with each other and the focus on the ill member may result in other family needs not being addressed. The message here is that "strong bonds" may result in the reduced capacity to deal well with chronic stress; that dealing with chronic physical illness may require a system approach that balances the sick member's needs with those of other family members. Perhaps a high level of closeness is not an advantage when dealing with a chronic process.

The question about the characteristics of interpersonal systems that protect against illness has produced a number of provocative studies. These studies are exciting in that they include measurement of physiologic variables that are known to play roles in both disease and the maintenance of health, including physiologic arousal manifested by significant increases in blood pressure, changes in serum hormone levels such as prolactin, epinephrine, norepinephrine, ACTH, and growth hormone, and changes in immune functioning as measured by a variety of sophisticated immunological assays. The two relationship processes most often measured are the level of conflict and the presence of a confiding relationship.

That the process of confiding may have positive impact on health status is suggested by Pennebaker and colleagues' demonstration that students asked to write for 20 minutes daily for four days regarding a deeply personal experience not previously shared, showed stronger immune responses than did a control group asked to write about trivial experiences (Pennebaker, Kiecolt-Glaser & Glaser, 1988). This intriguing work suggests that it may be the process of confiding that is helpful rather than the presence of a confiding relationship, although confiding in fantasy to an important other or to the professor (through the writing) cannot be ruled out. Indeed, a University of Nebraska study of healthy elderly persons demonstrated that the presence of a confiding relationship is associated with increased immune competence (Brody, 1992).

Kiecolt-Glaser and her colleagues have also reported that describing an emotional burden to a researcher strengthened the immune responses of volunteer subjects (Kiecolt-Glaser & Doherty, 1994–1995). Recent reports suggest that the presence of a confiding relationship with a spouse or other person protects against death from coronary artery disease in both vulnerable men and women (Ewart, Taylor, Kraemer & Agras, 1991; Ewart, 1993). Justice (1988) has reviewed numerous studies of social support and suggests that the ability to confide in a close other is at the core of the concept of social support.

Keicolt-Glaser and her colleagues report on what must be the most rigorous and beautifully designed work in this area. They paid 90 research volunteer couples to spend 24 hours on a research inpatient unit and monitored immune competence before and after a problem discussion task designed to involve the discussion of conflicts within the relationship (Keicolt-Glaser, Malarkey, Chee, Newton, Cacioppo, Mao & Glaser, 1993). They report that couples high on conflict demonstrate reduced immune functioning over 24 hours relative to couples low on conflict. They also found that the higher-conflict group developed significant increases in blood pressure, which remained elevated longer than in subjects with little conflict in their marriages. This finding replicates that published by Ewart and his colleagues (1991) with maritally distressed hypertensive patients. Finally, Malarkey, Kiecolt-Glaser, Pearl, and Glaser (1994) also report that hostile, conflicted behavior during the discussion task was followed by changes in pituitary and adrenal hormones. Kiecolt-Glaser indicates that the bulk of the evidence regarding both immune changes and blood pressure elevation support the idea that it is the negative or hostile behaviors rather than either avoidant or positive behaviors that are crucial (Kiecolt-Glaser & Doherty, 1994–1995). She thus echoes Ewart and his colleagues (1991) who write that "not being nasty matters more than being nice" (p. 155). This emphasis on hostile behaviors and physiologic arousal also mirrors the work of Gottman and his colleagues who report that greater physiologic arousal is a marker of distressed relationships and predicts the dissolution of those relationships (Gottman, Markman & Notarius, 1977; Gottman & Krokoff, 1989).

Burman and Margolin (1992) have published a rich and detailed review of the relationship between marital interactions and physical health and conclude that, despite gaps in our knowledge, the marital relationship is not another marker of social support, but "a conceptually distinct factor with potentially powerful implications for health outcomes" (p. 60).

These exciting studies and overviews hint of the potential rewards of studying the psychophysiologic aspects of relationship structures and processes. It is clear that much more needs to be done but areas like patterns of hostile exchange, confiding and/or the presence of confiding relationship, physiologic arousal, pituitary and adrenal responsiveness, and immune functions promise insights into important health matters. This research may also help us to better understand bereavement, grief, depression, and immune changes. Stein and his colleagues present a rich review of this area and conclude that diminished immune functioning is not a biologic marker of depression, but may relate to other variables associated with depression (Stein, Miller & Trestman, 1991). The work reviewed here suggests some of the aspects of depression that need to be investigated.

MARRIAGE AND MEANING

Most existential perspectives on human existence place the search for meaning at the center of theory. Yalom (1980), for example, discusses four ultimate concerns: death, freedom, isolation, and meaning.* The anxiety about death, the anxiety springing from the realization that each individual creates his or her own life structure, and the dread of an isolation more fundamental than isolation from others or parts of the self all lead to the central question, "If the structure of my life is of my own creation and if I must ultimately die—and alone, at that—what meaning has my life had?"

---

*See author's review of Yalom (1980), *Existential Psychotherapy*, in the Reading Notes on page 258.

Marris (1982) begins with this question and proposes that the core of meaning involves a crucial bond, a unique relationship of which the prototype is the mother-infant relationship. It is out of this relationship that a structure of meaning evolves. Marris prefers "structure of meaning" rather than "internal working model" or "assumptive world" because he wishes to suggest a broader process, indeed "an articulation and organization of purposes and emotional responses" (p. 192), as well as the perception of a relevant order in the world about us.

If, then, there is evidence that suggests that the quality of confiding may be a crucial factor in central relationships and that its absence may be involved in diminished life satisfaction, increased prevalence of depression and other psychiatric syndromes, and both increased mortality from coronary heart disease and reduced immune functioning, what is it about having a confiding relationship that is so powerful? I suggest that the presence of such a relationship in one's life is so important because it can provide the major sense of meaning and purpose to the lives of the participants. These unique relationships are relatively exclusive, claim priority, and are experienced as nurturing.

Marris believes that grief is more than a reaction to the loss of a loved one, because it centrally concerns the "disintegration of the whole structure of meaning dependent upon the relationship" (p. 195). Successful grieving is understood to involve transforming the meaning from the loved and lost person to a set of purposes, ideals, and things to care about.

I find Marris' thinking about central relationships and life meaning to be consistent with my emphasis on the search for healing. If such relationships are at the top of our unconscious priorities, if disturbances in these relationships increase the probability of psychiatric disturbances, if the presence and status of such relationships may influence immune mechanisms and other processes of physical health and illness, indeed, if the nature of such relationships is, for many, central to the very meaning of life, then it seems reasonable to believe that the search for healing may be a fundamental motivation in relationship formation.

3

Enduring Interactions and Collective Illusions

The foundations of my thinking and clinical work reflect the empirical tradition. Despite a primary commitment to private practice, I have been actively involved in medical or psychiatric research since medical school days. With the exception of my internship year, there has never been a year when I did not devote some part of my time to research.

I emphasize this because of the recent and fascinating challenge to this empirical tradition as it applies to human systems. Such basic issues as what a human system *is* and whether or not it can be reliably studied now fill the marriage and family literature. Do human systems have enduring interactional structures that exist independent of the process of observation or are such systems but the transient products of the act of observation in which the system and the observer cannot be distinguished? Is the search for a system of classifying marital and family structures a valid undertaking or does it represent the attempt by professionals to impose a value-laden theoretical straightjacket on a universe of uniqueness in which each couple and family is different from all others? Can professionals become experts regarding marriage and the family and use this expertise in helping others or should all forms of expertise be eschewed?

In order to discuss in subsequent chapters the theory of human systems that guides my assessment and therapy with couples, it seems necessary to deal with the challenge to empirical approaches to human systems brought about by constructivism. To do so will take us temporarily away from human systems to review briefly and selectively how this challenge has evolved.

HOW DO WE KNOW WHAT WE KNOW?

In the effort to introduce students to something of the contemporary dialectic between empiricism and constructivism as it applies to psychopathology, I have searched for a way to illustrate the perspective that such disorders are constructed in the mind of the observer, that they have no "out there" reality independent of the observer's mind. It has seemed to me that this could be a useful experience for beginners in psychiatry and other mental health professions, particularly at a time when the prevailing ideology emphasizes so strongly that many psychiatric disorders are brain diseases.

I would like my students to understand that the brain disease metaphor can be understood as the product of a period of particular emphasis in understanding psychopathology. This emphasis on biological variables has replaced earlier emphases on psychological and social variables, which had replaced a still earlier period of biological emphasis. Although much is learned during each historical period, the rotating emphases delay efforts at integrating across the domains. In other words, I would like students to hold on to (or develop) a significant attitude of doubt—doubt about even such strongly held conventions as the validity of current psychiatric nosology.

This pedagogic concern came back into my consciousness some time ago after reading Larry L. King's intriguing essay, "Redneck Blues" (1985). King writes about himself and the subculture of his origins. Let me quote liberally in the effort to communicate something of King's capacity for provocative description.

In describing "good" people who might properly be understood as Redneck, King writes:

> But even among a high percentage of these salts-of-the-earth lives a terrible reluctance toward even modest passes at social justice, a suspicious regard of the mind as an instrument of worth, a view of the world extending little farther than the ends of their noses, and only vague notions that they are small quills writing a large, if indifferent, history. (p. 86)

And again,

> Though broad generalities deserve their dangerous reputation, one hazards the judgment that always such

> unreconstructed Rednecks shall vote to the last in number for the George Wallaces or Lester Maddoxes or other dark ogres of their time; will fear God at least in the abstract and authority and change even more; will become shade-tree mechanics, factory robots, salesmen of small parts, peacetime soldiers or sailors; random serfs. (Yes, good neighbors, do you know what it is to envy the man who no longer carries the dinner bucket, and hope someday you'll reach his plateau: maybe shill for All-State?) The women of such men are beauticians and waitresses and laundry workers and notions-counter clerks and generally pregnant. Their children may be hauled in joust-about pickup trucks or an old Ford dangling baby booties, giant furry dice, toy lions, nodding doggies and plastered with down-home bumper stickers: "Honk If You Love Jesus," maybe, or "Goat Ropers Need Love Too." Almost certainly it's got a steady mortgage against it, and at least one impatient lien. (p. 88)

And, finally, in describing several families he knew when growing up, he writes,

> There was a hopelessness about them, a feckless wildness possible only in the truly surrendered, a community sense that their daddies didn't try as hard as some or, simply, had been born to such ill luck, silly judgments, whiskey thirsts, or general rowdiness as to preclude twitches of upward mobility. Such families were less likely than others to seek church; their breadwinners idled more; their children came barefoot to the rural school even in winter. They were more likely to produce domestic violence, blood feuds, boys who fought their teachers. They no longer cared and, not caring, might cheerfully flatten you or stab you in a playground fight or at one of the Saturday-night country dances held in rude plank homes along the creek banks. (p. 89)

What, however, would be the impact of King's material on students if I extracted it from its essay form and placed it in the familiar format of our diagnostic system? How much would dressing the material in the cloak of individual psychopathology change its implication for students? Would there be, as I might anticipate, a tendency to experience the material as not so much a commentary on a more-or-less well-defined subcultural group, but rather, as something more reflective of a mental disorder which an individual really "has," even brain disease? Would this experience facilitate students in holding diagnostic entities somewhat less firmly in their minds? Let me illustrate.

Exhibit 3.1 places some of King's observations in the familiar form of the *Diagnostic and Statistical Manual of Mental Disorders. Fourth Edition* (DSM-IV), (American Psychiatric Association, 1994). If one presents this reframing to beginning residents or graduate students before they read the essay and then asks them to think broadly and conjecture widely about the nature of the syndrome, a number of possibilities are discussed. These range from brain damage to early developmental arrest to severe and chaotic family dysfunction. What seems most clear is that the new frame clearly evokes images of psychopathology and that the same material presented in a different format leads to the construction of new meaning, one, I believe, very different from King's intent. In effect, presenting students with King's material in a different way leads them to construct a new meaning of that material.

If one is involved in marital and family research or therapy, it is difficult not to be aware of the ferment about the nature of reality and the importance of context, as well as their implications for clinical practice. If, however, a clinician does not read the marital and family lit-

---

EXHIBIT 3.1
Diagnostic Criteria for 415.80 King's Syndrome

A. A pervasive pattern of cognitive, affective, and behavioral characteristics beginning in early adolescence and present in a variety of contexts, as indicated by at least five of the following:
  (1) strong tendency to see world in "either-or" terms
  (2) failure in generalizing beyond personal experience
  (3) major reliance on projection, often with intense racism
  (4) absence of conventional ambition
  (5) frequent periods of anger and episodic fighting
  (6) underlying hopelessness and self-hate with only brief periods of sustained work and subsequent periods of indebtedness
  (7) tendency to drink heavily, especially beer

erature, he or she might not be aware of this current development in epistemology.

The philosophical debate about whether there is an objective reality independent of the observer has a long history, and its recent development requires understanding, as emphasized by Gergen (1985), of an ancient antipathy between two competing intellectual traditions. The exogenic tradition grounds all knowledge in observables. Its opposite, the endogenic tradition, emphasizes the interpretative nature of knowledge.

The exogenic or empirical tradition has been deeply ingrained into Western consciousness; it is a central part of how the world is experienced: There is a "real," out-there reality; identifiable entities possessing intrinsic properties do exist; their existence is not dependent on the presence of an observer.

Casti (1989) dates this debate to early in this century when relativity and quantum theorists began to doubt the Newtonian view. The issue started around the behavior of quantum objects like the electron that show characteristics of both a wave and a particle without being either. Dealing with this finding split physicists into two camps: the "romantic realists" and the "dogwork realists." Casti states that the romantic realists' perspective is currently dominant in physics. Its central premise is that an object's attributes are contextual in the sense that they depend upon the measurement situation and cannot be independently ascribed to the object. The object, the measurement device, and the observer are an indivisible whole and it is not possible to know what can be identified as solely the properties of the object.

The dogwork realists believe in an objective "out-there" reality. An object has intrinsic properties and the inevitable measurement problems result from the operation of hidden variables that, when identified, will allow complete identification of the object.

Casti takes the position that neither the objectivist nor the constructivist perspective can be refuted by experimental data; adoption of either is more like a matter of religious conviction.

Chessick (1990) traces another root of the current philosophical debate between mainstream realists and constructivists. Not a branch of physics, this root is hermeneutics, the act and science of interpretation.

Chessick concludes by stating that, if the hermeneutic approach is utilized, diagnoses and formulations in the practice of psychotherapy cannot be viewed as disease entities and scientific facts, but as temporary formations that change as the context changes. Naive realism ignores the major participation of the psychotherapist in the construction of that reality, but a radical hermeneutics may lead to relativism, nihilism, and hopeless skepticism. The answer for Chessick is to incorporate an as yet to be clarified hermeneutics into psychiatry.

It is fascinating to understand that in the last 100 years two very different sources can be found for the current dialectic regarding the nature of reality. One source, quantum physics, is in the very heartland of empirical science. The second source, modern methodological hermeneutics, originates in biblical study. Surely this divergence of sources speaks to the importance of the dialectic.

Constructivism itself, however, is split into two camps that share a common core: the belief that reality is invented rather than discovered. In constructivism, the invention occurs in the central nervous system of the observer as a fundamental attempt to evolve a "fit" with the environment. Cognitive psychology is a current example of this form of constructivism.

Social constructionism is the second constructivist perspective. Its central premise is interpersonal: Knowledge of the world is constructed as the result of interactions of persons in relationships. Thus, as Gergen (1985) emphasizes, the shift in explanatory locus from interior regions of the mind of the individual to the processes and structures of human relationships is "a wrenching, conceptual dislocation" (p. 271). Hoffman (1990) also states that, with the emphasis on a social interpretation of reality, the influences of language, family, and culture expand and the influence of the individual's central nervous system declines.

The dialectic between empiricism and constructivism is itself punctuated by intermediate positions. Noteworthy among these are the similar stances articulated by Watzlawick and Bruner. Watzlawick (1984) suggests that there are two fundamentally different aspects of what is called reality. "First order reality" involves the properties of objects and can be established by observation and experimentation. The facts thus obtained, however, give no reference points for the meaning of human existence. Watzlawick calls the aspect of reality in the framework of which meaning and value are attributed "second order reality." He states: "Relationships are not aspects of first order reality whose true nature can be determined scientifically; instead, they are pure constructs of the partners in the relationships, and as such they resist all objective verification" (p. 170).

Bruner (1986) also divides reality into two spheres—nature and human affairs. He suggests that an individual's experience is thus constituted by the experience of both nature and relationships. Knowledge of nature is more apt to be structured in the paradigmatic mode of logic and science, whereas knowledge of human affairs is structured by the narrative mode. The former is primarily concerned with causation; the latter with the drama of human interactions and their vicissitudes.

This philosophical discourse regarding the nature of reality has been expressed in the metaphor of the umpire.* In calling balls and strikes, the umpire reflecting the empiricist's position declares, "I call them the way they are." An umpire holding on to the empiricist's position, but aware of the influence of context, declares, "I call them the way I see them." The third umpire, endorsing a constructivist position, declares, "They're nothing until I call them." To this three-part metaphor, I would add a fourth component: the umpire operating from the perspective of social constructionism, who declares, "They're nothing until we talk about them."

With this brief review of the dialectic about the nature of reality as background, I would like to explore the impact of the dialectic upon psychiatry and other mental health disciplines. In doing so, I will not discuss (for reasons of space) what is arguably the greatest effect of this dialectic—the development of narrative theory and its growing impact on psychoanalysis and psychotherapy. Rather, I will focus only on another influential impact—the challenge within marital-family therapy and research to the empirical stance about human systems.

CONSTRUCTIVISM AND MARITAL AND FAMILY THERAPY AND RESEARCH

I shall introduce the challenge constructivism poses for the empirical tradition regarding marital and family therapy and research with a clinical vignette. The family is a two-parent family, Caucasian, Catholic, and affluent. They are involved with the developmental challenge of the older children leaving home, and during this period an "identified patient" has emerged. These characteristics in various combinations are present in many of the families I treat, but I chose this family because they illustrate clearly certain theoretical issues.

---

* I first heard this metaphor used by Carole Anderson (September, 1987). Doctor Anderson does not recall where she first heard it used, and I am unable to find a reference in the literature.

My initial impressions as they came into the office were that they radiated conventional success and that the women in this family were more decisive than the men. The impression of success had much to do with their clothes. The two women, mother and daughter, were both petite and stylishly dressed. Each wore a basic dark suit; the daughter's skirt was at the then popular mid-thigh level, and mother's was but an inch or two longer. The father and both sons were dressed in blazers and slacks, button-down shirts, and regimental striped ties. All five of them seemed to wear their clothes with a sense of casual familiarity.

The initial impression that the women were more decisive than the men arose from their individual responses to my suggestion that they sit wherever it looked comfortable, although one of the chairs contained my clipboard. Mother moved immediately to the chair on the left of the chair with my clipboard and daughter, Meg, moved quickly to sit on the near end of the sofa. During these decisive actions of mother and daughter, the father and two sons looked at each other and seemed momentarily at a loss about where to sit. "You boys sit on the sofa with Meg," Mother said, and, "Harold, sit in this chair next to me." The men moved promptly as if relieved to have their shared indecision resolved.

I told them that I appreciated their making the long trip to meet with me, and believed it essential for me to know them and they, me, if I were to be their son's therapist. The mother, Sara, responded by saying that they were pleased to have the opportunity because they were all very concerned about Jeff; then, as an apparent afterthought, she added that they had heard good things about me. Once again, I noted how readily she took the position of the family spokesperson.

Jeff was 19 and currently out of school, not working, and supported entirely by his family. His cocaine and marijuana use was associated with social withdrawal, extreme passivity—often, for example, spending several days in bed without eating—and some vague, disorganized thoughts about being caught between the "drug cartel" and "the forces of good." I had seen him eight times, mostly because his uncle, a prominent psychologist in town, had not only asked me to see Jeff, but picked him up and brought him to my office for each of his appointments. I doubted that Jeff would have appeared for his appointments without the uncle's efforts.

Jeff had talked a good deal about his family and consequently I was not without some impressions. The picture Jeff painted was that of several generations of strong women. Both of his grandmothers were alive and dominated their more passive husbands. Jeff saw this pattern in his parents. "My dad is a real salesman, people like and trust him. The family business is so successful, though, because of Mom. She's the comptroller, handles all the money, invests wisely, and is all caught up now in the effort to take the business public. She gets her way almost all the time—mostly, I think, because she's so often right. People see her as supersmart—but not warm like Dad."

Jeff went on to describe his sister, Meg, as much like Mother. "She's a freshman at Northwestern and already knows she is going to law school and then join the family business. When she makes up her mind, it's a done deal." The third child, Jason, was 15, a good student at a prestigious prep school, and seen by Jeff as a distancer. "Jason just maintains his own space. If Mom or Meg try to tell him what to do, he just smiles, backs off, and does whatever he wants."

Jeff's own role in the family was less clear to him. "Maybe," he said, "I'm the family black sheep. I screw up a lot and seem to disappoint my parents most of the time."

During the first 20 minutes of the 90-minute interview, the family focused almost entirely on their concerns about Jeff. Mother emphasized a "strong oppositional streak" exhibited by Jeff since childhood and specifically emphasized difficulty with early toilet training, enuresis until age 13, frequent school refusal during the first several grades, and academic problems "despite a high IQ." Father took a softer position, emphasizing Jeff's "easygoingness" and refusal to "be as intense as others would like him to be." Jason said nothing, but Meg was clear and decisive in her observations. "Jeff is a lot like Dad, but more so—and this really bothers Mother mostly and, to some extent, me."

Meg's comments offered the opportunity to expand the focus of the interview and to attempt to see Jeff's behavior more clearly in the context of the family system.

"Do you agree," I asked no one in particular, "that Jeff's behavior upsets Mother most of all?"

"You've got to understand, Doctor," Father responded, "just how intense Sara is. She always tries to mold and shape."

Mother interrupted, "Harold, that's not really relevant. We're here about Jeff and one of the problems is that you have never been firm with him—you let him get away with murder."

As the tense silence in the room grew, I asked, "Although everyone seems concerned, there is no agreement on how best to respond to Jeff?"

Meg responded, "Mother and I are from the kick-ass school, Dad is in the be-more-understanding camp, and Jason never takes a clear position."

I turned to Dad and said, "Sounds like you often end up more on Jeff's side?"

He colored slightly and stammered, "Well, I think—or it seems sometimes that there is a lot of intensity, a lot of suggestions about what to do. Sometimes it can be better to just go with the flow and see, kind of, what will happen if you don't push."

"If you had your way and we had gone with the flow," Sara interrupted, "we would still only have one store and be living in Rogers Park."

"Yeah," Dad said, "you're probably right—but, well, we were really talking about Jeff and our responses to him."

At this point, I turned to Jason and said, "Jason, you're awfully quiet—what do you see going on?"

He looked at me and without noticeable feeling said, "You've got it, right here. This is us."

Later in the interview I encouraged Jeff to share his observations about what was going on in the family. Although in our individual interviews he was usually clear and spoke in a way that was easy to hear, he was very different with his family present. "Well," he said softly, "it's hard to know—it's like how to approach—," and his voice became faint. "It's difficult to explain." He looked at no one and the silence seemed increasingly tense.

"Jeff," Sara said, "why can't you be clear? I don't have any idea what you're trying to say." Father stared at the floor,

Meg rolled her eyes, and Jason sat without change in his blank expression.

During the days the family was in town, I met briefly with each family member separately, interviewed the parents jointly to obtain a history of their marriage, and had a social work colleague meet with the parents to obtain a comprehensive, multigenerational family history, Jeff's developmental history, and a genetic inquiry focusing, in particular, on the presence of major psychiatric syndromes in first- and second-degree relatives. Although there is much that could be said about what I learned, for purposes of this presentation I wish to present the brief summary of these contacts that I dictated at the conclusion of the family visit.

Jeff's psychopathology cannot be understood without a major emphasis on family system variables that have played a role in both the etiology and the course of his symptoms. Although genetic factors may play a role, particularly in view of the loading for unipolar depression in first- and second-degree male relatives in both maternal and paternal lines, there are no conclusive genetic data linking his exquisite passive-aggressiveness, substance abuse, and tendency for cognitive slippage.

From a psychodynamic viewpoint, it seems clear that a central dynamic in Jeff's life is offering powerful others the possibility of gratification through his successes only to disappoint them before reaching the finish line. This relationship theme seems clearly related to his underlying anger at his parents and other authority figures.

Although a comprehensive psychodynamic formulation is not my present intent, observing Jeff in the context of his family makes clear certain psychodynamic themes. Jeff has not accomplished an appropriate level of separation-individuation; rather, his core sense of self is still fixated in his relationship with his parents. His periods of confusion about his own boundaries are manifested, in part, by his projective mechanisms. Being caught between the forces of good and evil reflects, I believe, both his tendency to think in preambivalent either-or dualities and his difficulty distinguishing what he thinks from what others think.

Jeff is currently unable to enter anything like a mature heterosexual relationship, and the few supportive relationships he has outside the family appear to have many of the characteristics of latency age friendships in that they focus on shared interests in sports and games.

To turn to the major focus of this note—Jeff in the context of his family—the various interviews have clarified an initial family formulation, the highlights of which I will summarize.

Jeff's parents, Sara and Harold, have a chronically conflicted marriage and Jeff was drawn into their conflict early in life and remains enmeshed with both parents.

Sara and Harold were drawn to each other during college days. Sara was attracted to Harold's warmth, outgoingness, and easygoing, laid-back style. He was very popular and she hoped to find in him some balance to her own intensity and her tendency to assume disproportionate levels of responsibility. He seemed also to have the ability to talk about his feelings and she hoped unconsciously to learn from Harold more about closeness and intimacy. In these ways, he seemed strong, much unlike her passive, henpecked father.

Harold was drawn to Sara's brilliance, decisiveness, and clear ability to manage. He felt he needed more of such traits, and in the early stages of their relationship he thought she was unlike his controlling and dominating mother.

Even before Jeff's birth, however, each came to see the other as difficult. Rather than finding him easygoing, Sara came to experience Harold as passive, indecisive, and weak. Harold experienced Sara as distancing and controlling. They shared religious values, a belief in the importance of family, and a mutual interest in the business they had created. There was, however, little, if any, sharing of private thoughts or deeper feelings.

Sara came to make most of the important decisions and Harold, while deferring to her ideas, came to resent her power. He was unwilling or unable to confront Sara directly, using instead passive-aggressive expressions, occasional episodes of excessive drinking, and openly flirtatious behaviors with younger women employees. For her part, Sara dealt with her disappointment and anger at Harold by spending more and more time in the business and retreating even further from him.

On the surface, Sara seems to have more to say about the definition of the marital relationship. In particular, she appears to have more to say about the amount and quality of their separateness and connectedness. Harold says he wants a closer relationship, one in which more is shared. He wants more affection, increased sexual activity, and more playfulness, but blames Sara for these deficiencies and experiences himself as the victim. He seems unaware of how his failure to deal directly with Sara is a significant part of the problem.

Jeff is and has been caught up for years in a complex, enmeshed relationship with his mother. The circular nature of this relationship quickly became apparent in the office. Jeff's failure to assert himself, disinclination to take responsibility, and failure to manage time and money encourage his mother to move in and take over. She does so, often with anger, and is experienced by Jeff as intrusive and dangerous. Consequently, he becomes even more passive and avoidant, Sara responds with even more taking over, and the circular interaction becomes more intense.

This enmeshed, highly choreographed mother-son interaction does serve a purpose in diverting attention away from the disappointment, pain, and anger that Sara and Harold share about their relationship. Harold, however, has a much more active role in this dysfunctional family triangle. Jeff's interaction with his mother causes her much pain and, at a certain level, this pleases Harold. From this perspective, Jeff's ability to distress Sara expresses Harold's underlying anger; Jeff is his father's surrogate, doing to Sara what Harold is unable to risk.

Both the enmeshed relationship with his mother and the role as surrogate for his father have kept Jeff from making appropriate progress in the direction of separation from his family. He is still a little boy, perhaps of latency age functionally; currently, his life has a drifting, timeless quality.

It is important to note that the family is faced with the developmental challenge of the children leaving home. Jeff's impending move to Dallas to attend college has been associated with the development of his symptoms and his assumption of the role of identified patient, thus blocking age-appropriate work on separating from the family. Meg's going to college removes from day-to-day family interactions a major source of gratification for Sara and Harold provided by Meg's successes in life. Jason's style of attachment to the family is more distant; he is the bystander. These losses increase the emphasis on the marriage as the major source of Sara and Harold's gratification. Their underlying dissatisfactions and conflicts make this emphasis threatening and Jeff's symptoms and their genuine concern about him allow them to avoid, at least in part, facing the ways in which their marriage fails them.

None of this has been helped by Jeff's siblings. Rather than finding support and encouragement from Meg and Jason, Jeff experiences Meg as a younger version of Mother. Clearly, and over much of Jeff's recallable life, Meg had done better than he. Within the family, in school, and in social relationships, Meg has been the competitive victor. Further, she is openly derisive of Jeff and sees his problems as lack of necessary willpower. For his part, Jason offers Jeff no support. His distancing style precludes an alliance, although he is not critical and condescending like Meg.

It is also noteworthy that Jeff's description of the transgenerational aspects of his parents' relationship is confirmed by other family members, who describe in various ways that the marital relationships of both sets of grandparents involve strong, dominant women and more passive, ineffectual men. Jeff's maternal grandmother is still a major force in the family. She lives close to the family, is the primary confidant of her daughter, Sara, and has invested capital in Sara's and Harold's company when such was needed for expansion. She is said to have little use for Harold, often calling him "pretty boy" behind his back. Jeff's paternal grandmother is described as both competitive with and critical of Sara, seeing her as bossy and cold.

The focus on pathology in this family should not preclude acknowledgment of the family's strengths. They are all very bright and competent problem-solvers outside the family. They work hard and accomplish much. With but few exceptions, family members appear to genuinely value the family, and although the caring is expressed, for the most part, indirectly through money and gifts, it is a strength. As with most distancing families, there is major emphasis on separateness, autonomy, and successful competition.

Communication within the family is clear with the exception of Jeff's use of indirectness, mostly with his mother and as a part of their enmeshed relationship. Family members can share a focus of attention; there is nothing to suggest a pattern of mystification. Although they are efficient problem-solvers, there is little in the way of negotiation, consensus-building, or ability for compromise. Most often their problem-solving reflects the relatively independent activity of Sara and Meg. Finally, and, once again, with the exception of Jeff, the family members share a basic group of religious values. Their Catholicism is important to them; they go to church together, partake of the sacraments, and play important roles in church-related organizations. These shared values and activities are one of the few sources of closeness for this family.

It seems clear from these findings that the family must be included in Jeff's treatment program. Jeff may be engaged in individual psychotherapy, but by itself this may not be enough. His psychopathology is so much a part of the family dynamics that the family can be understood as an external source of Jeff's resistance to change. Ultimately, I believe, Sara and Harold will have to resolve (if possible) their chronic marital conflict, for that conflict is what I see as the originating core of the dysfunctional family system in which Jeff's psychopathology plays an important role.

I believe that the clinical vignette and the brief formulation of the family dynamics and their relationship to Jeff's psychopathology will be familiar to most family therapists. Although clinicians of different theoretical persuasions might differ with some, even many, of my tentative conclusions, there would be broad agreement about the constructs and language used in the formulation. Triangles, enmeshed relationships, coalitions, distance-regulation, power, developmental stages, and other processes represent the language of empiricism as applied to families. During the 30 years that I have been involved in family research and therapy, this has been the only approach to understanding families—at least until recently. It is based upon the use of traditional scientific principles in family research and therapy and has resulted, I believe, in major advances in understanding crucial processes in human systems. It is, however, but one perspective, one stance about Jeff and his family.

Griffith and colleagues (Griffith, Griffith & Slovik, 1990) have recently discussed the importance of an epistemological stance—that is, the theoretical perspective from which an object, event, or process will be described. Since the constructivists have mounted such a provocative critique of the traditional empirical approach to studying human systems, and since I write from an empiricist's stance, it seems appropriate to begin with the assumptions that underlie the empirical stance and, following that, to offer something of how Jeff and his family might be viewed from a constructivist's stance.

Perhaps the most fundamental of the empiricist's assumptions about the nature of human systems involves the concept of structure. Structure is defined here as the more-or-less enduring patterns of interaction among the system's participants and between the system and the outside world. Interactional patterns most often operate out of the awareness of the system's participants. Once developed, they provide the system with a type of almost automatic responsiveness to many internal and external stimuli, and in this way provide the system with freedom to be more deliberate in dealing with truly novel events. Without more-or-less enduring interactional patterns, all events would require deliberate approaches each time they occur, a state of affairs that could quickly make life in groups impossible. Thus, empiricists not only believe that a human system's interactional structure is an important characteristic, but emphasize that it is essential for system survival.

A human system's interactional structure is thought of as "more-or-less" enduring. In this sense, structure is distinguished from process by a much slower rate of change (Rapaport, 1967). Change in interactional structure occurs most often in response to either developmental challenges, such as exits from and entries into the system, or severe stress, such as chronic severe illness or prolonged economic deprivation. Change in interactional structure is understood as either increasing or decreasing the system's adaptive competence.

There are other constructs concerning the interactional structures of human systems that are central to the empiricist's view. One is that hierarchy, power, and control are important variables in distinguishing different interactional structures.

All relatively enduring systems must elaborate "rules" that govern much of what goes on within a system. One set of rules concerns how decisions are to be made, how conflicts are to be resolved, and how authority is to be vested. Although the rules may call for the dominance of a particular family member, or a relatively equal sharing of power, there is no avoiding the issue of power without inviting a chaos that threatens the survival of the system.

A second construct is that different interactional structures have different adaptive implications. Some structures work better in certain contexts than do others. Although the issue is far from settled, some empiricists believe that in certain highly stressful contexts, an interactional structure involving relative egalitarianism, the open expression of a wide range of affects, and reliance on decision-making by consensus, may not be highly adaptive (Reiss, Gonzalez & Kramer, 1986). There are circumstances in which one participant must take over and, at least temporarily, operate with disproportionate power. "If the train is coming and your car is stalled on the tracks, someone must take charge," a mother said during an interview probing family decision-making.

A third construct is that a human system's interactional structure plays an important role in the course of its participants' lives. Some structures encourage high levels of both separateness-autonomy and connectedness-intimacy in their participants; other structures facilitate the development of psychopathology in its members—the disorders of both separateness-autonomy and connectedness-intimacy. Thus, most empiricists believe that a given interactional structure has predictive implications for the lives of its members.

This view of human systems, with its central construct of more-or-less enduring interactional structures, includes the idea that a nosology of human systems is possible. Although currently there is no broadly accepted nosology of either marital or family systems, the shared belief among many empiricists is that such nosologies are not only possible, but desirable.

Empiricists also believe that human systems can be reliably studied from without. Although acknowledging that observing a system introduces a possible contaminant, empiricists believe that there are strategies for minimizing this effect. It is possible, for example, to vary the metaphorical distance between observer and system by the choice of observational instrument. A mail survey probing family members' opinions about family rituals maintains much greater observer-system distance than does living with a family in order to study their rituals.

All of these broadly-held beliefs about human systems are based on the assumption that a human system's interactional structure is the same when the system is unobserved as it is when observed. Clearly there is no way to test this assumption; it is a matter of belief. I believed that what I observed of Jeff's family in my office was, to a very considerable degree, present outside the office. Although coming to the office to see a professional about a family member's disturbance may accentuate or minimize certain features of the interactional structure, most empiricists believe it does not change the basic pattern itself. I believe that Sara's dominance, Harold's difficulty in openly opposing her, the underlying conflict between the two, Jeff's enmeshed, circular interactions with Sara and his service as Harold's surrogate, and the other features of their interactional pattern operate outside my office. In that sense the interactional structure is relatively stable and what I noted in my office is not solely a product of the moments I shared with them. All of this, however, is an assumption: It can be neither proved nor disproved.

Until recent years, I would not have thought it necessary to acknowledge these basic assumptions on which the empirical approach to understanding human systems is based. Indeed, I doubt that I would have thought about it at all; rather, I would have assumed everybody agreed that interactional structures existed when unobserved, that they endured outside the therapist's office or research laboratory.

The challenge to this assumption began to appear in leading family therapy journals some years ago when a small number of influential writers began to question the basic nature of human systems and whether such systems existed unobserved. This view of families starts with the position that observer and family are inseparable; together, they form a system in which clearly distinguishing which is family and which is observer is impossible; thus, objectivity is not possible.

In this view, human systems are produced by social conversation, hence the designation "linguistic systems." At their core, they represent the participants' efforts to establish agreed-upon meanings. As such, human systems are always fluid, changing, transient. Human systems do not "make" problems; problems "make" human systems. There are no enduring interactional structures, no coalitions, power struggles, triangles, enmeshment, or scapegoats. Further, there are no normative structures, no dysfunctional families, no possible typologies; there are only, in Hoffman's wonderful phrase, "collective illusions" (Hoffman, 1985).

The distinctions between this view of families and the empirical view are clarified by the descriptions of the type of family therapy emanating from the constructivist's stance. Family therapy ("therapeutic conversation") centrally involves the therapist's attempts to facilitate conversation in which new meanings may evolve. The principal "technique" is circular or reflexive questioning in which the aim is to facilitate an ever-expanding range of new questions from which new meanings can be established. Answers are not sought, nor is consensus a goal. The therapist joins the system as free from preconceptions as possible. There is no attempt, therefore, to identify the problem, make a diagnosis, or in any way fit the family into a theoretical framework. The therapist strives not to be the expert and there are no interpretations, behavioral prescriptions, or communication training.

Constructivists would disagree with my brief formulation of Jeff's family and might respond to it as a clear example of a presumptuous "expert" forcing the family into an outdated theoretical straitjacket. They would emphasize that I was now a part of the system, and distinguishing what reflected my involvement from that of the family would be impossible. The interviewer-family system might be very different with another interviewer with a different theoretical lens, constructivists believe; they would assert that the system processes occurring in my office would not occur in a different context and without my contribution.

Further, they might believe that if anything good came out of my involvement with Jeff and his family, it was despite my theoretical orientation. Perhaps there were segments of the interview in which the use of circular questions ("Do you agree that Jeff's behavior upsets Mother most of all? Who is least distressed by Jeff's behavior? When Mother is upset about Jeff, who is best able to make her feel better?") had led to discussions that changed the family's understanding.

The challenge provided by constructivism to the empiricist's answer to the question, "What is a human system?" is, I believe, valuable because it encourages empiricists to examine their basic assumptions about the essential nature of human systems. In particular, this challenge addresses the assumption that human systems have more-or-less enduring interactional structures—a central construct of the empiricist's epistemological stance. In addition, however, the constructivist's challenge encourages a reexamination of the ways in which the observational context, including centrally the person and the theoretical beliefs of the observer, influences the behavior of the system under observation.

For many empiricists, the assumption that a human system has a relatively enduring interactional structure is fortified by their ability to successfully predict certain outcomes for the system's participants. The reasoning is that if what is observed in the clinician's office is but a transient, linguistic system—if the system's interactional characteristics are not relatively enduring—how could those system characteristics have predictive power?

As an example of a marital-family system's predictive power, I would note the Timberlawn Research Foundation's longitudinal study (Lewis, 1989) in which the characteristics of a young couple's marriage, assessed prenatally, predict subsequent infant-mother attachment behaviors. Another clinical example involves the longitudinal study of disturbed adolescents by the UCLA family research group (Doane, West, Goldstein, Rodnick, & Jones, 1981) in which measures of parental cognitive deviance and critical affects predict the development of more severe psychopathology in the adolescents, years later. These findings, as well as many others, lead empiricists to believe that their assumptions about the basic nature of human systems are valid.

Fraenkel (1995) has recently suggested that the debate has often been framed as being between those holding a nomothetic position and those subscribing to an idiographic perspective. This way of looking at that which I have referred to as the empirical-constructivist dialectic is helpful in that it places at the center of the debate the issues of the universal and the particular. One theoretical stance focuses either on those behaviors that can be reliably identified across a wide variety of human systems and the other on those behaviors unique for a particular system.

Fraenkel's framing of this challenge to the more traditional perspective (empirical, nomothetic) by the radical perspective (constructivist, idiographic) encourages the clinical use of both perspectives. As a way of illustration, I will focus on a class or category of marital relationships well-known to marital therapists. Dominant-submissive relationships are common in both clinical and research volunteer samples. Their prevalence in the general population is unknown, but male-dominated marital relationships are often espoused as the norm by certain ethnic groups and some lower middle class, blue collar groups.

At the center of dominant-submissive relationships is unequal power. One spouse has greater influence, usually across a broad range of topics, but most importantly, in defining what the relationship is to be. In later chapters (5 and 10), I will argue that the central issues in the definition of a relationship are the constructs of separateness and connectedness. To the extent that one participant has greater influence in establishing how much of what types of both separateness and connectedness are to be the norm for the relationship, the relationship can be called dominant-submissive.

Within this general type of a relationship structure, there are, however, many ways in which couples differ. The dominance can be absolute, dictatorial, and the result of threat, intimidation, or violence, or it can be soft and subtle, with genuine concern for the welfare of the less powerful partner. The submissive spouse may be childlike and find comfort in a parental spouse or be a person with considerable power and autonomy outside the relationship. The dominant-submissive relationship may be complementary in that each spouse is basically satisfied with the arrangement or there may be considerable conflict. When present, the conflict can be subtle and present with all sorts of passive-aggressive mechanisms or it can be severe, with frequent exchanges of disgust and contempt. There may be much closeness in the form of shared values, interests, and friends or quite separate lives may be the rule. Some dominant-submissive marital structures involve a third party who is triangulated into the relationship. Often this is a child, but it may be a parent, good friend, or lover. There is often the sense that the third party is on one side—often that of the less powerful spouse.

These examples only begin to suggest the ways in which dominant-submissive relationships may differ. There are enough ways that such couples may differ so that the observation that the relationship is dominant-submissive is the beginning, not the ending, of the therapist's search for understanding.

The empiricist's approach to understanding human systems generally, and marital and family systems specifically, is never complete. Doubt is always present. Understanding the omnipresent and powerful forces of transference leads often to questions about how much of the couple's behavior in the office or the research laboratory is responsive to the person of the therapist or researcher, real or imagined. That such doubt is part of all we do is a given. That does not seem, however, sufficient reason to give up the search for reliability and predictability—to throw the baby out with the bathwater.

Minuchin (1992) summed it up cogently in his discussion of expertise:

> Therapy is a temporary arrangement. Hierarchies are mutually organized for a period of time and for a "more or less" specific purpose. Temporary as it is, the arrangement would be a sham if the therapist were not an expert—that is, a person of informed uncertainty. (p. 7)

It is not, however, that my work is uninfluenced by the tenets of constructivism. An example is my emphasis on each spouse's subjective reality rather than on divisive searches for the truth. This topic is elaborated in Chapters 6 and 10.

4

Competent Marriages and the Continuum of Marital Competence

In this chapter the reader is introduced to the work of the Timberlawn Research Foundation's findings on well-functioning marriages and families. Two brief case vignettes are used as examples of some of the issues involved.

> They were not spectacular. Their life together was more quiet and steady than anything else. She taught English at a local school and he was a midlevel manager for a printing company. They shared many interests, including jogging, camping, and the opera. They were active in their mainstream Protestant church and, although they did not consider themselves unusually religious, many of the day-to-day rituals that expressed something fundamental about them were religious.
> They disagreed about very little. He was more conservative than she and occasionally they voted differently. When their two daughters were young, she tended to be the more lenient of the two. They agreed on what was important in life, on their friends, and on all those everyday issues like money and sex that are so often the presenting edges of deeper issues. Their quarrels were infrequent and most often involved those occasions when he needed some distance and she wished for closeness. For the most part, these periods of conflict lasted several hours, or at most, half a day.

They had a small circle of friends with whom they went to dinner and the opera. With some, birthday gifts were exchanged and anniversaries celebrated. He had several male friends with whom he shared an interest in sports and season tickets to the local pro football games. She had three friends from college, and with two of them tennis and lunch was a weekly ritual.

They led a Sunday school class at church, were active in the opera society, and belonged to a runners' club. Although their life together was busy, they both enjoyed quiet evenings at home reading biographies and history.

Their daughters were grown and educated. The older girl was an intensive care nurse engaged to a young physician. The younger daughter, who had recently married a graduate student, was a paralegal in a large law firm. There were many opportunities for family gatherings. Sunday night cookouts were frequent, family vacations not rare, and mother and daughters talked on the phone every several days.

They considered themselves very fortunate in that their life together had not been punctuated by tragedy. The individual physical health of each was good and their economic circumstances relatively secure. Although their parents were deceased, they had lived full lives and died without undue suffering.

The couple had worked out a system of making decisions and dividing responsibilities that was acceptable to each. If asked, they would most likely say that their relationship was an equal one with neither more dominant. They talked things over easily and agreed on most issues. They occasionally needed a compromise solution to some problem and each seemed willing to accept those occasions. Although it did not happen frequently, there were occasions when they talked about deeply personal feelings, including fears and fantasies. This was most likely to occur during periods of special sharing—a long walk on a deserted beach or the evening of their daughter's wedding, for example.

What, however, about passion? Was it ever an important part of the relationship? Does it still exist in one form or another in this stable, quiet, middle-aged couple? The answers to both questions are affirmative.

Competent Marriages and the Continuum of Marital Competence

>Passion has been and is a part of their relationship, although it has changed considerably from the earlier days when they made urgent, wild love on the den floor after their dinner guests had left. There are, however, still moments. These moments are more likely to seem somewhat choreographed—in bed Sunday morning after coffee and the paper, mid-afternoon after a half day in the sun while on a beach vacation, or late at night in a fine hotel while watching a porno flick—these and other contexts often led to passion, although not quite the spontaneous and wildly eruptive sort of earlier days.

This first couple's relationship has a particular style. It is laid back, steady, and without much of the dramatic. Contrast this style with that of another couple:

>Their life together was an active, vibrant sort of thing. They were both high-level managers in different national consulting firms and each was constantly on the go. They had an art-filled condominium close to the top of a fancy highrise overlooking the city. They usually said goodbye to each other at the airport around dawn on Monday mornings. He said, "We break our asses, though, to get back to town Friday nights. Our deal is that the first one home cooks—and it's fine food, wine, candlelight. Usually it's 11 or so before we start—and although each of us is dead tired—the romantic coming together sort of infuses us with energy."
>
>She responded, "It is very special. We usually have only Saturdays and Sundays together—and we make the most of them. Saturday we sleep late, often make love after breakfast, and the afternoon is for errands. Saturday night we go out to dinner and see a movie or play. Sunday morning we breakfast in bed over *The New York Times* and talk and talk. Sunday afternoons we do whatever we feel like. Maybe cycle around the lake, take a picnic to the park, or catch another movie. Sunday night we cook at home—then it is usually up at 4:00 A.M. on Monday and off to the airport."
>
>They have no children, by design. She said that she had been the oldest of eight and "got all the mothering out of my system." They were both invested heavily in their careers.

Each made a six-figure income and together they decided on investments. Both in their late 40s, they have already accumulated a sizeable nest egg. When asked what their dreams were for the future, they discussed going as high as possible in their work and eventually retiring. "Heavy emphasis on travel, art, theater," he said. "I bet we'll always be on the go," she added.

They seemed to agree on most things. Conflicts were rare. The balance of two days of intense involvement with each other and five days of separateness seemed to satisfy both of them. They were not conventionally religious. Life was a gift, they said, and it was their responsibility to make the most of it. Her roots were Irish Catholic and his were reform Judaism, but there was little about their life together that appeared to reflect either orientation.

"Neither of our families understands or approves of our lifestyle," he said, "and we see them only three or four times a year." "We love them," she added, "and in a way I think they're proud of our success. But understand? Accept how we live? No chance."

When seen together they seemed connected by an intense bond. They touched frequently and spoke with a personal shorthand that suggested something of their exclusiveness. Each was warm and engaging, but it was clear that their relationship was the center of their lives. They knew many people, occasionally went to big parties—but all of their capacities for closeness and intimacy were vested in their relationship. It was as if they were newlyweds still caught up in a shared infatuation—but they had been married for 22 years.

These two marriages seem on the surface to be very different. One is quiet, stable, and, in many ways, quite traditional. The other is much more career-oriented, but beyond that it is more intense, vibrant, and fast-moving. The first couple have two daughters, teach at their Sunday school, and have a circle of close friends. The second couple decided against having children, are not involved in traditional religious worship, and seem to have little need for either close friends or extended family.

These brief descriptions of two marriages are deliberately selected to emphasize their differences. Each of the marriages may evoke a distinct set of feelings and assumptions in observers. In part, the observers' responses may reflect value orientations about what marriages "should be:" how the observer values stability versus change, predictability versus uncertainty, security versus adventure, and safety versus danger. For some observers, the first couple's marriage might represent a safe haven in an uncertain world; for others, it might seem to be a boring, even dreary, sameness. For some observers the second marriage might be seen as self-indulgent and without sufficient grounding. Others would value its excitement and the fact that each spouse appears to so thoroughly satisfy the other.

The descriptions may also raise other issues. Some would doubt that either description is accurate. This position, shared by many therapists, would question the stability and relative absence of conflict in the first couple and doubt that the second couple could find such high levels of satisfaction in a relationship that, apart from their careers, appears to be so self-involved. In part, disbelief can reflect how limited the field of observation is for many individuals. Most persons know well only a few marriages. An individual observes closely his or her parents' marriage and, perhaps, also knows a good deal about several other marriages. All told, an in-depth view of more than three or four marriages is unusual.

An individual's view of this small number of marriages is embedded in a context created by the media's selective reporting of the dramatic, the abusive, and the tragic. If the three or four marriages one knows reasonably well are not particularly happy, it is easy to develop cynicism and pessimism about all marriages. For therapists, this tendency can be strengthened by their own careers that focus on the pathology of human relationships.

Another factor aiding the growth of disbelief about the validity of the brief descriptions of the two marriages is the tendency of many to be drawn to and surround one's self with couples who have about the same level of marital functioning as one's own marriage. If chronic conflict, infidelity, and other symptoms of marital dysfunction are part of one's life, there is a high likelihood that one's friends will have at least some of the same. The entire world of marriage can come to be equated with what goes on in one's narrow social orbit.

Disbelief may also involve a defensive function. To the extent that one believes that all or most marriages are as unsatisfactory as one's own, there may be less pain. It is, after all, all that one can expect. If one accepts as valid the descriptions presented above, there may be even more reason to be unhappy with one's own marriage. Better not to believe.

Beyond the issues of desirability and believability, there are other issues, such as, who is to judge the quality of a marriage? What criteria are to be used? How are the inevitable value judgements to be dealt with? What role does the context in which the marriage is embedded play—particularly the economic, ethnic, cultural, and religious contributions? Can nontraditional marriages—gay and lesbian, for example—be evaluated using the same criteria?

These and other complex issues are faced by marital-family researchers who are interested in the study of competent or well-functioning human systems. There are others, however, who believe the issues I have noted make it unwise to attempt to define the characteristics of competent systems. They prefer to emphasize the unique balance of strengths and liabilities each marriage or family may possess.

I have argued that from an empirical perspective it is both possible and desirable to identify the characteristics of competent marriages and families and that doing so results in information of value to couples, families, therapists, and all those interested in human systems. For over 25 years at the Timberlawn Research Foundation, we have been involved in systematic studies of couples and families that function very well. Our earlier work was cross-sectional in that it studied two very different samples of families at one point in time (Lewis, Beavers, Gossett & Phillips, 1976; Lewis, 1978a, 1986; Lewis & Looney, 1983).

The two samples, an upper-middle-class Caucasian group and a lower income African-American group, were studied with individual, marital, and family interviews, psychological tests, value surveys, and marital and family interactional testing. Competence was defined as facilitating the healthy growth of children and stabilizing or enhancing parental psychological health. It was apparent that, despite pronounced demographic differences between the two samples, there were striking similarities in how the most competent families in each sample talked within the family, solved problems, and shared feelings. Their value systems were remarkably alike as measured by a standard value survey.

All of this was not anticipated—we had hypothesized more differences and fewer similarities. We debated whether to study other groups of families such as, for example, upper-middle-class African-Americans, lower-income Caucasians, or Hispanic families of a particular social class, or to turn our research in the direction of longitudinal studies. The latter offered an opportunity to study young families over time in order to better understand how marital and family competence develops. This is the track we took and it is now 10 years since we started the study of young couples expecting their first child. We have collected data periodically and reported our findings in one book and a series of papers (Lewis, 1989, 1988a, 1988b; Lewis, Owen & Cox, 1988; Lewis & Owen, 1996). The findings have been well-received and the methodologies have been used by other investigators in studies that range from exploring the role of family variables on successful renal dialysis to the impact of family competence in buffering the effect of a genetic diathesis for schizophrenia (Steidl, Findelstein, Wexler, Feigenbaum, Kitsen, Kliger & Quinlan, 1980; Tienari, Sorri, Lahti, Naarala, Wahlberg, Ronkko, Pohjola & Moring, 1985).

Rather than reviewing these research projects and the large amount of data they have produced, it seems more relevant for the purposes of this book to discuss those findings that relate specifically to the parental marriages. I will emphasize in particular those findings that offer insight into the concept of competent or well-functioning marriages.

COMPETENT MARRIAGES

The overview presented here evolves from observations of three different samples of research volunteers. The 102 couples studied have been analyzed from multiple perspectives, either at one point in time or on multiple occasions over a period 10 years. The couples studied in our earlier descriptive studies all had one or more children in adolescence, and were either middle to upper middle class or lower-income working class. One sample was Caucasian, the other African-American. The longitudinal sample involved young couples in their late 20s at the start of the project. They were Caucasian and middle to upper middle class. This sample was studied initially during a major family transition—the transition to parenthood.

As will become obvious in Chapter 5, a (perhaps, *the*) central issue in any longstanding, emotionally important dyadic relationship is the definition of the relationship. Two aspects of the definition are crucial. The first is *what* the definition is to be, and the second is *how* the relationship comes to be defined. Thus, one issue is the content of the definition and the other is the process of arriving at the definition.

The central issue in the definition of the relationship involves the balance of separateness and connectedness. "How much of what kind of separateness, and how much of what kind of connectedness will characterize the relationship?" is the key question. If this issue is decided by the couple in a way that satisfies both participants, there is a very strong likelihood that there will not be chronic underlying conflict. Agreement on this issue not only reduces the chances of chronic conflict, but increases the probability that each participant will experience the relationship structure as satisfactory.

The second issue involves the "how" of relationship formation. Under optimal circumstances, both participants will have a hand in negotiating the balance of separateness and connectedness, and the outcome will feel satisfactory both because of its actual balance and the fact that each person played a role in defining the balance.

The balance itself may take only one of several forms: high separateness and high connectedness, high separateness and low connectedness, low separateness and high connectedness, or low separateness and low connectedness.

In our research, we have found it useful to approach the level and quality of connectedness by exploring the dimensions of commitment, closeness, and intimacy. Commitment is concerned with the primacy of the relationship. A high level of commitment is said to be present if there is no other relationship that commands comparable emotional significance for either participant. A low level of commitment is present if other relationships have greater priority for one or both participants.

Closeness is defined as the level of sharing. Here the reference is to shared values, interests, activities, and friends. Closeness also includes a shared high level of satisfaction in the couple's sexual relationship.

Intimacy is considered to be present if the participants share highly personal material about which there is a sense of vulnerability. Private thoughts, feelings, fears, memories, fantasies, and hopes are the most frequent forms of this very personal material. Intimacy is clearly contingent upon having sufficient trust in each other to overcome the fears of what this level of self-disclosure might bring.

Separateness is defined in two ways. The first involves the capacity of each participant to experience himself or herself as a separate person. This is most clearly reflected in the capacity to accept the ways in which one is different from one's partner. The second aspect of separateness is the capacity for autonomous functioning—the ability to take care of one's self, to act independently, and to accept the consequences of one's actions.

In many ways, power is the most important variable in regard to the definition of the relationship. Power is understood as interpersonal influence, persuasive ability, or the ability to control another person. If one person has more power than the other, he or she has the ability to define unilaterally the basic structure of the relationship, to impose his or her will on the other, and, most importantly, to decide on the balance of separateness and connectedness.

There are but a few basic patterns of power distribution noted in research or clinical samples: egalitarian, respectful leadership, mild to moderate dominance, severe dominance, conflicted, and chaotic. These patterns can be understood as a continuum of power, with overlap between contiguous types.

Couples who have negotiated a relationship structure that provides an environment facilitating continued psychological maturation of both participants have competent marriages. In regard to the what and how of the definition of competent relationships the following may be said: These relationships are found to have high levels of separateness (autonomy) and high levels of connectedness (commitment and closeness). Intimacy may or may not be present. If it is present, there is a high likelihood that the relationship is competent; if it is not present, the relationship may be either competent or dysfunctional.

The structure of the competent relationship is the result of a negotiated process taking place over months or several years and to which both participants have made relatively equal contributions. The negotiation almost always occurs around specific issues, such as decisions about relationships with friends and extended family, money, sexuality, and the like. Rarely, if ever, is the overall balance of separateness and connectedness directly negotiated. Indeed, the process of negotiation is subtle, usually out of awareness.

Thus, in competent marriages both partners have considerable power. The pattern may be either egalitarian or respectful leadership; it is not a dominant-submissive, chronically conflicted, or chaotic distribution.

The basic relationship structure of competent marriages described briefly above can be understood as increasing the probabilities that other characteristics of such relationships will naturally follow. One of the more important of these is partners' respect for one another's subjective reality. If the participants have a relatively equal relationship and have evolved a mutually satisfactory balance of separateness and connectedness, there is a heightened likelihood that each person will respect the other's subjective reality. They will listen attentively to each other, be clear about whether they wish to explore some experience or are asking for advice, and in the former instance will facilitate each other's exploration without changing the subject, suggesting solutions, or passing judgement. It is through the process of helping each other explore particular experiences more thoroughly without imposing a structure of one's own that new meanings can be co-created and a deep level of intimacy achieved. It is during such explorations that the speaker may come to feel deeply understood. It is also during such explorations that the couple's discussion most clearly resembles something of a formal psychotherapeutic process.

Couples with dysfunctional relationships are often caught up in conflicts about "the truth": "That's not what *really* happened—," and similar statements are frequent. In competent marriages, there appears to be a well-developed and shared ability to recognize the less frequent occasions in which *the truth* is important ("The tax deadline is tomorrow. We've got to get the form to the mailbox") and those more frequent occasions when subjective reality is far more important than the truth. In this way, it seems that competent couples have adopted a tenet of constructivism: Reality is constructed either in the mind of the observer or in his or her conversations with important others.

Perhaps in part because each participant respects the subjective world of the other and often takes an empathic position regarding it, competent couples are more open about feelings. Each participant is usually clear about expressing feelings and there are few, if any, rules proscribing the expression of certain feelings. In particular, there is considerable likelihood that feelings of vulnerability can be shared.

For all these reasons, there is no chronic conflict in competent marriages. When enduring conflict is found in a relationship, it is most apt to stem from disagreement about the definition of the relationship. Specific issues such as sex, money, or inlaws may be the immediate focus, but usually beneath these issues is a basic disagreement about the balance of separateness and connectedness. Since the participants in competent marriages have negotiated a balance acceptable to both, this underlying conflict is not present. Acute disagreements and conflicts do arise, however, but are usually short-lived. Most often they occur around the issue of synchrony—those times when one participant wants separateness and the other desires some form of connectedness. These periods wherein one participant is not "there" for the other are usually brief, and prolonged conflict and escalation are rare.

Another related characteristic of competent marriages is a high level of effective problem-solving. Because they share power, agree about the basic structure of their relationship, respect each other's subject reality, express feelings openly, and have no enduring conflict, the participants approach problems in ways that remain focused rather than spread to other subjects in an escalating pattern. These couples search for a consensus, construct compromises, and, on some occasions, agree to differ without rancor. Their ability to negotiate is well-developed and as a consequence each participant is apt to feel that solutions involve something of what each desired.

Other characteristics of competent marriages include a high level of agreement about basic values, combined with the ability to respect what differences there are. For the most part, stress and change are dealt with effectively. Many competent couples have good skills in gathering information and using the services of experts. The basic egalitarian, open structure of their relationship allows for considerable flexibility. In our study of the transition to parenthood, for example, these couples did not experience this transition as a crisis (Lewis, 1989). Although strain was present, the couple did not have to restructure their relationship; they remained pretty much as before.

Couples who had evolved a competent relationship before the birth of their first child were also found to have a greater probability of secure infant-parent attachments when the infant was one year of age. This effect of the parents' relationship (as measured prenatally) on the security of attachment was not mediated by the psychological health of the parents, but appears to be a direct influence.

Parenting for competent couples is usually sensitive, and when the children are older, parenting appears to involve both high levels of empathic responsiveness and the setting and maintenance of clear, firm limits. Parents with competent marriages appear to incorporate the child into the family system without establishing a dysfunctional triangle in which one parent is excluded from the relationship of the other parent and the child. We have seen in other less competent couples what we believe to be the early forerunner of later dysfunctional triangles. Thus, in the early parenting of their infants, competent couples appear to demonstrate some of the same processes that we observed in competent couples with adolescent children. At the heart of this observation is the centrality of the parents' relationship. Children are nourished and loved, but no child is more important to either parent than is his or her spouse. I believe it is this feature of the parents' relationship that provides children the opportunity to develop in healthy ways, unfettered by parental needs for a special relationship with the child, basically used to compensate for what maybe missing in the parental marriage.

There is considerable variation among competent couples regarding religion, rituals, sexuality, and relationships with the outside world. We have studied couples rated as competent for whom religious beliefs and practices were at the center of the relationship. Other couples with equally competent relationships had no formal religious activities, were uncertain about the existence of God, and did not believe in life after death. These couples shared many values concerning respect for life, treating others fairly, maintaining honor in relationships, and other precepts that are often thought of as religious in source. For these couples, however, the precepts were not associated with traditional religious belief systems.

Most of the rituals of competent marriages and families express symbolically their strong ties to each other. Holidays, birthdays, anniversaries and other major occasions are often associated with particular rituals. Daily routines, particularly those involving mealtimes and bedtimes, often have a ritualized component. It is in the development and enactment of their rituals that such couples give moving testimony to the specialness of their relationship.

Competent couples vary considerably regarding their sexual practices. For some, sexuality is at the center of the relationship. Lovemaking and intercourse occur frequently and are associated with high levels of shared satisfaction. For other competent couples, sexuality is a more peripheral phenomenon in their relationship. Intercourse is relatively infrequent but highly satisfactory.

There is also considerable variation in how competent couples relate to the world about them. Most often, they are very involved with friends, extended family, and organizations. There are those, however, who are much less involved with the world. They do not seek a network of friends with whom to share their lives; rather, the major focus of day-to-day living is with each other.

This brief overview of the major characteristics of competent marriages only begins to describe these fascinating relationships. Much of what is described here has been reported by other investigators and therapists and I have reviewed these similarities in another publication, and will not repeat that review here (Lewis, 1989, pp. 10–16).

In closing this section, I return to the two couples described briefly in the opening pages of this chapter. Although the couples seemed to have very different kinds of marriages, both couples can be understood as having competent marriages. This is so because each couple demonstrated the following characteristics of competent marriages:

1. A balance of high levels of separateness (autonomy) and high levels of connectedness (commitment, closeness, and intimacy) at the center of their relationship structure.

2. Each spouse had relatively equal power and shared in the establishment of the balance of separateness and connectedness.

3. There was no chronic conflict about the basic structure of the relationship. When present, conflicts tended to be brief and resolved without escalation.

4. In each relationship, the partners' respect for each other's subjective reality was well developed.

5. A broad range of feelings were clearly expressed and often responded to empathically.

6. Problem-solving was effective and negotiation skills clearly apparent.

With these fundamentals in place in their relationships, competent couples are usually able to work out differences, deal with inevitable changes, agree on religious orientation, develop meaningful rituals, decide what role sexuality will play in their lives, and decide together how they will relate to the surrounding world. This type of relationship also appears to offer children raised by the couple an interpersonal context conducive to healthy development.

THE CONTINUUM OF MARITAL COMPETENCE

If one thinks in terms of individual, marital, or family competence, it is important to make explicit on just what values the idea of competence is based. I take the position that marital competence is based on two cardinal values: facilitating the continued maturation of both spouses and creating a psychological climate that increases the probability that children raised by the couple will develop along psychologically healthy lines.

It is important to emphasize that both "maturation" and "psychological health" involve the capacity for both separateness-autonomy and closeness-intimacy. A marriage is considered competent to the extent that the relationship structure increases the likelihood that both cardinal tasks are accomplished—that spouses and children are encouraged to develop the capacities for both relating closely to others and functioning autonomously.

As indicated earlier in this chapter, not all students of marriage agree either that the concept of marital competence is useful or that it should be based on these particular cardinal tasks.

There are other serious objections to the concept of competence. One is that its use can lead to minimizing the effects of the context in which the system is located. Socioeconomic deprivation surely influences what is possible. It is neither wise nor fair to expect those couples struggling for economic survival to be primarily concerned with psychological development. Putting food on the table, keeping a roof overhead, finding adequate healthcare—the list of more important priorities could go on and on. I am in agreement with this perspective. It not only makes sense, but expresses the importance given to context by all of those interested in human systems—in particular those systems that comprise the context for individual growth and development.

Thus, my colleagues and I were astounded to find that two-parent African-American families who were near the poverty level could (and did) evolve relationship structures that facilitated both close relationships and individual autonomy (Lewis & Looney, 1983). They were much more similar to their crosstown, affluent neighbors than they were different. The crucial issue may involve numbers. Our research did not answer how prevalent competent families are in these two vastly different socioeconomic contexts.

Ethnic traditions also shape family structures and in some instances may dictate forms of marriage that are not conducive to healthy development. In particular, those traditions that support male-dominated marriages may place some wives at increased risk for psychopathology.

Cohort effects can also mold relationship structures. The loss of employment during the Great Depression moved many men into marginal positions in their marriages and families. In some such situations, the wives took over, and there is evidence that this change in marital-family structure was associated with positive effects for girls and negative effects for young sons (Elder, 1974).

Any sort of stress, particularly if chronic, also ultimately impacts on what is possible in human systems. Chronic illness, for example, has been well studied. Having a child with serious congenital defects may seriously erode marital quality. For all of these and other reasons, the informed awareness of the clinician and researcher is important. I teach, for example, that the clinician must identify the marital structure and then immediately ask herself or himself, "What is there about this couple's context that helps me understand the couple's relationship structure?" It is apparent that if clinicians are going to use the concept of competence they must be sensitive to context.

In the preceding section of this chapter, I described briefly some of the characteristics of competent marriages, emphasizing that a similar relationship structure often exists in couples whose marital styles are very different. There are four other global types of relationship structures, each of which is comprised of several distinct types. Before describing these other four relationship structures and their within-group variants, the issue of the Continuum of Marital Competence needs to be addressed.

The idea that five basic types of marital structures form a continuum of competence is, perhaps, the most controversial aspect of this approach to thinking about marriages and their assessment and treatment. The underlying logic of the continuum seems reasonably clear. If competent marriages provide the optimal structure with which to accomplish the two cardinal tasks, it holds that other types of marital structures should be found that fail to provide the context that optimally facilitates maturation of the spouses, the healthy development of children, or both. To the extent that a marital structure fails either or both tasks, it can be considered dysfunctional. Further, the more extensive the failure, the greater the level of dysfunction.*

---

* The reader should be reminded that, in addition to the contextual factors noted above, there are many other influences on both child and adult development. Some of these influences are biological and others represent the impact of earlier developmental experiences. This broader view—biopsychosocial in kind—does not detract from the utility of the Continuum of Marital Competence. It does, however, require clinicians to be sensitive to the role of other influences in understanding what is possible for a particular couple.

It is important to point out that the empirical foundation for the Continuum of Marital Competence is incomplete and, in the instance of the transition to parenthood, support for the continuum is only partial (Lewis, 1989). Despite this caveat, I believe the Continuum of Marital Competence has clinical utility, particularly as a construct that provides clinicians with an initial orientation about both the severity of marital dysfunction and the types of interventions to be considered.

Competent but Pained Marriages

> They were at every soccer game, recital, and PTA meeting, and it took some time to realize that they were never without one of their children. Helen and Jack shared a deep commitment to their family and this commitment was clear in their approach to parenting. They were firm and authoritative, but gave their children much leeway in making decisions. They combined their straightforward manner of parenting with a great deal of emotional support for their three children. The children, in turn, seemed to be flourishing. They were all active in extracurricular activities, made excellent grades, and had many friends.
>
> Both exploratory interviews and psychological tests revealed the absence of developmental abnormalities or symptomatic states. Each child seemed well-put-together psychologically. Individual interviews and psychological tests also revealed that Helen and Jack were functioning at normal levels psychologically. Jack's interviewer noted that he was matter-of-fact, moderately compulsive, and did not readily express a wide range of affect—all of which suggested a moderate degree of emotional constriction, which, however, was not considered abnormal. Helen's interview revealed an energetic and bright woman who was moderately obese and somewhat preoccupied with her appearance. Once again, however, it was noted that she had many personality strengths, including better than average relationship skills.
>
> It was only when the focus turned to the marriage that Helen and Jack's problems became clear. Helen said that Jack was an excellent provider, a stable and reliable com-

panion, and a devoted father. He was, however, emotionally, a very remote person. He neither expressed deeper feelings of his own nor was he interested in exploring Helen's feelings. As a consequence, Helen often felt lonely and, at times, unloved. There were occasions when she thought about other men and what life might be like with a more accessible man. Helen wondered, too, if her overeating was "some kind of compensation for my emotional hunger."

Jack also found the marriage something less than what he would like. He commented on what a wonderful mother Helen was to their three children and how well-liked and effective she was in the community. "But," he said, "with me she's kind of sour. She focuses mostly on how unavailable I am emotionally, without, I think, any awareness that her sour, bitter ways make it hard for me to feel close to her."

Helen and Jack articulate clearly the central dynamic of the competent but pained marriage: their inability to jointly construct a relationship structure that includes the sharing of more deeply personal feelings, thoughts, hopes, dreams, and fears. Each is aware of the deficit, but sees only what the other contributes to the failure. At most, each gives only lip service to the ways in which he or she is partly responsible for the deficit.

Helen and Jack work well together at outside tasks. Their shared investment in their children is obvious. They fail, however, to achieve a more intimate level of relating and each assigns responsibility to the other. What is of paramount importance, however, is that neither Helen nor Jack bring the children into their underlying problem. In other couples, one or both spouses make a confidant of a child by forming a triangle that is often harmful to the child. Confining their problem to their relationship allows the children's development to proceed unencumbered by inappropriate roles in such triangles.

Thus, in the competent but pained marriage the relationship structure does not facilitate further maturation of either spouse. Although having generally normal levels of individual health, neither spouse learns to relate at an intimate level. By constraining the conflict to their relationship and providing their children with high levels of parenting, Helen and Jack do facilitate their children's growth along healthy lines. This is the basic finding from our early research: Competent but pained couples successfully accomplish one of the two cardinal tasks.

They raise healthy children but do not facilitate further maturation of the spouses.

There are other signs of the failure of the couple to achieve an intimate level of communicating and of their tendency to blame each other for the failure. They are less open affectively; rather, they are mostly polite to each other, and in this way may fail to provide the children with a model of the spontaneous expression of a wide range of affect. When they are seen as a family, it is the quality of affective constriction that is obvious, particularly when contrasted with highly competent couples.

Competent but pained couples have many strengths and do much to insure a strong family system. It is in the affective realm that they fail. As a consequence there is much of each other's subjective reality that never gets expressed. They know each other less well than do the spouses in more competent marriages. Their relationship fails to heal.

Dominant-Submissive Marriages

It is helpful to think of dominant-submissive marriages as a group that varies along two dimensions: the level of dominance and the quality of response to that dominance. The level of dominance ranges from mild to severe; the quality of response ranges from acceptance to passive-aggressiveness to open conflict. The quality of the dominant-submissive marriage can be understood as ranging from high levels of competence (mild dominance with acceptance) to low levels of competence (moderate to severe dominance associated with open conflict).

The mild dominant-submissive marriage in which the submissive spouse readily accepts the less powerful role is closely aligned to the competent marriage in which one spouse provides most of the leadership. The difference involves the level of respect the more powerful spouse demonstrates for the subjective reality of the less powerful spouse. In the competent marriage with one spouse the clear leader, there are high levels of respect for the other's feelings, opinions, and experiences. In the mild dominant-submissive marriage with acceptance by the other spouse, there are more occasions in which the less powerful spouse's subjective reality is not taken into consideration.

Nevertheless, the mild dominance with acceptance type of marriage often provides children with conditions reasonably suitable for healthy development. This type of relationship does not, however, facilitate the continued maturation of the spouses. The less powerful spouse often does not develop high levels of autonomy; the more powerful spouse does not learn to share his or her personal world. Control, however subtly manifested, remains so important that the expression of vulnerability is avoided.

At a midlevel of dominant-submissive structures are those relationships usually demonstrating moderate dominance, and passive-aggressive responses by the less powerful spouse. Although no reliable statistics are available, widely held jokes about passive-aggressive mechanisms (not remembering to fill the car with gas, not recording checks written, chronic lateness, etc.) suggest that this is a common relationship dynamic. The less powerful spouse is able to neutralize much of the dominant spouse's power by using mechanisms that avoid direct confrontations. Although such power maneuvers may serve as real irritants, they do not often change a dominant-submissive relationship to one in which power is more equally shared. The pattern of a dominant, controlling spouse with a disorganized, forgetful partner is commonly presented in comedy.

Unless children are drawn into the stereotyped hyperadequate-inadequate dance, they are not usually seriously harmed by this type of parental relationship. The exceptions include the incorporation of very constricted gender roles, more often those of controlling men and helpless women, although controlling women and helpless men are also noted.

When children are directly drawn into the choreographed interactions, the results can be harmful. I recall the evening my wife and I were invited to dinner at the home of a former resident. Their 10-year-old son answered the door and showed us to the living room. "My father is mixing drinks in the kitchen and will be with you soon," he announced with a formality unusual for one his age. He turned and went upstairs where he was easily heard chastising his mother with these words, "*Mother*, why can't you get ready on time for your own party? You are always late." It does not take much speculation to anticipate something of how this boy may relate to women when he grows up.

The spouses in moderate dominant-submissive marriages in which passive-aggressive mechanisms predominate do not usually demonstrate continued maturation. The dominant spouse is generally unable or unwilling to give up his or her controlling ways and, as a consequence, cannot express the anxieties, doubts, hopes, and fears that constitute so much of life's richness. The need for control, usually fear-based, robs him or her of much that is richly human. The disorganized, forgetful spouse accepts a very limited identity in which his or her overall competence is an open question. Sometimes, when such marriages end through death or divorce, others express surprise that the disorganized, forgetful spouse demonstrates clear competence. It is only then that it becomes obvious that disorganization and forgetfulness were passive-aggressive mechanisms used to deal with a powerful spouse, rather than stable personality traits.

The moderate or, more likely, severe dominant-submissive relationship is pathological in its impact on the spouses and the children being raised by them. To be in a human system in which all decisions are made by a powerful other either strongly inhibits the development of individual autonomy or provokes a rebelliousness that, whatever its adaptive consequences within the relationship, may have adverse effects if internalized and present in all interactions with authority figures.

An intriguing question is whether it is adaptive for the less powerful spouse to actively oppose the controlling mechanisms of his or her dominant partner. Once again, value judgements are involved. For the less powerful spouse to battle actively may in some situations assist that spouse to maintain or achieve increased maturity. For children in such a family, the consequences are less clear. Gottman's demonstration of the negative psychophysiologic and behavioral consequences of exposure to parental strife suggests that it is conflict that is the important harmful variable (Gottman & Katz, 1989). Conflict, as noted in Chapter 3, also appears to be involved in both adverse immune and vascular effects for spouses.

In addition to the key variables of the level of dominance and the quality of response, there are other factors that may influence dominant-submissive relationship systems. One such factor is whether or not the less powerful spouse engages the assistance of a third person in the struggle with the controlling spouse. Such oppositional triangles may be helpful to the less powerful spouse, but, in the case of a child or children brought into the struggle, the developmental consequences can be destructive. The pattern of a dominant-submissive marriage with a child triangulated into the conflict is not infrequent in the family context of adolescents with severe behavioral disturbances. We have noted what appears to be the forerunner of such oppositional conflicts in the videotaped play sessions of year-old infants and their parents (Lewis, 1989).

The following vignette illustrates some of the observations about dominant-submissive marriages.

> Allen came from a long line of small-town physicians who were experienced by others as competent but controlling. It was no surprise when he married Julie, the daughter of the attorney-mayor of the small town in which they both lived. Julie was attractive, soft in the way of many Old South women, and very traditional in her values. Allen and Julie settled into a routine that was comfortable for both, a way of life in which Allen defined unilaterally most aspects of their life. Some years later when I saw them as a couple, Julie said, "In those early days I wasn't bothered by the fact that the extent of my decision-making was whether we'd have fish or chicken for dinner. Allen made almost all of the other decisions."
>
> As their three children grew up, Julie became unhappy with her childlike position in the family. Gradually, she began to express her dissatisfaction with passive-aggressive mechanisms involving lateness (Allen was very compulsive about time), acts of fiscal irresponsibility (Allen was frugal and believed in a "no-frills" approach to life), and increasing disorganization in her approach to housekeeping (Allen was insistent about order and cleanliness).
>
> Several years of passive-aggressiveness were soon supplemented by the development of psychiatric symptoms. Julie began to drink in the afternoons and after several drinks became openly confrontive and hostile with Allen. She also began to complain of depression and, as that appeared to intensify, Julie would spend increasing time in bed. In addition, Julie encouraged their third child, a daughter, to become her confidante. Much of what they discussed revolved around Julie's anger and critical observations about Allen. As this daughter entered adolescence, she developed increasing evidence of a serious behavioral disturbance involving declining school performance, the use of street drugs, and, somewhat later, a pattern of sexual promiscuity. When this daughter was 17, she was admitted to a psychiatric hospital, at which time Julie and Allen were referred to me.

Julie and Allen's situation is fairly typical for the very dysfunctional level of dominant-submissive relationships. The rigid relational structure became increasingly unsatisfactory to Julie, who responded initially with passive-aggressive tactics. Later, she developed depressive symptomatology and drinking problems, both of which can be understood as signals of increasing despair, messages designed to change the relationship with Allen, and as expressions of rage meant to bring him pain. Finally, she brought her young daughter into the conflict, and they formed an intense coalition aimed at opposing Allen's rigidity, controllingness, and near-absolute power. The daughter's participation in this triangle became one of the causative factors in the development of her severe behavioral disturbance.

Thus, dominant-submissive marriages demonstrate considerable variation. At one extreme are those relationship structures that can facilitate the children's healthy development and, perhaps, have but modest negative impact on the spouses' maturation. At the other extreme are those dominant-submissive relationships that have a high probability of both interfering with normal development of all concerned and playing a role in the development of serious psychopathology. My clinical experience suggests that it is the submissive spouse or the child caught up in the harmful triangle who is most likely to develop a symptomatic state.

Conflicted Marriages

Although all marriages contain conflict, some marriages are characterized by seemingly unresolvable conflict. It is as if continued or intermittent conflict is a central feature of the relationship structure. In this sense, conflicted marriages do not present what appear to be incidental moments or periods of conflict; rather, the conflict has an essential, ever-present quality.

Another way of expressing this defining characteristic is that the basic underlying conflict is about the fundamental definition of the relationship. If each couple must decide what their relationship is to be and, in particular, what balance of separateness-autonomy and connectedness-intimacy is to prevail, chronically conflicted couples have been unable to agree and each spouse doggedly persists in pursuing his or her own definition.

A second crucial aspect of the dynamics of this type of relationship structure involves shared, intense, and usually unconscious fears of connecting too closely. Most often, there is a clear history that illuminates these fears—a history of childhood abuse, or destructive parental dominance. Both spouses have ample reasons to distrust, to avoid relationships they do not control, and to maintain distance in all important relationships.

Other important characteristics of these relationships involve whether the chronic conflict is on the surface much of the time or whether periods of conflict punctuate phases of relative peace. Feldman (1979) has described the latter type and emphasizes the distance regulation aspects of conflict. Periods of conflict are understood as producing distance following a period in which the spouses experienced some level of closeness to each other. The distance produced by the conflict is understood to provide relief from the fears induced by the closeness. At some point, one or both participants experience loneliness and gradually the spouses move closer to each other. These cycles of closeness-conflict and distance-loneliness are often apparent to clinicians. Inquiring about the hours or days preceding the conflict may lead to evidence of a preceding period of unusual closeness.

Some chronically conflicted couples fight about a single subject (e.g., sex, money, etc.). It is as if they have unconsciously agreed on the battlefield for their distance-producing conflicts. Other such couples disagree about most life domains and bring to the clinician's office a different conflictual topic each session.

Gottman (1994) has studied physiologic arousal during and following marital conflict and presents evidence suggesting that the nature of the physiologic arousal predicts the future of the relationship. He also reports that the expression of contempt by one or both participants is an ominous sign.*

Chronically conflicted relationships may last for the lifetime of the participants. Even in these days of easy divorce, some such couples stay together. Although many factors may be involved, I believe that the enduring nature of many such relationships is related to the couples' underlying fears of closeness and their unwillingness or inability to chance relationships in which such fears are not shared.

---

*See my review of Gottman (1994), *Why Marriages Succeed or Fail*, in the Reading Notes on page 248.

There are probably more data about the harmfulness of marital conflict than there are about any other single characteristic of marriages. Much of the research, however, focuses on periods of conflict induced experimentally in the laboratory without appropriate consideration of whether such induced disagreements are related to patterns of occasional conflict outside the laboratory or are reflections of the more deep-seated structural conflict described above. Regardless of these issues it seems clear to clinicians that chronically conflicted marriages are destructive to all concerned. Neither spouse is encouraged to overcome the underlying fears of closeness; each remains locked into a defensive, distance-producing stance. In some such relationships, manipulation and dishonesty prevail. Children may be brought into the endless conflict—sometimes in stable coalitions with parents, but frequently playing one side against the other.

If severe enough, such marriages form the template for a family system that produces sociopathy. Closeness is to be distrusted, so that lying, cheating, and manipulating are common.

> Although bright and articulate enough to finish graduate school, Arnold came to be understood as an extremely narcissistic, exploitative man whose callous disregard of others was most prominently displayed in his relationships with women. "Anything goes" was his life theme and he appears genuinely surprised when confronted with any rules.
>
> He came to my attention at age 31 following his hospitalization for cocaine abuse, but also in the attempt to avoid imprisonment for selling drugs. As part of my consultation, I interviewed his parents. They were urbane and with the sort of sophistication that may come to some in academic life. He was an associate professor of history and she was an associate professor of English literature at the same local college.
>
> Their relationship was severely conflicted and there were few, if any, periods of peace and closeness. They were open in their viciousness and there was about them something of the quality of Martha and George in *Who's Afraid of Virginia Wolf?* (Albee, 1963). In the single interview I had with them, it was not possible to document thoroughly the source of their shared fear of closeness. There were hints, however, of an incestuous relationship she had experienced with her father, and his exposure to a sadistic, dominating, alcoholic father.

They described Arnold as manipulative, untrustworthy, and insensitive to his impact on others and said that he had been that way "since birth." They had no understanding of how his shifting coalitions with them throughout his life may have played a causative role. Rather, they discussed with apparent pleasure how closely he resembled "scoundrels" in both lines of their relatives. They speculated about genetic factors in criminal behavior and did so as if they were discussing a character from Russian fiction. Neither parent voiced any concern about Arnold, his difficulties, or his future; rather, they thought him "most interesting" and "not the usual run of the mill."

Severely Dysfunctional Marriage

There are some marriages that are so patently destructive to all concerned that they can be considered severely dysfunctional. There are three types of such relationships that weigh the scales heavily against anything like normal individual development. The three types are the totally alienated marriage, the psychotic marriage, and the chaotic marriage.

The Totally Alienated Marriage

The totally alienated marriage is one dominated by extreme distance. The spouses lead totally separate lives and appear to share only living quarters. They do not fight and often treat each other with civility and politeness. They talk about only the most superficial subjects, never personal beliefs and feelings. Most often each focuses almost exclusively on career, and both are apt to be successful in vocations that involve only a minimum of emphasis on relationships. They may function with high levels of individual autonomy, but appear devoid of either relationship skills or the need to relate.

This form of alienated marriage can vary in severity, but is usually considered satisfactory by both participants. As a consequence, clinicians do not often see such couples. I have seen but a handful and then at the request of internists or family physicians who are treating one of the spouses for a serious illness and note the total lack of emotional support from the spouse.

Not surprisingly, couples with the most severe forms of alienation rarely have children. Some with less severe forms do have sexual relationships occasionally and produce children. The clearest descriptions of these marriages I have encountered come from the young adult children who enter either individual or couples therapy around their problems establishing emotionally meaningful relationships. In these families, the total emphasis is on separateness, autonomy, and achievement and often the children do well in these areas but are handicapped relationally.

The Psychotic Marriage

The psychotic marriage is a particular form of a severe dominant-submissive relationship in which the dominant spouse is psychotic. His or her distortions and delusions are accepted by the less powerful spouse. These marriages involve pervasive distrust of the outside world and, in particular, of those whose views do not match their own. Often, there is a primitive religious cast to the shared underlying beliefs. Sometimes, this cast is clearly grandiose in the sense that the more clearly psychotic spouse believes that he or she has a worldshaking role to play that will forever change the course of human affairs. In particular, evil will be punished and only the small band of believers will prevail.

Children born to such couples may be indoctrinated into the psychosis and come to share their parents' extensive projections. The family seals itself off from the world with the exception of a small circle of believers. In that circle, the more psychotic and dominant spouse may be accepted as a very special and powerful person.

I have seen only several such couples and those when I was involved with an adolescent inpatient treatment service in a psychiatric hospital. The adolescents from such families were referred by an agency, often the school system, because of bizarre behavior; when examined, they were often found to be psychotic. The parents were totally uncooperative, and were able to obtain their child's release against advice. During these brief intervals, however, it was possible to see something of what I have termed the psychotic marriage. Clearly such a marriage does not facilitate normal development for either spouse or for their children. The dependent spouse adopts the psychotic stance of his or her spouse, and the children often do the same. Both individual autonomy and connectedness of any but the most limited type are severely compromised.

The Chaotic Marriage

The chaotic marriage is characterized by a diffuseness of boundaries. There are times when the spouses seem to have fused their individual identities into an amorphous entity. At other times, such couples appear to be in different universes and their conversations are disjointed, fragmented, and most often lack any observable coherence. It is as if each spouse were rendering a monologue that was not in the slightest way responsive to what the other spouse was talking about. Thus, there appears to be a fundamental inability to maintain a shared focus of attention. The paradox for the viewer is that such couples often insist that they have no disagreements—they are completely together on all issues—and, yet, observing them conversing with each other suggests a great distance between them.

Many of these spouses appear to have relatively primitive personality organizations. Their self-concepts are diffuse and they use primitive defense mechanisms. Under these circumstances, it is well to keep in mind the circular nature of the relationship between primitive personality organizations and chaotic relationship systems. Each influences the other and, as in other circular processes, how each got started is often not easy to know.

Children born to such marriages often display clear deficits in relating to others, major reliance on schizoid defenses, and qualities that mark them as queer or bizarre in school and other public settings.

Many of the characteristics of chaotic marriages and families were described during early phases in the growth of the marital-family disciplines when a major focus was the study of families containing one or more schizophrenic individuals. Although I doubt that there is anything specific to the schizophrenias in chaotic marriages and families, they are human systems that seriously impede the development of both separateness-autonomy and connectedness-intimacy in all those involved.

In writing "all those involved," I exaggerate because such a statement fails to attend the continuing interest in so-called "invulnerable" children (Anthony & Cohler, 1987). There are children—perhaps as many as 10 percent—who, despite growing up in severely dysfunctional families, appear to have achieved normal or outstanding levels of psychological functioning. We do not yet understand the confluence of biological, developmental, psychodynamic, and family variables that make possible escape from their more predictable destiny, but achieving such understanding will be important for the insights it will provide into all human development.

I have presented here a brief description of 10 marital types that can be arranged on a continuum of competence. Competence is defined as the facilitation of maturation for the spouses and the encouragement of healthy development in children. The continuum itself is presented in Exhibit 4.1.

There are no data from studies of representative populations that might inform as to the prevalence of each type. Competent marriages are not rare in research volunteer samples, so I doubt that they are hard to find in the general population. Competent but pained and mild dominant-submissive marriages are more common in research volunteer samples and my guess is that the same is so in the general population. Severe dominant-submissive and conflicted marriages are commonly seen by clinicians who either treat couples or children and they likely represent the two most common types of dysfunctional marriages. There is no way of knowing how often they would be seen in representative samples, but I would guess they constitute about one-fifth or so of all marriages. The severely dysfunctional marriages are much less common—perhaps less than 10 percent of the universe of marriages.

One's vantage point clearly influences how many of what types of marriages one sees. Because of this, it is easy to assume that certain marital types are more prevalent than they really are. Clinicians may come to believe that dominant-submissive and conflicted marriages are all there are unless they have also studied competent marriages.

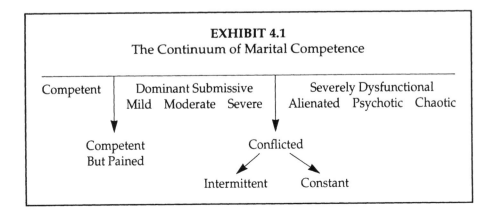

As I will discuss in describing my approach to marital therapy, there appear to be advantages in treatment planning for those clinicians who tailor their interventions to the nature of the system pathology. The Continuum of Marital Competence is one approach to distinguishing those couples with mild to moderate dysfunction from those with more severe system pathology. Although this continuum must be considered an evolving construct, its use as one part of a careful assessment can be helpful.

5

A Theory of Marital Systems

It is difficult, perhaps impossible, to be without a theory. Clinical theories may be quite simple—almost to the point of mocking the complexity of human behavior—or so complex that they are unintelligible to all but the originator. Haley (1980) suggests that clinical theories are judged on their utility rather than on their comprehensiveness and that they must be useful to the average clinician. Perhaps of equal importance is how explicit the clinician's theory is. Theories that operate out of awareness, without the grounding of empirical validation, are most dangerous because they often are comprised of value judgements, biases, and other idiosyncratic processes. They also are often so diffuse and ambiguous that "proof" of their validity can be found in any and all data.

In this chapter I describe briefly the theory of marital systems that guides my assessment and therapy. The theory itself continues to evolve as I test it in my clinical work and am challenged to rethink its premises both by my patients and by the publications of colleagues. I shall cite those colleagues whose work has contributed to my understanding of marital systems, but in no way do I claim to review comprehensively all the relevant literature.

Before I describe the theory, there are a few general principles about human systems that are a part of many systems theories. Those that have been most relevant for me are outlined in Exhibit 5.1.

There are also several phrases that need definition. These include:

1. *Metaphorical distance:* the affective-cognitive position taken regarding the subjective experience of another; may range from great distance (e.g., inattentiveness, changing the subject, suggesting actions) to moderate distance (e.g., intellectual understanding), to very little or no distance (e.g., experiencing that which the other experiences, empathy, merger, "being there").

EXHIBIT 5.1
Important Characteristics of Human Systems

1. Human systems have a *relational structure,* which is the characteristic, repetitive patterns of interaction. This structure can be *flexible* (responsive to changes in the system's participants or of the system's context), *rigid* (relatively unresponsive to change), or *chaotic* (usually unpredictable). These characteristics of the relational structure (flexibility, rigidity, chaos) have implications for the survival of the system and the developmental course of system members.

2. The essential nature of a human system can be predicted only in part from the characteristics of the system members. (A system is more than the sum of its parts.)

3. The essential nature of a human system can be understood as evolving from a small group of underlying beliefs, paradigms, or values that are shared by system members. A system's relational structure both expresses and preserves the underlying shared beliefs.

4. A system member's behavior is understood as invariably shaped by his or her interactions with other members of the system. A particular behavior is thus understood as both cause and effect within the system.

5. This systems view of individual behavior minimizes the role of linear causality and thus poses problems for individualistic approaches to concepts such as free will, autonomy, and responsibility.

6. There is no broadly accepted typology of human systems, although there is much agreement that certain characteristics of human systems are of importance. These characteristics include the distribution of power within the system, the nature of coalitions within the system, role assignments, the levels of closeness and separateness encouraged within the system, the boundary with the system's surround, problem-solving effectiveness, communication clarity, respect for subjective reality and thus, differences within the system, affect regulation, level of conflict, and conflict management.

2. *Separateness-autonomy:* the experience of one's self as separate or at some distance from the experience of others; an ability to act alone and independently, to take care of one's self; may be associated with feelings of freedom, solitude, isolation, or loneliness.

3. *Connectedness-intimacy:* the experience of one's self as close to or merged with another as, for example, experiencing what another is experiencing; the ability to be in a relationship; may be associated with feelings of togetherness, sameness, or oneness.

BASIC PREMISES OF THE THEORY OF MARITAL SYSTEMS

The 15 premises of the theory of marital systems are presented in Exhibit 5.2 and discussed at greater length below.

EXHIBIT 5.2
Theoretical Constructs Regarding Dyadic Relationships

1. Separateness-autonomy and connectedness-intimacy are basic human behavior systems coexisting in each individual.

2. Separateness-autonomy and connectedness-intimacy have biologic, developmental, and social determinants.

3. Each individual can be understood as having a more-or-less stable balance of separateness-autonomy and connectedness-intimacy that may be altered in response to life circumstances or developmental challenges.

4. Psychological maturity or health involves the capacity for both separateness-autonomy and connectedness-intimacy.

5. Both separateness-autonomy and connectedness-intimacy may be associated with underlying, frequently unconscious fears.

6. For most individuals, it is possible to identify a central problematic relationship from childhood that is a source of the underlying fears.

7. Individuals are drawn to specific others for many reasons, including the unconscious attempt to repair the central problematic relationship from childhood.

8. The central task of relationship formation is the definition of the relationship—in particular, establishing a balance of separateness-autonomy and connectedness-intimacy that is reasonably comfortable (relatively free from fear) for both participants.

9. Affects and their communication are central to the establishment of the balance of separateness-autonomy and connectedness-intimacy that characterizes the relationship.

10. The balance of separateness-autonomy and connectedness-intimacy in the relationship is subtly "negotiated" around five issues: closeness (sharing), commitment (priority), intimacy (vulnerability), separateness, and power.

11. Out of the negotiation of these five issues, repetitive interactional patterns develop that come to serve as rules that regulate actual and metaphorical distance in the relationship. Over time, these interactional patterns become relatively stable and are considered the *relational structure.*

12. Although any relational structure may persist and be experienced as satisfactory by the participants, certain structures facilitate the continued healthy development of the participants and other structures do not.

13. Certain parental relational structures increase the probability of healthy psychological development of children raised by the couple and other structures do not.

14. Dyadic relational structures undergo a developmental course that often involves changes in the balance of separateness-autonomy and connectedness-intimacy.

15. Marital relational structures both reflect underlying value systems and memorialize them over time.

1. Separateness-Autonomy and Connectedness-Intimacy: Two Basic Human Behavior Systems

This premise states that these two behavior systems are separate and coexist in each individual rather than representing the opposite poles of one behavior system. Thus, it should be possible to identify individuals who manifest well-developed functioning in both systems, greater development in one system relative to the other, or little development in either system.

These two systems are believed to be fundamental in the sense that they are deeply rooted, with lengthy lineages in evolutionary time. As will be obvious in the discussion of the next premise, it is believed that the strength of these two behavior systems in individuals is determined by the complex interplay of genetic programming, developmental experiences, and family, ethnic, and social variables. Although I do not believe that the following constructs are identical to these two systems, it is likely that there is considerable overlap between the two basic systems and those of extraversion-introversion, approach-withdrawal, and agency-community.

My belief in the separateness of these two systems is not meant to suggest that they do not influence each other. Rather, they are found to have systematic and lawful relationships.

Finally, I believe that the central role played by these two systems in human behavior is the construct that most effectively links a rich variety of theories of individual development and functioning and major theories of small interpersonal systems, such as marital and family systems. From object relations theory and attachment theory to marital-family systems, these two fundamental behavior systems offer many opportunities for theoretical bridges.

2. Separateness-Autonomy and Connectedness-Intimacy: Biologic, Developmental, and Social Determinants

This premise states that the factors that determine the strength of the two systems are multiple and complex. The biologic, developmental, and social determinants are discussed below.

Biologic Determinants

There is little question, for example, that both systems have biologic roots. In his classic discussion of attachment, Bowlby (1973, 1980, 1982) emphasized that the ability to connect with one's offspring has survival value. Those who connect well will provide more protection for their progeny and more of the progeny will survive. Over many generations, those who connect well will be more represented genetically in each generation and those biologic mechanisms, whatever they may be, will endure over time. The same type of evolutionary logic applies to the capacity for separateness-autonomy: Individuals better able to take care of *themselves* will survive in greater numbers and will be overrepresented in subsequent generations.

Although we do not know the biologic mechanisms involved in either behavior system, there is a wide range of speculations. One group of speculations involves temperament—those hard-wired behavioral characteristics present at birth and subsequently modified to some extent by later experiences. If one examines, for example, the overall types of temperament described by Chess and Thomas (1984), it seems apparent that the easy child, the difficult child, and the slow-to-warm-up child can be understood as having different balances of separateness-autonomy and connectedness-intimacy. Cloninger's recent work involves dimensions of temperament such as novelty-seeking, harm-avoidance, and reward-dependence—all of which can be understood to suggest directly, particular balances of separateness-autonomy and connectedness-intimacy (Cloninger, Svrakic & Przybeck, 1993).

Although it is far too rich to review in detail here, mention must be made of the work of Kagan and his associates on the physiology and psychology of behavioral inhibition in children (Kagan, Reznick & Snidman, 1987; Kagan, Gibbons, Johnson, Reznick & Snidman, 1990; Kagan, Reznick, Snidman, Gibbons & Johnson, 1988). Their studies have examined the longitudinal courses of both extremely shy and very sociable children through the first seven years of life and they present evidence of an association between behavioral inhibition and lower thresholds of physiologic processes that originate in the limbic lobe. They note that the literature suggests that studies of monozygotic and dizygotic twins reveal that those characteristics yielding the best evidence for heritability involve the approach to or withdrawal from the unfamiliar. It is clear that Kagan believes that the temperamental disposition to be inhibited or uninhibited in early childhood is biologically based, but that, when consideration is given to the many variables influencing personality, temperamental disposition "probably contributes no more than 10% to the variation in the adult characteristics our society values" (Kagan et al., 1990, p. 174).

There is also much to suggest that yet-to-be-understood biologic aspects of affective development may play a role in the biology of these two behavior systems. This commonsense belief grows out of the role expressions of affect play in signaling both the wish for separateness and the wish for connectedness. As far back as we know, creatures have used multiple affective expressions to signal others to approach or leave. Although the development of language has placed a primary expressive responsibility on words, there is much use of the earlier nonverbal mechanisms. We grunt, groan, cry, laugh, threaten, and implore with facial expressions, postures, movements, and all the paralinguistic mechanisms at our disposal. All of these have many functions but none are more important than serving as distance regulation signals.

Lazarus (1993) has presented a relational theory of affects. Each of 15 affects is thought to arise from a different relational theme involving the person and his or her environment. Lazarus takes the position that the particular emotion experienced depends upon the person's thoughts about the encounter, particularly the harms and benefits involved. It seems apparent that the harms and benefits involved can be translated into distance regulation language.

Our understanding of the biology of affects is in its infancy. Reviewing a few of the possibilities suggested by research may hint at the complexity that is certainly involved. Davidson and his colleagues present evidence that positive and negative affects are associated with left- and right-sided cerebral activation, respectively (Davidson, Ekman, Saron, Senulis & Friesen, 1990). They suggest that positive emotions are associated generally with approach, and negative emotions with withdrawal. Dawson and her co-workers investigated affective behavior and frontal lobe activity in the infants of depressed and nondepressed mothers (Dawson, Klinger, Panagiotides, Hill & Spicker, 1992). They found evidence of reduced left-frontal activity during playful interactions with their mothers in the infants of symptomatic mothers, along with a failure to find right-frontal activation during maternal separation. Fox (1991) has presented a model of affective arousal that specifically involves the decision about approach or withdrawal leading to asymmetric activation of the two frontal regions. George and colleagues have recently presented evidence from brain-imaging techniques that extend the knowledge derived from earlier brain electrical studies (George, Ketter, Parekh, Horwitz, Herscovitch & Post, 1995).

In addition to the now firm evidence for cerebral asymmetry of the affects involving approach and withdrawal, there is mounting evidence to support sex differences in the biology of affects. A multitude of studies were recently reviewed in *The New York Times* and, in particular, I note those studies suggesting that there are sex differences in how well various emotions are recognized from facial expressions (Kolata, 1995). It appears that men, for example, have difficulty recognizing sadness in women's facial expressions, but no difficulty in recognizing sadness on the faces of other men or happiness on the faces of women.

Brothers (1989) suggests that empathy is a concept with great potential ability for bridging neural and psychological data. He reviews some of the clinical syndromes in which there are deficits in the ability to perceive the emotions of others, and includes autism and alexithymia. He notes that Ross (1981) has published evidence that certain right hemispheric lesions result in deficits in either producing or comprehending affective communication. It appears also, from the studies of twins, that empathy is further developed in infant girls than in infant boys, and that empathy appears to have a modest hereditary component (Zahn-Waxler, Robinson & Emde, 1992).

There are also suggestions that certain hormones may be associated with separateness-autonomy and connectedness-intimacy. Oxytocin has been designated the "cuddle hormone" because it is associated in experimental animals with social attachments (Angier, 1991). Mehlman and his colleagues demonstrated that, in free-ranging primates, affiliative behaviors were associated with high levels of cerebrospinal fluid derivatives of serotonin, and low levels were associated with more aggression and risk-taking (Mehlman, Higley, Faucher, Lilly, Taub, Vickers, Suomi & Linnoila, 1995). They note that the chemical variables appear to account for 20–40 percent of the variance in these behaviors, suggesting the multiplicity of factors involved.

The multiplicity of biologic factors that may play roles in both separateness-autonomy and connectedness-intimacy is only now being recognized. Clearly these are complex matters involving temperament, affective development, particular portions of the brain, gender differences, and, perhaps, various hormones and neurotransmitters. A few of these biological mechanisms are under some degree of genetic control. In trying to understand the strength of a particular individual's behavior systems for separateness and connectedness, the clinician must keep in mind that some of what is observed may represent differences in underlying biologic mechanisms.

Developmental Determinants

When the focus is turned to how developmental experiences can influence the strengths of the child's separateness-autonomy and connectedness-intimacy behavior systems, we enter another area of great complexity. The literature on early development is voluminous and, in addition to early psychoanalytic theoretical emphases, recent decades have brought a huge outpouring of empirical studies. These research findings have reaffirmed the central importance for subsequent development of the first several years of life. Empirical findings have also brought into question some of the earlier theoretical constructs, such as the hypothesized earliest periods of infantile symbiosis and autism. Indeed, it appears that from birth on, the infant is highly interactive with his or her environment (Stern, 1985).

The leadership role in the empirical approach to early development has been assumed by attachment researchers. Starting with Bowlby's theory of attachment and taking vigor from Mary Ainsworth's development of a measurement procedure—the Strange Situation test—the field of attachment research has exploded with studies and new findings (Bowlby, 1972, 1980, 1982; Ainsworth, 1989).

The Strange Situation test is based on a series of separations and reunions in a standard setting. Infants from one to two years of age are observed insofar as to their capacity to explore the toys in the room, their protest when mother leaves, and the quality of their reunion behavior when mother returns. Four types of attachment behaviors have been described: secure, insecure-anxious, insecure-avoidant, and disorganized. These types of attachment behaviors have intriguing, predictive powers for the child's subsequent developmental course through childhood and into adolescence.

There is a good deal of data that demonstrate that the infant's attachment behaviors are correlated with the quality of mothering the infant has received. There are also data that suggest that mothers of securely attached infants are more likely to report positive experiences of their own as children with their mothers than are the mothers of insecurely attached infants (Ainsworth, 1989). There are also data, including some from the Timberlawn Research Foundation's Young Family Project, demonstrating that the quality of the mother's marriage, rated before the infant's birth, influences the type of attachment behavior her infant develops (Lewis, 1989).

There has been much interest in looking at adult romantic relationships through the lens of attachment. The theory involves the establishment in the infant of an internal working model as a result of early attachment experiences. From this working model, a group of expectations about the self in relationships flow and, unless altered by later intense relationship experiences, they can form the template for adult relationships. Those who study this facet of attachment search for descriptions of adult relationships that parallel the basic types of infant attachment. They also explore the correspondence of retrospective accounts of early attachment and descriptions of current romantic relationships (Hazen & Shaver, 1987; Cohn, Silver, Cowan, Cowan & Pearson, 1992; Feeney & Noller, 1990; Bartholomew & Horowitz, 1991). Although there are methodological issues to be resolved, on balance this type of inquiry has yielded positive correspondences between infant and adult styles of attachment.

The aspect of attachment research that is most relevant for this theory of marital relationship is the inclusion in the Strange Situation test of measures of separateness-autonomy (the child's ability to move away from the mother and explore the surround) and connectedness-intimacy (both the quality of the infant's protest upon separation from the mother and the quality of his or her reunion behavior). Although it appears that reunion behaviors are most heavily weighted in arriving at attachment classification, it should be possible to obtain an early measure of the strength of both behavior systems through use of the Strange Situation paradigm. To my knowledge, however, Strange Situation data have not been analyzed in such a manner. Regardless, the revolution in the empirical study of early development brought about by attachment research has solidified the importance of crucial early experiences for the individual's subsequent development, including his or her balance of separateness-autonomy and connectedness-intimacy.

Social Determinants

The third major determinant of the strength of these two behavior systems is the family in which the child spends his or her formative years. Families vary tremendously regarding their emphasis on separateness and connectedness. In some families, the emphasis is heavily skewed toward separateness, autonomy, and successful individual competition. In other families, the skew is in the opposite direction and relationships, closeness, and being intensely connected are paramount. For some families, both separateness and connectedness are emphasized and family members often learn the importance of context in facilitating behaviors that invite separateness or connectedness.

There are many family variables that operate in concert to establish the emphases on separateness and connectedness. Perhaps at the core are shared underlying belief systems and values that reflect positions on universal issues. Although I will discuss this topic later in some detail, I refer here to such issues as: What is the basic nature of humankind? Is it dangerous to get close to others? What is the nature of the world? Is it orderly and knowable and can it be mastered through knowledge? Or is it random and do destiny and fate prevail to the extent that individual effort at mastery is of little consequence and need not be emphasized?

Shared family belief systems are most often not conscious constructs. If family members are asked about them, they may or may not acknowledge their importance. Often, the observer infers the underlying belief from the family's rules that govern relationships within the family. In observing family discussions, there are a small number of variables that may provide particular insights into the family's emphases on separateness-autonomy and connectedness-intimacy.

Those variables that facilitate the development of separateness-autonomy include:

1. Acceptance of individual differences

2. An insistence that family members speak clearly and honestly about their thoughts and feelings

3. Encouragement (most often by parental example) of the process of going out into the world

4. A focus on family members' areas of competence

5. Permission and/or encouragement to compete both within and outside the family

Those variables that facilitate the development of connectedness-intimacy include:

1. Encouragement of the sharing of a wide range of feelings

2. An acceptance of sharing vulnerabilities within the family

3. Encouragement of the development of high levels of empathy both for others in the family and for those outside the family

4. The modeling (most often by the parents) of open affection

5. Encouragement of friendships outside the family

These family processes are but examples used to illustrate some of the many ways in which what goes on in the family can play a crucial role in establishing the strength of the individual's behavior systems for separateness-autonomy and connectedness-intimacy. It is also most often through the family that individuals incorporate particular religious, ethnic, or social class influences on these behavior systems.

My brief discussions of these three categories of variables (biological, developmental, and social) that influence the development of the individual's capacity for separateness-autonomy and connectedness-intimacy is not meant to be inclusive; rather, it is to illustrate the complexity involved. It is, however, even more complex than I suggest because not only are there many other variables involved, but all the variables interact with each other and do so most often in ways that are difficult to know. If the idea of interaction is tested even in a simple way, the results are suggestive. One illustration is the work of Mangelsdorf and colleagues on the interaction of infant temperament and maternal personality (Mangelsdorf, Gunnar, Kestenbaum, Lang & Andreas, 1990). Neither infant proneness-to-distress nor maternal personality independently predicted attachment outcome, but attachment was predicted by the interaction of this temperament variable and maternal personality. Mangelsdorf suggests that these findings support a "goodness-of-fit" model of attachment.

From a different perspective, Maziade and colleagues examined the interaction of temperament in seven-year-olds and family functioning in predicting adolescent psychopathology (Maziade, Caron, Cote, Merette, Bernier, Laplante, Boutin & Thivierge, 1990). All adolescents in their study with difficult temperaments at age 7 and dysfunctional families were symptomatic at age 16. Once again, it was the interaction that was crucial.

I use the work of Mangelsdorf and Maziade to illustrate the importance of even simple interactions between variables. When we think about the development of the individual's behavior systems for separateness-autonomy and connectedness-intimacy, there may be a dozen or more important variables involved, all of which interact with each other in ways we can only begin to imagine.

3. The Balance of Separateness-Autonomy and Connectedness-Intimacy

Each individual can be understood as having a more-or-less stable balance of separateness-autonomy and connectedness-intimacy that may be altered in response to life circumstances or developmental challenges.

The use of the phrase "more-or-less" signifies the presence of a significant qualification to this premise. The issue is to what extent the individual's life is understood as continuous and how much emphasis is given to discontinuities over the life course. Continuity is basic to the concept of personality itself in that it speaks to the relatively enduring ways the individual experiences himself or herself and the world.

On the other hand, discontinuities—defined as distinct changes—appear to occur with surprising frequency. Some individuals mellow as they age and others discover a quality of assertiveness heretofore missing. Marriage can change one for better or worse. Parenthood can lead to the discovery of qualities hidden from view before a child is born. Some losses lead to chronic depression. Chronic unemployment can change the individual's relationships with important others as well as with the self. Experiences in the Armed Forces during war-time can leave lasting impact—sometimes for the better, but sometimes for the worse. A religious conversion, a near fatal illness or accident, the adoption of a new belief system—the list could go on and on.

Thus, it appears that life has some continuity (although we may read in more than there "really" is), but discontinuities are very common. When it comes to the premise that each individual has a more-or-less stable balance of separateness-autonomy and connectedness-intimacy, there are simply no data that I know of to either support or disprove the premise. My including it as one of the premises is based on my clinical work and my observation that the premise has utility.

It is almost always possible to help individuals formulate their own estimates of the strength of each of these behavioral systems. They sometimes emphasize continuity ("I've been shy, a loner since I can remember. I had no trouble getting things done and I could take care of myself—but never got too close to anyone"). Others describe discontinuities ("As a kid I was horribly insecure and avoided relationships. The Navy fixed that—it taught me how to be part of a team, how to relate to others—and my confidence soared").

Thus far, I have discussed these two behavior systems as if they were relatively independent of each other. They are not, of course, and they influence each other in complex ways. Common examples involve the individual who overcomes the inability to relate closely to others, in part, as a consequence of successful individual functioning. On the other hand the confidence in one's self growing out of a deeply meaningful and successful relationship may inspire the individual to experiment with higher levels of individual autonomy than ever before.

4. Psychological Maturity or Health

Psychological maturity or health involves the capacity for both separateness-autonomy and connectedness-intimacy.

This premise addresses this culture's traditional emphasis on separateness-autonomy as the major construct in psychological health. Within psychoanalytic-psychodynamic circles, the literature of recent decades has been filled with theories supporting separation-individuation as the organizing metaphor in thinking about healthy development and psychological maturity. Provoked by confrontations from feminist writers and augmented by increasing recognition of ethnocentrism, a gradual shift has taken place. The shift involves an increasing emphasis on the capacity for relationships, and therefore, connectedness-intimacy, as equal in importance to separateness-autonomy in the definition of health.

Thus, this premise states that for both men and women to be considered healthy or well functioning, there should be evidence of the capacities for both separateness-autonomy and connectedness-intimacy. This premise is not meant to minimize the importance of data suggesting that there likely are sex differences of a biologic nature in the roots of these two behavior systems. Rather, it is to emphasize that the ideal of health and maturation for both sexes involves transcending to whatever degree possible whatever biologic factors influence the capacity for either separateness-autonomy or connectedness-intimacy.

5. Underlying Fears

Both separateness-autonomy and connectedness-intimacy may be associated with underlying, frequently unconscious fears.

Fears of separateness and fears of closeness are considered ubiquitous, but we have very little empirical data. The deficiency is most marked regarding representative samples. In psychotherapy, it is usually easy to help patients organize diverse experiences around themes of loss, aloneness, abandonment, separation and/or being invaded, and merger with loss of sense of self, or around themes involving aggression and death. From such crystallizations, patients can develop insight and metaphors that organize their experiences. In this way, they may come to feel an increasing sense of mastery. Whether or not such themes would arise from exploratory interviews with nonclinical samples is unknown—at least, I am not aware of any such studies.

And yet there is every reason to believe that such fears are deeply ingrained in human experience. Yalom (1980), for example, in his discussion of the ultimate concerns of existential theory, presents the viewpoint that these concerns are fundamental. They are believed to be a part of each person, but are usually more hidden than concerns about dependency, anger, and the like. Yalom's four ultimate concerns—death, freedom, isolation, and meaninglessness—can be understood as having much to do with separateness and connectedness. Death, for example, can be understood as either separation from important others or reunion with deceased loved ones. Freedom, as defined by Yalom, relates to the absence of external structure—the awareness that one constructs his or her own world, that there is nothing "there" but what one constructs. In this regard, freedom is a statement of one's essential aloneness. Existential isolation refers to the final, unbridgeable gap that exists between self and the world. Meaninglessness springs from the awareness that life is of one's own making, that in that construction one is essentially alone, and that death awaits.

It seems clear that the underlying emphasis in Yalom's four ultimate concerns involves fears associated with separateness. Many have agreed that separateness is the fundamental fear. Being cast out, exiled, and abandoned have been the ultimate punishment. As Tracy Kidder wrote in *Old Friends* (1993), separateness is the universal problem: "The original punishment, the ultimate vulnerability, the enemy of meaning" (p. 345).

Bowlby (1973, 1980, 1982) has written that intense reactions to early separation from mother have had survival value through the ages. Hofer (1984) has suggested that dyadic relationships have regulatory functions for the participants and that separation may lead to loss of physiologic regulation. Silverman's work with subliminal stimulation involving merger statements in which a broad variety of functions show improvement following presentation of such stimuli may also speak to the centrality of both the fear of separation and the longing for connection (Silverman, Lachmann & Milich, 1982).

In psychotherapeutic work, fears of connection (in the form of closeness, commitment, or intimacy) are at least as frequent as—if not more frequent than—fears of separateness. Once again, however, we are on thin ice in regard to the prevalence of such fears in nonclinical samples and, if they are broadly present, to whether or not they can be retrieved with interviews.

With all the gaps in our knowledge about underlying, frequently unconscious fears, there is still sufficient clinical knowledge and theoretical prominence to accord such fears an important place in a theory of marital systems.

6. A Central Relationship from Childhood

For most individuals it is possible to identify a central problematic relationship from childhood that is the source of the underlying fears.

This premise reaches back to the individual's family-of-origin experiences to locate the source of the fears of separateness-autonomy or connectedness-intimacy. Once again I am not aware of systematic data from representative samples that inform as to the prevalence of a central problematic relationship from childhood. The problems of retrieving such memories and their interpretation are legion. Main and her associates, for example, have developed an interview technique (The Adult Attachment Interview) to retrieve the nature of adults' early attachments to their parents (Main & Goldwyn, 1988; Main, Kaplan & Cassidy, 1985). The scoring of the Interview relies more on the subject's ability to tell a coherent story than it does on the actual content of the memories. Our research at Timberlawn Research Foundation demonstrates that women's memories of their fathers change during the early years of parenthood, and the change is associated with here-and-now problems the women's husbands are experiencing (Lewis & Owen, 1995).

Despite the absence of a solid base of empirical knowledge of representative samples, patients in many forms of psychotherapy (including marital therapy) almost always present a central problematic relationship from childhood. The problematic relationship issues range from most severe (sexual abuse, physical abuse, extreme neglect) to those that appear more subtle (excessive demands, highly contingent affection, subtle parental favoritism for another sibling).

Following recent leads in psychotherapy research, it is useful to develop a three-part synopsis of the problematic relationship. The first part focuses on what it was that the individual wanted from the important person from childhood (e.g., affection, affirmation, protection). The second part involves how that important person responded to the wish (e.g., with disregard, inconsistency, outright rejection). The third part of the synopsis focuses on how the individual responded to the important other's response (e.g., with continued effort, retreat into self, blaming self). This gives the central problematic relationship from childhood an interactional cast that lends itself to the search for parallels in here-and-now adult relationships.

These early problematic relationships can be seen as resulting in fears, fears that may operate across a wide variety of adult relationships. The fears may lead to avoidance of relationships, or to relationships that can be understood as tests of the individual's childhood hypothesis, or to relationships that heal in the sense of diminishing or extinguishing the fears.

Some patients do not report a central problematic relationship from childhood. Often, however, what they report is the absence of an early family milieu that emphasizes either connectedness-intimacy or separateness-autonomy. Most often this involves families that emphasize separateness but not connectedness. Children growing up in these families may not fear connecting closely with others; rather they have not learned how to do so. Many such individuals are more readily able to learn how to relate closely than are those with clear reasons to fear closeness.

7. Attraction to Specific Others

Individuals are drawn to specific others for many reasons, including the unconscious attempt to repair the central problematic relationship from childhood.

One of the most intriguing observations of longitudinal research is that some persons have adult experiences that undo the harmful effects of central problematic relationships from childhood. Most, if not all, of such healing experiences appear to involve new connections—with a confidant, a therapist, or a new belief system. The most frequently observed turning point in the lives of individuals, however, is entering into a stable marriage in which there are both low levels of conflict and the opportunity for confiding. I have summarized in Chapter 2 and in another publication (Lewis, 1996) some of the studies that suggest that relationships with low levels of conflict and the presence of confiding have implications for both the psychological and physical health of the participants.

Kernberg (1991) discusses two levels of the unconscious search involved in marriage. One is primarily oedipal in the sense that each partner searches for the ideal opposite sex partner with whom sex and tenderness may be experienced. Kernberg also suggests that for women, the lover represents the pre-Oedipal mother who satisfies her dependency needs and is tolerant of her sexual intimacy with the symbolic Oedipal object.

There are, in addition, more specific dynamics involving the unconscious wish to repair the dominant pathogenic relationship from the past and "the temptation to repeat them in terms of unfulfilled aggressive and revengeful needs" (Kernberg, 1991, p. 50). The actual reenactment with the lover is the result of this inner struggle between the forces of repair and repeat. Each partner tends to induce in the other, through projective identification, the past Oedipal or pre-Oedipal conflicts around aggression. It thus appears that the repair-repeat dilemma is, for Kernberg, decided by the severity of the conflict with the early object, the amount of unresolved aggression, and the strength of the unconscious wish for vengeance.

That healing marriages occur is without question. Once we move beyond their documented occurrence, however, we know very little. How frequently they occur is not known. Whether they represent lucky occurrences like fortunate spins of the marital roulette wheel or are lawful in the sense of resulting from factors that can be learned is also unknown.

Rutter (1988) has discussed whether or not the healing process is likely to be found in the presence of certain characteristics of the individual (e.g., planfulness), in the presence of certain characteristics of the spouse (e.g., absence of serious psychopathology), or in the nature of the relationship itself (e.g., confiding). He finds support for all three possibilities.

If one takes as a starting place Meissner's (1978) transference theory of marriage, the emphasis would fall on the unconscious motivation to repeat the central problematic relationship from childhood with the spouse. Healing would occur when the transference was not allowed to unfold.

I prefer to believe that the search for healing experiences—both those in which one is the healer and those in which one is healed—are important and neglected aspects of basic human motivation. Searles (1975) has been one of the few voices proclaiming the important dynamic of the need to heal, and he suggests that the dynamic begins with the infant's wish to relieve the mother's anxiety about their interaction.

It is possible, however, that there are yet-to-be-discovered aspects of an individual's psychological makeup that load the scales in the direction of repeating rather than repairing the childhood injury. It is tempting to think that severity of psychopathology may play a role, with the most disturbed tending to repeat and those with lesser disturbances tending to repair—although several studies found this not to be the case (Rutter, 1988).

Notwithstanding our lack of convincing empirical data, I find it useful in working with couples to posit marital dysfunction as failed healing. In doing so, the emphasis is on the issues of separateness-autonomy and connectedness-intimacy. Statements like, "You hoped to find a relationship in which you felt safe from abandonment" or "You wanted a relationship in which you could feel safe from your fears of intrusion by a powerful other" are common organizing themes. In this, as in other therapeutic work, the emphasis moves from identifying the wish to identifying the way in which the individual gets in the way of the gratification of such wishes.

It is known that individuals are attracted to each other for multiple reasons. Appearance, personality features, similar backgrounds and values, stage of life, and other reasons are all involved. In this clinical theory of marital systems the major focus is on those unconscious factors in mate selection that reflect the underlying search for a healing experience.

On a few occasions, the search for healing is not apparent in the clinical material and, indeed, the data suggest the opposite dynamic: the unconscious selection of a spouse because he or she will *not* interfere with a pathological fixation on a childhood object. The woman still tied to a charismatic father, who selects a methodical man with little interest in or ability to help her emerge from her father-fixation is an example. Here the dynamic is not healing, but rather a prolongation of the early relationship.

8. Definition of the Relationship

The central task of relationship formation is the definition of the relationship, in particular establishing a balance of separateness-autonomy and connectedness-intimacy that is reasonably comfortable (relatively fear from fear) for both participants.

In the early stages of a relationship of emotional intensity, with a hoped-for indefinite future, the process of establishing the basic relationship dimensions begins. Each person brings to the process of definition a number of desires. Some of these are conscious and reflect experiences in particular family, ethnic, and class cultures. Popular stereotypes from the media may play decisive roles. In addition, unconscious factors are involved and these reflect another wide range of experiences. In the preceding premise, the unconscious wish for a healing experience was hypothesized as a significant part of the choice of a partner. The characteristics of the chosen partner may include the general characteristics of effective therapists (e.g., empathy, warmth, and genuineness), but specific qualities that are corrective for particular deficiencies in one's sense of self are also sought.

So often, neither partner is actually what the other thought during the early intoxicated phase of the relationship. Perhaps as a consequence, each partner tries to define the relationship by attempting to change his or her partner.

The process of defining the relationship usually occurs around everyday issues and there is rarely conscious awareness that discussions and disagreements about money, in-laws, sex, time, space, and all the other daily issues are actually about the "big" questions: "What kind of relationship are we to have?" "How much of what kind of closeness and separateness can we agree upon?" "How is the nature of the relationship to be decided?"

At the core of the relationship's definition are the issues of separateness-autonomy and connectedness-intimacy. If the spouses come easily to an agreement about the amount and quality of these two dimensions of their relationship, the developmental course of the relationship is very apt to go smoothly. If one participant imposes his or her wishes on the other participant, the developmental course of the relationship may be somewhat difficult. If the participants cannot agree and each continues in the attempt to unilaterally define these two dimensions, there is apt to be chronic conflict or termination of the relationship.

Although biological, developmental, and family factors can influence each participant's attempt to define the relationship, often his or her efforts can be understood as driven by fear. Each person attempts to negotiate a balance of separateness-autonomy and connectedness-intimacy that is relatively free from fear. When both partners are highly satisfied with the relationship, it is safe to assume that they have found a balance of these two dimensions that is relatively free from fear for both of them. This balance may be skewed in the direction of either separateness-autonomy or connectedness-intimacy and may seem unusual to the outside observer, but it "works" for both partners because it does not impinge too heavily on the fears of either.

The idea that central to relationship formation and key marital dynamics is the balance of separateness-autonomy and connectedness-intimacy has preoccupied many students for many years. Those whose descriptions have been particularly helpful to me include Rausch and his colleagues, Kantor and Lehr, Napier, Jacobson and Margolin, Jacobson, Fogarty, Johnson and Greenberg, and Feldman. (Rausch, Barry, Hertel, and Swain (1974), Kantor and Lehr (1975), Napier (1988), Jacobson and Margolin (1979), Jacobson (1989), Fogarty (1976), Johnson and Greenberg (1994), and Feldman (1979).*

9. Affects and Their Communication

Affects and their communication are central to the establishment of the balance of separateness-autonomy and connectedness-intimacy that characterizes the relationship.

---

* See my reviews of Kantor and Lehr (1975), *Inside the Family*; Napier (1988), *The Fragile Bond*; and Johnson and Greenberg (1994), *The Heart of the Matter*, (Eds.), in the Reading Notes on pages 251, 252, and 250–251, respectively.

Affect is considered to be the primary organizing force in social interactions. Most commonly, it is through the expression of affect that the individual signals his or her wish to approach or retreat from another. The expression of affect also signals another either to come closer or to retreat. Earlier in this chapter, I noted several of the studies that suggest something of the biological, developmental, and social roots of an individual's affective systems.

Within a culture, the expression of certain affects signals the wish for increased closeness. Sadness and fear are examples. Other affects signal the wish for increased distance. Disgust and anger are examples. The response of the other—particularly in relationships of emotional importance—to the expression of affect is crucial for the quality of the relationship. Disregarding an important other's affective signals often leads to despair and conflict. Responding to the expressed affects by recognizing them accurately and letting the sender know that the feelings are understood is crucial to the empathic process. Other terms are sometimes used to describe this level of empathy. Examples are attunement and mirroring. Deeper levels of empathy involve actually experiencing the affects of the other.

When two individuals share a deeply felt affective experience, there is often a feeling of intense closeness, bonding, or oneness. Such affective experiences are the hallmark of psychological intimacy and may lead to a profound sense of new meaning for the partners.

Recently, Goleman (1995) has brought together a large group of studies regarding the importance of affect. He has coined the phrase "emotional intelligence." At the heart of this multifactorial construct is the ability of the individual to be in touch with his or her feelings from moment to moment while being sensitive to the feelings of others. From this perspective, psychotherapists come to know individuals with vast differences in emotional intelligence. Some of these differences almost certainly reflect hard-wired biological variations. Other differences, however, are better understood as reflecting ego-defensive operations related to unresolved feelings from adverse childhood experiences. The differences may also reflect widely divergent family experiences regarding the expression of and response to feelings. Thus, the psychotherapist must consider a wide array of factors that can influence the couple's capacity to express and respond to a wide array of affects.

10. Negotiating Around Five Issues

The balance of separateness-autonomy and connectedness-intimacy in the relationship is subtly "negotiated" around five issues: closeness (sharing), commitment (priority), intimacy (vulnerability), separateness, and power.

In the research at Timberlawn Research Foundation, we have found that collecting data regarding each of these five issues provides an overview of the balance of separateness-autonomy and connectedness-intimacy. Berman and Lief (1975) identified these same five issues as crucial for relationship formation. Couples must face important questions regarding these issues, questions that can hardly be avoided.

The issue of *closeness* is defined here in terms of how much of their lives the spouses are to share. Will they come to agree on basic values? How many interests and activities will they share? Will they share the same level of investment in parenting if they decide to have children? Will they have many shared friends? Will they share satisfaction in their sexual life? There is considerable variation among couples in this sharing perspective on closeness. Some spouses share very little of their lives and others appear to share so extensively that it is difficult to find areas of separateness.

Commitment refers to the emotional priority of the relationship for both participants. At a practical level, the question is whether there is any other person who is more important to either spouse than each is to the other. The other person may be a child, parent, sibling, friend, or lover, and if the relationship with that person has greater emotional significance than the marital relationship, there is a problem with commitment.

Although many couples seen in therapy indicate high levels of commitment, there are those couples in which each spouse has another relationship of higher emotional priority. Couples in which one spouse has less commitment to the marriage than the other spouse are also common in clinical samples.

Intimacy is defined here more narrowly than it usually is by other students of relationships. Waring (1988), for example, has been one of the most productive investigators of intimacy, but starts his work from a much broader definition of intimacy than do I.* Intimacy as used here

---

* See my review of Waring (1988), *Enhancing Marital Intimacy*, in the Reading Notes on pp. 257–258.

is the ability to share vulnerabilities. When each spouse participates in reciprocal sharing of vulnerabilities, the relationship is considered to be intimate.

Vulnerabilities involve those secret wishes, fears, hopes, dreams, and fantasies that are usually kept private for fear that exposing them will result in some negative, harmful response. When couples are intimate, it is often noted by them as one of the most important aspects of their relationship.

Clearly, intimacy involves being in touch with one's own inner world and trusting that sharing that world will not turn out badly. How common intimacy is in contemporary life is not known. Wynne and Wynne (1986) believe it is quite rare—a luxury of sorts—that eludes most couples. In our research volunteer samples, we find that 20 to 25 percent of middle and upper middle class couples had intimate relationships, but intimacy was much less frequent in economically-deprived couples (Lewis & Looney, 1983).

Separateness speaks to the ability of the spouses to accept the ways in which they differ from each other. To accept the ways in which the other has different values, interests, activities, and friends acknowledges differences and is the first step toward respect for each other's subjective reality.

The capacity of the spouses to agree on the ways in which they differ, to accept the ways in which they will be separate in contrast to fighting over what is "right" or "the truth," is an important determinant of how much separateness and connectedness will prevail in their relationship. Accepting the ways in which each partner differs from the other facilitates the development of greater levels of connectedness and sets the stage for intimacy.

Power is the most important variable in the couple's attempts to define their relationship. This is so because if one spouse has greater power he or she may prevail in unilateral decisions as to how much of what kind of closeness, commitment, intimacy, and separateness will characterize the relationship. Thus, the subtle negotiation of the balance of separateness-autonomy and connectedness-intimacy is intensely political. Marriage is, as emphasized by Rose (1983), usually the most political experience of an individual's life. She states that marriages fail not just because people fall out of love but, more often, due to failure in their joint political process.

In the attempt to define the relationship, both participants bring to the process all of those power tactics developed in earlier life. For some, those tactics are overtly aggressive; for others, they are better described as passive-aggressive; for some, the tactics are deliberately manipulative. For many, however, power tactics are primarily persuasive, even charismatic. As noted before, the surface issues are everyday disagreements, and the cumulative outcome sets the tenor of the relationship more than any other single factor.

Thus, the position taken here is that spouses cannot *not* deal with power. It is a "given"—every human system must establish some sort of organizational structure and, in the doing, each participant strives to influence the other to accept an organizational structure in keeping with his or her individual needs and fears.

11. Repetitive Interactional Patterns and the Development of Relational Structure

Out of the negotiation of these five issues, repetitive interactional patterns develop that come to serve as rules that regulate actual and metaphorical distance in the relationship. Over time, these interactional patterns become relatively stable and are considered the relational structure.

As the term is used here, I wish to emphasize those interactional patterns that regulate separateness and connectedness in the relationship. These patterns or rules govern the circumstances in which greater separateness-autonomy or greater connectedness-intimacy is to be acceptable to both participants. The rules provide operating guidelines that inform as to the circumstances in which one person may move toward or away from the other physically. The rules, however, have a more important function than the regulation of physical space: they also regulate metaphorical space.

A key issue in regulating metaphorical space concerns the sharing of subjective experiences. What are the circumstances in which inner experience is disclosed? What are the rules regarding the kind of response to be made to the inner experience of the other? When is help in exploring that experience indicated? When is giving advice the preferred response? There are a large number of such issues regarding closeness to or distance from the subjective experience of an important other. Because of the complexity, it would not be possible to deal with each interchange as a new experience. Some sort of structure is required, a system of rules that provide general guidelines.

This relational structure is relatively stable. One way of looking at the developmental phases of a marriage, however, it to look at those periods that make changing the rules either necessary or adaptive. Thus, both the intensity and quality of separateness and connectedness within the relationship can change because of developmental challenges or because of stressful life events.

A common clinical observation in couples who come for assessment and therapy after some years of a stable, satisfactory marriage is that one partner is involved in a unilateral attempt to change the rules governing separateness-autonomy and connectedness-intimacy. The conflict involves either how acceptable the new rules are to the other partner or whether it is acceptable that one partner tries to change the rules unilaterally.

12. Relational Structures Either Facilitate or Fail to Facilitate Continuing Healthy Development

Although any relational structure may persist and be experienced as satisfactory by the participants, certain structures facilitate the continued healthy development of the participants and others do not.

It is a remarkable irony that individuals select mates and participate in the establishment of a relational structure that may come to haunt them. A basic premise of this theory of marital systems is that relational structures have profound importance for the life of the participants. At one extreme are those structures that encourage the continued healthy development of both participants. At the other extreme are relational structures that facilitate the development of serious psychopathology in one or both participants. In the middle ground are relationships that neither encourage growth nor facilitate psychopathology; rather, they more-or-less assist each participant to maintain his or her psychological status quo.

The relationship of individual development, health, and maturity to the interpersonal context in which the individual lives his or her life is, at the minimum, circular. Individual psychological health increases the probability of relationship competence, and relationship competence increases the probability of individual health.

The questions about relational structures that facilitate healthy development cannot be answered completely. In Chapter 4, I discussed the characteristics of competent marriages as revealed in the research studies at Timberlawn Research Foundation, and those observations are a starting place to search for a thorough understanding of healing relationships.

As discussed in Chapter 4, however, relational structures have even broader implications for the participants. There is a growing body of empirical data suggesting that the nature of one's primary emotional bond influences physical health. At this relatively early stage of research, it appears two relationship variables may be involved in the interface with physical health. One involves the level of conflict; the other, whether or not the relationship is confiding. If there are relatively low levels of conflict and the capacity to exchange confidences exists, there is a good likelihood of better physiologic regulation of blood pressure and enhanced immune functioning.

In Chapter 4, I also commented briefly on the correlation of satisfaction with one's marriage and both overall life satisfaction and the sense of meaning in one's life.

It is important, however, to recognize that marital satisfaction measures are not without their problems. For the most part, this reflects the observation that individuals can be satisfied with relationships seen by outside experts as significantly dysfunctional.

13. Parental Relationship Structures and the Psychological Development of Children

Certain parental relational structures increase the probability of healthy psychological development of children raised by the couple and other parental relational structures do not.

Three relationships are crucial for shaping the healthy development of the child in the family. One is the mother-child relationship; the second is the father-child relationship; and the third is the parents' relationship with one another. The more recently evolved concept that the nature of the parents' relationship has a powerful impact on the child's development has received increasing support from systematic longitudinal family research. I will illustrate this empirical documentation of what therapists have known for years at a clinical level with examples from our own research.

The parents relational structure as studied during the mother's first pregnancy predicts infant-mother attachment behaviors at age one year and at other developmental markers for the child. Further, this effect appears to operate separately from the influence of either mother's or father's personality (Lewis, 1989). In those instances of marital dysfunction (measured prenatally), it is also possible at one year to observe triangular interactions involving infant, mother, and father that appear to parallel dysfunctional family triangles observed clinically with some symptomatic adolescents and their parents.

Thus, the important stage of marital development involving the incorporation of the child into the family in a healthy way is clearly threatened by preexisting marital dysfunction. This research and that of other family researchers adds a beginning empirical foundation to the observations of clinicians regarding the importance of a stable and satisfactory parental marital relationship as a safeguard against the development of destructive crossgenerational alliances.

14. Developmental Course of Marital Relationship Structures

Marital relational structures undergo a developmental course that often includes changes in the levels of separateness-autonomy and connectedness-intimacy.

For several decades, great credence has been placed in the concept that development occurs in an orderly way. Whether one is discussing the development of individuals, marriages, or families, there has been broad acceptance of this premise. How much the presumed orderliness of development is a reflection of the needs of observers to impose upon complex processes occurring over time a much simplified organizing scheme is not known. Empirical support can be found at the level of the individual for both continuity and discontinuity of developmental processes, but it is well to note that empirical support for the orderly development of marital and family systems is extremely rare. In the absence of empirical support, theoretical models of system development have arisen, some of which emphasize periods of crisis, conflict, and resolution as necessary and normal developmental processes.

Once again, I wish to illustrate something of the greater complexity that may be involved by briefly summarizing some of the research at the Timberlawn Research Foundation (Lewis, 1989). We studied couples' marital relationships both prior to and following the birth of their first child, a time calling for major accommodations in the marriage. We found that some types of relational structures were remarkably stable during the transition to parenthood, with no signs of crisis, conflict, and resolution. Other types of relational structures (those with significant conflict before the baby was born) did appear to go through crisis, increased conflict, and resolution. Further, the resolution was of an unpredictable nature that ranged from dissolution of the marriage to continued conflict to significant conflict resolution. This piece of rare empirical research suggests what makes intuitive sense: The nature of a couple's adaptation to parenting is clearly influenced by how well they had established a relational structure that was highly satisfactory to both before their child was born.

Despite the relative lack of empirical data regarding the orderly development of marital and family systems, clinical work with couples and families reinforce the utility of developmental formats. Over and over, couples come for help at times in which some alteration in the balance of separateness-autonomy and connectedness-intimacy appears either required or desired. Thus, clinicians need to be sensitive to those situations in which developmental challenges are not being met and the marriage is becoming increasingly conflicted or alienated.

15. Underlying Value Systems

Marital relational structures both reflect underlying value systems and memorialize them over time.

There is growing interest in the idea that marital relational structures reflect jointly held values that are often not openly articulated. Couples may be able to articulate their shared values spontaneously, or may acknowledge such values only when such are presented to them, or may deny important values when presented with them despite behaving as if such values were present.

When to this problem of validating a couple's values is added the complexity arising from a failure of the participants to realize consciously that the values are shared and are a central part of the relationship, the task of studying marital values systematically may seem overwhelming.

Reiss (1981) has written cogently about underlying, shared family paradigms (values) and suggests that the presence of particular paradigms must most often be inferred from both the way the spouses treat each other and the way they relate to the outside world.

There is also the problem of which values to consider. In my interviews with couples, I most often use Spiegel's (1982) modification of the Kluckhohns' (1951) key values (as slightly modified by this author). The modified Spiegel list of values is presented in Exhibit 5.3.

I also use the Rokeach Value Survey, a forced ranking of terminal values and a similar ranking of instrumental values (Rokeach & Ball-Rokeach, 1989). I search for significant areas of agreement and disagreement about the relative importance of different values. I may ask couples to discuss their differences regarding values in which they differ greatly.

From the perspective of the theory of marital relational structures presented here, I am particularly interested in knowing how much each spouse values separateness, independence, individuality, and autonomy as contrasted with connectedness, relatedness, closeness, and intimacy. It is also useful to know where the emphasis each spouse places on such values has arisen—particularly whether these values have been passed on over many generations or have arisen out of each spouse's own life experiences.

Finally, it is important to recognize that almost regardless of what individuals say about their values, it is the ways in which they relate to each other and to the world that not only reflect their values but carry them forward into the future. It is, of course, not what parents tell their children that is internalized by the children as much as the ways in which the parents relate to each other, to the children, and to the world.

These 15 premises comprise the foundation for my approach to the assessment and treatment of couples, which I describe in the chapters that follow.

EXHIBIT 5.3
Important Value Orientations*

Time

I. Our perspective of time is influenced by an emphasis on:
   A. Past: Focus on ancestors and family traditions
   B. Present: Focus on current day-to-day issues
   C. Future: Focus on long-term goals that take time to achieve

Activity

II. The preferred pattern of action in interpersonal relations is influenced by an emphasis on:
   A. Doing: Focus on getting things done
   B. Being: Focus on spontaneous expression of feelings and actions
   C. Being-in-becoming: Focus on the development of different aspects of the person in a rounded and integrated fashion

Relational Orientation

III. The preferred way of relating in groups is influenced by an emphasis on:
   A. Individual: Focus on autonomy and independence
   B. Collateral: Focus on a shared responsibility to a collectivity such as the family, community, or the larger society
   C. Lineal: Focus on a hierarchical orientation

Man–Nature Orientation

IV. The way people relate to the natural world is influenced by an emphasis on:
   A. Harmony-with-nature: Focus on adapting to nature
   B. Mastery-over-nature: Focus on controlling nature
   C. Subjugated-to-nature: Focus on accepting nature

Relationship with the Supernatural

V. The way people think about the supernatural is influenced by an emphasis on:
   A. The belief in a personal God
   B. The belief in an orderly universe
   C. The belief in fate, chance, or randomness

Basic Nature of Humanity

VI. The attitudes held about the innate good or evil in human behavior is influenced by an emphasis on:
   A. Good: Focus on the belief that people are born good
   B. Evil: Focus on the belief that people are born bad
   C. Neutral/Mixed: Focus on the belief that people are born neither good nor evil, but more likely a blank slate to be developed

Gender

VII. The way people think about gender roles is influenced by an emphasis on:
   A. The belief that men are naturally stronger than women
   B. The belief that women are naturally stronger than men
   C. The belief that neither men nor women are naturally stronger

* Modified from Spiegel, (1982). An ecological model of ethnic families. In M. McGoldrick, J.K. Pearce, & J. Giordano (Eds.), *Ethnicity and Family Therapy*. New York: Guilford Press. Used with permission.

6

Assessment: First Contacts

They were referred by her therapist, who said that the husband was very powerful and needed a "strong man" that he could look up to—that prior attempts at couples therapy had failed either because he wasn't confronted enough or because he had been dismissive of women therapists. The wife was described as a capable professional who was moderately depressed and trying to learn greater assertiveness.

As I thought about this information I found myself wondering how much of the wife's therapist's brief synopsis I would come to agree with. Would the husband be as powerful as the therapist suggested? How much of her conclusions reflected issues of her own—issues I recalled as her former training director? As a resident, she was a very competent diagnostician and had developed unusual skills in the prescription of psychotropic drugs. As a beginning therapist, she struggled, successfully at times, to manage her tendency to be directive and to overmanage her patients' lives. She was seen by other residents as bright and capable, and I suspected she was more admired than liked. In her supervision with me, she resisted taping her sessions and struggled about minor administrative issues.

I saw her vulnerable only once. She lost a close election for the chief residency to an affable and very popular young man. She came to me hurting and struggling not to reveal too much of her fierce competitiveness and the injury she felt in not winning.

I knew something of her deprived childhood from her autobiographical statement written when she applied for the residency. I had interviewed her at that time and felt much admiration for her bootstrapping her way up without family assistance, from junior college to nursing school to pre-med courses while working nights as a nurse, and finally to medical school. She had taken charge of her life and done what few do. Along the way, perhaps she had little time or inclination to learn the nuances of relating closely to others. Life had been a struggle for survival, and she had not only survived but, I thought, done, remarkably well.

I start with this information about the referring doctor because the assessment process begins with the initial information. It is impossible not to be influenced by it and one's thinking can often be skewed by that information. I prefer not to have any information until I have seen the couple one or two times and then, information from others has a greater opportunity to be more helpful than mischievous. My former resident knew about my position on this, but when she called, it was clear that she wanted me to know beforehand that she thought the husband was more the problem than the wife, that she wanted me to be "strong" with him, and that the wife needed to become more assertive with this domineering husband.

All of this may be so—my former resident might be right on target—but her formulation is a construction (just as mine will be) and into that construction there is often projected much of the therapist. Many clinicians either selectively see or selectively avoid those themes that have personal relevance. How much of her view of this couple included her struggles to overcome earlier oppression, achieve competence and status, and compete successfully in a professional world? At a different level, what does her referring this couple to me, accompanied by the mandate to be strong with the husband, say about the undercurrents of our relationship? Certainly, there is much left over from her days as a resident and the ways in which we both helped and failed each other. And so I wondered with much curiosity how the couple would present themselves.

> I did not have to wait long. He called and when I got back to him he began a telltale series of negotiations about an initial appointment. First, he wanted to see me privately—before I saw the two of them together. When I declined, he asked for evening or weekend appointments. I indicated that such was not possible and suggested several possible times on a date 10 days in the future. He refused these and countered with a date and time two weeks in the future. I told him I was at the medical school on that afternoon—and so it went. We finally

> agreed on a day and time and he then asked if I took insurance assignments. I said I didn't but that I tried to help patients retrieve as much of their fees as their policies allowed.
>
> After more requests to make an exception in their case—all of which would have set up special arrangements for them—I indicated that it seemed there was a good deal getting in the way of making an initial appointment and that I was wondering if something else was involved. He denied this and we settled on the day and time.

I found this telephone conversation tedious and began to think of him as controlling and difficult. He was a successful professional not tied to a rigid schedule. I suspected that his maneuvering about the insurance assignment was tactical in some way other than the money involved. His and his wife's income almost certainly were far more than adequate and of this talk about appointment times, seeing him alone, and accepting the insurance assignment seemed like an elaborate set of opening chess moves. I wondered what dynamics were behind it. Was he as power oriented and controlling as he seemed (and as my former resident suggested) or was he anxious about meeting with a senior professional, perhaps even fearful about being accepted? I also wondered what my former resident had told them about me. Had she said something to encourage his going through with the appointment—something that had impinged upon an old anxiety or fear of his?

This kind of silent musing is for me a necessary sort of internal processing that helps me deal with an early negative reaction about a patient or couple. With this man, the movement in my thoughts from thinking of him as power-seeking and controlling to considering him as anxious and afraid represents the kind of recasting that gets me off a defensive edge and allows me to have a better chance of meeting him, and them, with a more neutral and open set.

> They arrived 40 minutes early for their appointment. The receptionist reported that he seemed anxious and, although the wife sat and read, he paced about, went into the library, and generally appeared to be casing the place out. He asked if I were available and she told him I was with some-

one and should break at 2 P.M., the scheduled time for their appointment.

Although being 40 minutes early is not always a sign of anxiety, it frequently is. His pacing and taking everything in can also reflect underlying anxiety. On the other hand, my office is in a research building and there are psychiatric, psychologic, and medical journals on every table. There are pictures on many walls of past and present community leaders who have served on the Foundation's board. There is a bulletin board in clear view with newspaper and magazine articles about the Foundation's research. Young graduate students are here and there. There is a small kitchen-copying room open to the main waiting area and sometimes staff and students are seated at a table drinking coffee and talking. The ambiance is informal, and I am one of only several who wear a coat and tie. The scene is not at all like a typical doctor's office; rather it more resembles an academic setting. I point all of this out because my new patient's behavior may be a direct response to a setting that is unfamiliar to him—it may not necessarily be a deeply personal anxiety, although it could reflect both anxiety and the newness of the setting.

> I walked to the area in which they were sitting and introduced myself, shaking hands with each of them. We walked together the 40 or so feet to the entrance of my office and went in.
> My office is large and filled with books and art. At one end is a large writing table and in one corner are a television monitor and VCR. The major area contains a leather sofa and three comfortable chairs. This sitting area is arranged around a low table—and all of this is on an oriental rug. The lighting is from several lamps, and the large windows that look out on a peaceful patio area are covered with vertical blinds. There are often fresh-cut flowers arranged in an antique glass urinal on a low bookcase in front of the windows. One end of the room is entirely filled with books. Around my writing table are scores of manuscripts, reprints, and books—most of them in piles on the floor. There are usually some canvas briefcases (each containing a chapter or article in process) arranged against a far wall.

All of this is important because the office is a representation of myself and how I work. It is immediately taken in by those who enter it for the first time. It is part of the patient's or couple's diagnostic efforts—their efforts to label me, to place me in a particular category, to be able to think, "Oh, yes, I've dealt with this type before." Their diagnostic process is usually intense and designed to reduce uncertainty. It is as intriguing a process as the clinician's initial efforts to understand what patients and couples bring to the office, although it may not be as structured or systematic as the clinician's efforts.

The stimulus impact of the clinician's presence and of his or her office cannot be overestimated. It is important, for example, for me to keep in mind that I am older than most therapists. My hair is grey. Most of the year, I am deeply tanned from being outside in the Texas sun a part of each day. I am a large man—six feet four inches and 200 pounds.

Further, I really enjoy clinical work and suspect it shows. I am more active verbally with couples than in the individual therapy I do—but I've heard often enough that one of the things that can come across to people right from the start is that I seem to have a high level of interest in them and in their stories.

All of this and more form a complex set of stimuli that new patients are confronted with at the time of our initial face-to-face contact. The clinician's awareness of his or her stimulus impact is important in that much of what might otherwise be considered enduring traits of patients can more clearly be understood as responses to the clinician's presence and office. State explanations are not only generally kinder than trait explanations, but are more apt to be correct.

"Did you have much trouble locating me?"

"No," he said, "your secretary's directions were good—and recently I was at the cemetery next door for a funeral—so I kind of knew about where you were."

"We came very early," she said with a small smile, "because Ken has a thing about being late. We get to the airport an hour and a half before boarding time—and then just sit there waiting."

"Are you really that different about time?" I asked to neither of them in particular.

He responded, "Well, sort of—you see—"

She interrupted him and said, "Ken is very compulsive, very controlling, and a real perfectionist. He makes my life very difficult."

I nodded and said, "It sounds like the two of you aren't in agreement on certain aspects of your relationship—"

This opening 30 seconds of conversation was, I thought, remarkable. Had I just witnessed in a microcosm a fundamental piece of their dynamics? I reviewed quickly and silently the several points that seemed most important to me. He took the lead in responding to my question about the Foundation's out-of-the-way location, but within a few seconds she was at him—and with a smile. My attempt to depersonalize it—to make of their differences about time a neutral fact led, once again, to his response that was quickly interrupted by her describing him as compulsive, controlling, and a perfectionist. "He makes my life difficult" was her statement—and that intrigued me because here in the first 30 seconds of the first appointment she had taken the more powerful position both by defining him as the problem (and she as victim) and by interrupting him and taking charge of the direction of the interview.

If she seems so powerful in these first 30 seconds, how is it that she also experiences herself as victimized by his behavior? Is it that she maintains a fiction of his power, all the while being more the aggressor than he? Or is it that here—in the office and in the presence of an older man, a presumed expert—she can risk a retaliating aggression toward her husband, a kind of behavior too dangerous for her without the presumption of protection from a third party?

My last statement, "It sounds like the two of you aren't in agreement on certain aspects of your relationship—" was a reflection designed to open up the conversation to include how else they differed. This type of intervention is—like reflexive questions—designed to broaden the focus of inquiry and, for the clinician, to invite the unknown.

"Oh my God, Doctor, you're a master of understatement," she responded without obvious rancor.

"The problem is," he said with a sideways nod of his head and just the hint of high authority, "we have always been too damn different. From the start we have been apples and oranges. It's not just time—although we are different about time—but about space, money, self-discipline. We disagree about sex, God, how to raise children—even what books to read. Furthermore, we've always been that different."

"And you've been married how long?" I asked.

"Twenty-seven years," she said. "I'm eligible for parole."

"For 27 years you've lived together with these profound differences—somehow staying together. Now, for some reason I don't understand, it seems to be all coming apart." With that I looked at them as if to reinforce the paradox. Why is something now coming apart that worked for so long?

"Doctor, you should understand that Jill, our youngest, just got married. Now it's just Ken and me. Further, his company is beginning to hint they want him out—early retirement is their euphemism. All of a sudden the ground rules have been changed—and neither Ken nor I are in charge."

"Oh," I said, "there's lots going on. Let me see if I'm beginning to get the picture. You two have always had many differences—but, somehow it worked. Now, Jill, your youngest, is gone and Ken may be nudged out. That will leave just the two of you. Marj, you'll still have your law practice, but, Ken, what will your life be like—and what will your life together be like if they retire you?"

Ken glanced at Marj, sighed, and softly said, "I'm not ready to lay it down. All my life work has been where it's at. Now, well—it may be I've gone as far as I will go. I don't know, I can't imagine how I'll live. What will I do each morning? Marj's law practice is booming and it's like I'm over the hill, or almost so."

The silence was painful. Ken was clearly talking about his pain, but Marj made no reach toward him; rather, they both stared at me silently.

"Son-of-a-gun," I uttered, "Ken, it sounds like you may be about to lose something that has always been at the center of your life. That clearly hurts a whole lot."

Ken teared up and Marj looked away. Finally, he said, "The problem is really complicated. I was sort of promised the presidency four or five years ago. Then, the Chairman died suddenly and very quickly I was out—no longer an insider, no longer the heir-apparent. It also involves Marj. I really focused on the job and, well, sort of promised her that if she didn't bitch too much, someday we'd sit together at the head table—someday she'd be the first lady. Now, well, it's clear that won't happen."

I sighed and looked at them. "Darn. It's not just the loss of Ken's dream, but, Marj, he says there was an understanding—the head table—you've lost too. Both of you must be struggling with the end of a dream—a dream that didn't turn out the way it was supposed to—"

Marj looked hard at me and said, "Please understand. I've always been ready to trade having more of Ken for the head table. It's hard for me because I made the trade-off years ago—the head table for less of Ken. It wasn't a good trade-off for me; it was a very bad or sick thing for me to agree to—although, of course, we never talked about it. I can't excuse myself, though. I bought into Ken's dream and despite how well my career has gone, the pot of gold at the end of things was sitting with Ken at the head table—a Fortune 500 Company, the Plaza, the company digs in Europe, all that stuff. I made a bad decision and then—well, even what was supposed to be the payoff fell through. It's like you sell your soul and don't get the pieces of gold. And, yes, I probably blame Ken. I shouldn't—he didn't know Ted's aneurysm would burst—but at some irrational level I do blame Ken."

I felt moved by their story. What a rotten deal for both of them. How painful, how sad—to put all your chips on one number and lose. How could they not be angry with each other, with fate, with God? And yet, as I stepped back from my painful identification with them, questions came to mind. What factors made it possible or necessary for them to accept the trade-off—a lack of closeness for the promise of being at the head table? How much of their interactional pattern here in the office, a pattern in which she seems to be the aggressor, is a recent development—perhaps in response to the failed dream of the head table? Until the end of that shared dream, was he more dominant in defining their relationship? How does Jill's leaving play into the dynamics of their relationship? At a different level, is there some possibility that behind the scenes Ken is as depressed as Marj and may need an antidepressant?

These and other questions flood my mind. The initial exploration with them has led to a beginning understanding of their current situation and some clues as to the relationship problems that have been there for a longer period. The issue I face at this point is whether to continue the initial exploration in a way that may lead to new understandings for them or whether to veer off and begin the more structured aspects of my assessment procedure. I am more apt to veer off if I note that we have moved to what seems like a great deal of pain for one or both of them. With Ken and Marj I had seen and heard pain—but not of the quality that seems potentially disruptive, so I decided to continue the initial exploration. I wished to do so, however, by having one or both of them select the direction of the exploration. One technique for doing so is to present them with another brief summary and then follow their responses to the summary.

> "Okay, I reflected, "let me see if I'm beginning to understand. You two have always been very different about many things, but the relationship has not been seriously troubled until more recently. Jill has left and that's a loss. However, there's been a different kind of loss—the loss of your shared dream of Ken becoming company president and the two of you having some years at the head table. Ken, it sounds like you lost out through no fault of yours—rather because of the death of the Chairman. You've been very work-oriented and now they're nudging you into early retirement. What will you do? Is your career really over so early? How does one deal with the disappointment and anger? Marj, you bought into the dream and accepted the trade-off of less of Ken for the head table. Now it appears you have neither and you're plenty angry and struggling with some depression. You say you shouldn't hold Ken responsible for all of this—but at some level you say you do.
>
> If I have it reasonably in mind, you folks have lost a great deal recently."

There was a long silence and Ken and Marj looked at each other with what I took to be unspoken questions of each other. I suspected there was more to be said and they were trying to decide whether to say it.

"You have it right, Doctor," Marj said quietly, "but there's more to it. You focus on our loss of the shared dream and the loss of Jill. There's more in the way of loss. You see—"

Ken reached over and took her hand and when she began to cry he gave her a tissue. "Marj is a twin," he said. "Her twin, Marie, and she have always been extremely close and, well, Marie has an inoperable cancer. Marj just learned several months ago, and losing Marie is like losing a part of herself."

Marj blew her nose and wiped her tears away. "Marie has been my soulmate. In some ways I've leaned on her too much. Even as kids she was the more outgoing, more dynamic one. She and her family live only three blocks from us and for years I've seen her every day."

Here was more of the puzzle. Marj's trade-off of closeness with Ken for a seat at the head table was made possible, in part, because of her closeness to her twin, Marie. That relationship provided her with the intense emotional bond that she and Ken did not have. In fact, it is possible that unconsciously she selected Ken because he would not push for a kind of closeness that might take from her relationship with Marie.

Further, she describes herself as dependent on Marie and now is facing not just the loss of the special closeness but also the loss of a person upon whom she was clearly dependent. All of this may help explain why she has become more angry with Ken—blaming him (irrationally, she said earlier) for what feels to her like losing everything. On the other hand, Ken has been able to devote most of his energies and self-esteem to his career, and now that seems to be ending at the same time that Marj seems more angry than ever before and yet may need from him a kind of closeness that he has never provided. At some level, he may need more now from Marj than ever before and, at the same time, feel from her an entirely new set of demands.

There were only 10 to 15 minutes left in this initial interview, and I decided to summarize again briefly and then outline a plan of assessment.

"You have told me a great deal about yourselves and your relationship in this short time. We'll be coming to the end of this appointment soon and several of the points you've made need emphasis. First, this is a period of painful losses for the two of you. In addition to the natural loss of your youngest child leaving, there are several unusual losses that seem to have upset your relationship's equilibrium. The first is the loss of the shared dream about the head table and all that has been sacrificed for it. The second is the upcoming loss of Marie, which would be dreadful under any circumstances but is especially difficult both because you, Marj, depended so much on her and because she played an important role in making the lack of closeness between you and Ken more palatable. If Marie's cancer takes her—and it sounds like it will—and with Jill gone, and maybe your forced retirement, Ken, everything emotionally will be on the shoulders of the relationship between the two of you. It sounds to me that the relationship has never had that kind of responsibility and I'd guess that both of you must have some doubts about whether it's up to it."

They were both silent and seemed to share a long wave of sadness. Ken finally said, "That's quite a summary—it feels right."

Marj looked at me with tears rolling down her cheeks and said, "Losses—Jill, the dream, Marie—and can we, maybe for the first time, be enough for each other? It is sad and scary."

"It *has* to be," I said, and after more silence, "Let me talk with you about my approach to trying to be helpful. Although I think your current situation is reasonably clear, there is much more I need to know about both of you and about your relationship. I need to understand better all that has gone into getting you to where you are. I have four or five major areas that I need to explore with you—mostly together, but I'd like to have one or two individual interviews with each of you. There are also several paper-and-pencil things to be completed and, perhaps, we'll videotape a conversation so the three of us can look at it together. At some point I'll feel that I have a good enough overview to discuss some treatment alternatives for you to decide about."

They nodded and Ken asked, "When can we start?"

I asked them to discuss this first interview and how they felt about working with me and call in the next day or two and we'd set up some appointments if that was their wish. "Fit" was important, however, and if either of them wasn't comfortable with me or my approach we needed to talk about it. Perhaps another therapist might be more suitable.

If they decided to work with me, they might also think about any questions they had about me and my experience. Within certain limits, I thought they had a right to know something about me. I also discussed my fees and other administrative aspects of couples therapy. They seemed pleased and said they'd call me the following day.

These segments are from a fairly typical first interview with a couple. I hope in such an interview to arrive at an initial formulation of where they are and of why a particular type of relationship had "worked" for them for years and now no longer does. I also wanted to begin the process of alliance formation, to have them leave with each feeling that I listened attentively and could hear both sides of their story. I wanted to model both respect for their subjective reality and a variety of empathic processes. I wanted also to introduce them to interpersonal language—the attempt to describe and/or translate their labeling each other with undesirable traits to interactional language that emphasizes the context.

All of this I believe to be fairly mainstream marital-family therapy. It focuses on context, affect, exploration, and, most of all, the therapist hanging loose and following the couple's narrative or narratives. It searches for the organizing theme or metaphor of their joint presentation. It looks for the inevitable differences in points of origin, causal sequences, and levels of responsibility. Having followed this sort of format and having summarized my observations and initial thoughts, I indicated that I have more to learn and, indeed, a format or structure I wish to impose on our meetings.

This is a monumental step for the therapist to take. It is an acknowledgement of his or her expertise, a statement of "I know what I need to know and, as a result, here are the directions in which we need to turn." It is, of course, an exercise of power in that it defines, for the immediate future, where the therapeutic relationship is going, what it is we are to discuss, and who is to decide about the content and direction of our talks.

The therapist's use of power is nowhere more passionately debated than in the field of marital-family therapy. The constructivists' challenge to traditional marital-family therapist expertise-based power fills our most prestigious journals. The essence of that challenge involves the belief that since the observer-therapist is inseparable from the system being observed or treated, no objectivity is possible, nor is there any data-based expertise. As a consequence, marital-family therapists should strive for egalitarian relationships with individuals, couples, and families and search only for ways to assist them to explore and discover new meanings. All efforts of therapists to define themselves as experts with important theories and techniques are to be eschewed. Therapy is but a particular form of conversation in which circular questions are the high priests and interpretations the devil's agents.

I am much opposed to this perspective. I believe in expertise. I want a vascular surgeon (not an internist, however capable) to remove my aneurysm. I want a highly trained therapist to listen to my associations, confront my interactions with my wife, and raise appropriate existential issues. I want my therapist to know something of where I've been, what I value, and what I hope for. In all of this, I am willing to cede power to get help. Know me, value me, and I will follow you deep into the valley.

The challenge to authority based on expertise has a long history and the marital-family psychotherapeutic arena has been recently revitalized by the challenge of constructivism (see Chapter 3). Because of the need for clarity about an issue as important as the use of power by the therapist, I outline briefly below my current position.

1. Power is a crucial variable in all enduring, emotionally important relationships. This is not because the need for power is necessarily a fundamental human motivation, but because any system must be organized and, power is required in the process of organization. Said another way, the participants in the system must define their relationship and, in particular, how much of what types of separateness and connectedness are to prevail. This definition and the processes used to achieve it are central to the structure of the relationship.

2. In the psychotherapeutic relationship, the therapist usually starts with the greater power. This power is based upon the presumption of knowledge-based expertise and is sanctioned by governmental bodies. There is no escaping the issue of power; rather, the critical decisions involve the therapist's approaches to the appropriate uses of power in the service of the patient's needs. Under all but a few clinical circumstances, the therapist should strive to minimize his or her power and facilitate the patient's empowerment.*

---

* An insightful example of the dramatic role of power in the therapeutic relationship is presented in the play (Bennett, 1992) and the movie, *The Madness of King George*. The mad King's therapist must use all of his power to treat the King successfully and, once the King is restored, must return to the clearly less powerful and traditional role of subject relating to King. This example highlights the fact that even in relatively brief psychotherapeutic relationships there is no escaping the issue power.

3. The therapist's disavowal of power is a powerful tactic. In its ability to confuse patients and perturb systems, it is usually more powerful than its opposite, the deliberate assumption of a powerful position. The use of such extreme positions is only rarely in the patient's or system's best interests. To those readers familiar with the debate about power, it will be clear that my position reflects the orientation of Haley (1981) and Minuchin (1992). Some 40 years ago, Haley suggested to his research colleagues that usually two persons work out areas of their life together in which each is in control and this is satisfactory to both. When, however, the two persons cannot agree about who is to determine the kind of relationship they are to have, chronic conflict ensues.

Later, Haley (1981) described his belief that power was a central issue in human life in that each person had to decide how much power he or she would allow another to have. At the same time, Haley says, postulating an inner need of the individual to control others is naive. He appears to attempt to escape this contradiction by moving to the level of the system and postulating that "all learning creatures are compelled to organize" (p. 23); they cannot not organize. In the process of organizing, a hierarchy is produced; when it is not, the participants will struggle with one another.

In describing the hypnotic relationship, Haley (1981) suggested that all behavior exchanged between two people can be said to define the type of relationship they will have together.

Haley (1969) also writes about the complexity of understanding power in relationships by describing Christ's use of the surrender tactic. The vanquished wolf's exposure of the jugular vein is the prototype for many human maneuvers that emphasize the use of helplessness as a way of determining what will happen next. It is being in control of what is to happen next that demarcates the individual's power. Haley concludes that Christ's recommendation to turn the other cheek is a strategic tactic that leads to either victory or extermination. It is strategic in the sense that Christ did not use it personally; rather, He answered criticism not only with criticism, but with threats. As Christ was very aggressive, Haley doubts that He originated the surrender tactic; rather, He codified it such that it became a central tactic for Gandhi and Martin Luther King.

Minuchin has always emphasized the importance of power, authority, and control in understanding relationships. In responding to the constructivists' challenge, Minuchin (1992) points out that the constructivists, in their equating of expertise with power and their developing interventions that avoid control, are only creating a different use of power. Therapeutic hierarchies are temporary arrangements that would be a sham if the therapist were not an expert ("a person of informed uncertainty") (p. 7).

He quotes the poet, Wendell Berry. "I have a land. I walk on my land. I step on a stone. I kick the stone. The stone rolls away." Bateson, Berry complained, "takes his intellectual shovel, and neatly piles the stone, land, and walking all back inside my brain" (Minuchin, 1992, p. 7).

Haley's and Minuchin's perspectives on the inevitability of dealing with organization, power, and control in human systems have been challenged most energetically by Hoffman (1985). She objects to the use of "normative ideas of what a family should be like" (p. 389), and supports abandoning the "expert-dummy model" (p. 390) to search for collaboration rather than hierarchy in the therapist-patient relationship. She would set a context for change rather than specify a change, reduce the therapist's instrumentality, provide circular models of marital-family problems, and display nonjudgemental attitudes. I would agree with emphasizing the importance of these concepts, but point out that none of them negate understanding that power is an important variable in human systems. One cannot go "beyond power and control" (p. 381) if this means avoiding the significance of power in organizing human systems.

Amundson, Stewart, and Valentine (1993) write of the temptations of power and certainty, and use a colonial metaphor to describe occasions when the therapist's "expert" knowledge blinds him or her to what is going on in the therapist's office. These writers emphasize that power is misused most particularly in the definition of the problem. They support the idea that problem definition must be a collaborative process. They contrast a "therapy of certainty" with a "therapy of curiosity" in which a critical differentiating variable is the therapist's use of power.

Towns (1994) writes about the role of power and emphasizes the contributions of Foucault (1982). She suggests that part of the constructivists' difficulty with power as a relevant construct in marital-family systems is their overly narrow definition. Towns asserts that their negative, "control from the top down" (p. 163) definition of power makes it difficult to integrate power and circular causality. Only a broader definition of power in which actions are emphasized (over motivations) makes it possible to understand power in the context of circular causality.

There is no one who writes more persuasively about the role of power in marital therapy than Jacobson (1983). He states that "the therapist helps to decide what the problem is, what caused the problem, how to treat the problem, and what constitutes a 'cure' " (p. 12). In these processes, "the therapist inevitably reflects his or her values and political positions inherent in all important clinical decisions"(p. 14).

Perhaps Rose said it most cogently:

> ... like Mill, I believe marriage to be the primary political experience in which most of us engage as adults, and so I am interested in the management of power between men and women in that microcosmic relationship. Whatever the balance, every marriage is based upon some understanding, articulated or not, about the relative importance, the priority of desires, between its two partners. Marriages go bad not when love fades—love can modulate into affection without driving two people apart—but when this understanding about the balance of power breaks down, when the weaker member feels exploited or the stronger feels unrewarded for his or her strength. (p. 7)

There is much more that might be said about the therapist's use of power but, for present purposes, I wish to turn to the reasons for my use of power in imposing a particular structure on the process of data collection. First of all, I do so because I have an explicit theory of marital relationships (outlined in Chapter 5) and need to collect clinical data following the format of that theory. Doing so increases the likelihood that treatment will be based on the clinical data rather than solely on my hidden values and biases. I will also construct a clinical formulation of the relationship emphasizing both its problems and its strengths. The clinical data are the basic building blocks for this formulation.

A second reason for imposing a particular assessment structure is that it reflects a careful, measured, and, I hope, thoughtful attitude. It emphasizes a relatively thorough review of the couple's life together. As such, it provokes memories and, for many, asks them to discuss aspects of their relationship that may have faded from consciousness.

A third reason involves my observation that quite often the assessment procedure has therapeutic impact. It is not rare for participants to comment on new learning about themselves or each other. "I'd never heard him acknowledge before how deeply wounded he was by the episode. It made me stop and wonder if I haven't assumed that he couldn't be hurt," one wife said of her remote, controlling husband.

It also quickly becomes obvious that my detailed review of each participant's experiences in his or her family of origin, the explicit definition of the most problematic relationship each had as a child, and the efforts to clarify the dynamics of that relationship all have something to do with my evolving view of their relationship. In response to questions about the transgenerational aspects of marital relationships, I may comment, "Oh, I think there are unconscious reasons that help us to understand whom we marry and the kind of relationship that results. Most of us are searching for a healing experience of some sort." For many, such information is neither new nor particularly impactful; for others, however, a chain of new learning begins.

Another reason involves the ways in which a highly organized assessment may serve as a holding structure that both contains escalating rage or despair and offers hope. There are exceptions, however. On rare occasions, I have experienced several couples who withdrew from the process without explanation—they only called and left the message. I have wondered if the reasons involved their unwillingness to accept the structure of my assessment.

On several other occasions there has been an explicit effort by one of the partners to impose his or her structure on the assessment. Deciding how much to divert the assessment process temporarily in order to deal with such concerns is a sensitive issue. Occasionally, also, the couple will appear to divert the process—usually by cycles of arguing or blaming. Most often, I interfere directly with such interactions by saying something like, "Well, it's time to stop arguing and get back to the areas we need to explore."

As can be readily inferred from these exceptions to the holding function of the assessment procedure, the structure of my inquiry can also be understood as an experiment in much the same way that a psychoanalyst may make an interpretation in an early session in order to note whether the patient responds with deeper exploration or increased defensiveness. The structure of my assessment can elicit useful information about the couple's response to the outside world—particularly to external authority and control.

Finally, my use of this type of detailed assessment process also involves my needs. I am by nature both curious and deliberate. I distrust what seem to be simple, often faddish, explanations of complex interactions. I also believe that many couples arrive for help at crucial periods in their lives together and deserve a careful, thoughtful response. The stakes are often high, and the lives of many people may be significantly influenced by what does or does not occur in the therapist's office. For these reasons, the systematic approach I have developed suits me. It is congruent with my experience of myself.

The assessment procedure also involves the opportunity to begin a teaching process. I hope to demonstrate listening skills, empathic responsiveness, the importance of affective messages, respect for subjective reality, and the identification of major themes. I want to model careful listening to each spouse's complaints in a way that indicates respect for his or her subjective reality. I use reflections and brief summaries, and pay much attention to feelings. I avoid the use of questions, especially those that narrow down, rather than open up, a theme or story.

After the initial explanation of each spouse's complaints, I will summarize the two usually markedly differing realities with a statement that accepts both of them, maintaining the attitude that such differences are inevitable. I hope during these initial assessment interviews not only to demonstrate listening skills that facilitate self-exploration but to introduce several basic concepts. One such concept is that reality is largely constructed in the mind of each individual. Thus, from the start of the assessment process, the concept of constructed realities is introduced.

A second concept is to substitute whenever possible the language of *state* for the language of *trait*. Initial attempts to accomplish this involve confronting the spouses' use of "never" and "always." I use questions like, "What are the circumstances in which he is least likely to withdraw from you?" "When is she most able to control her anger toward you?" "Tell me about those times when he seems most sensitive to your fears." These requests and questions are meant to begin the process of changing the ways in which the participants view their dilemma, from a process of blaming each other based on undesirable personality traits to an appreciation of the role of context in the sense of here-and-now circumstances. "So—it is after several nights of your working late at the office and not being available to him," I said to a wife, "that he is most apt to seem angry and withdrawn." This is the type of summary statement that is meant to begin the process of converting a trait to a state perspective.

A third fundamental concept that I try to introduce is that of circular causality. Whenever possible, it is useful to point out the basic circular nature of many interactions. "Let's see if I'm getting the picture: It is after you've had to work late and then experience him as angry and withdrawn that you're most apt to take an additional assignment at work that often means getting home late? Getting home late seems to lead to angry withdrawal and angry withdrawal leads to getting home late?"

These three concepts—an awareness of the subjective nature of reality, a preference for state over trait explanations, and an understanding of circular causality—are often observed in highly functional marriages. I believe they also represent ways of viewing the world endorsed by many therapists. They also are processes that increase the likelihood that two persons can achieve greater closeness. If one respects the other's way of seeing things, emphasizes the importance of circumstances in the behavior of the other, and understands that one's own behavior can be both cause and effect, there is less likelihood of feeling victimized and blaming the other for one's situation. Over time, this can lead to greater closeness. Indeed, resistance to the gradual acceptance of these concepts and the persistence of victimization and blaming are understood as the shared inability to give up a mutual projection system. In such circumstances, the therapist needs to think through whether the magnitude of each spouse's underlying fears of closeness has been sufficiently appreciated.

Thus, the initial contact with the couple is important for many reasons and the therapist must be watchful that information from the referral source and the initial telephone contacts do not activate personal biases that may skew the initial assessment procedure. First, the initial interview begins the process of alliance building; second, it provides the opportunity to demonstrate crucial communication skills; and, third, it begins the process of data collection, particularly about the couple's current dilemma.

From the start, the therapist must deal with the issue of power and how it can be best used in the service of successful therapy. He or she also begins the process of introducing key theoretical constructs, and I have suggested that important consideration be given to three ideas: (1) that subjective reality is usually more important than the truth; (2) that state explanations are usually more useful than trait explanations; and (3) that circular causality provides more intervention opportunities than linear causality.

Before turning to the more structured portions of my assessment, I would like to emphasize again the intellectual challenge and pleasure I experience in the initial contact with the couple. There is a sense of real adventure, of beginning a process in which the outcome is unknown but which may lead to substantial improvement in the quality of their life together.

7

Assessment: A Structured Approach

On the day after Marj and Ken's initial interview, Marj called and said they'd like to go ahead with the assessment. They both liked the idea that I would do a formal assessment, and liked my fairness—that I seemed to want to see both sides. Marj remarked that other therapists they'd seen seemed to take sides more: "It was usually my side they took—Ken can really be a pompous ass at times—but I think he picked up on their turnoff of him and that sunk the whole effort."

When they arrived for their next appointment I told them I was glad they had decided to go ahead with the assessment and then began to explore how they felt about the initial interview and their impressions of me.

> Ken took the lead, "I felt good about the first session—and good about you. I like the idea of collecting and analyzing data and talking about various options. The others we've seen didn't appear to have a game plan. If they did, it wasn't clear to me."
>
> Marj said, "I like the assessment part, too—and, as you know from our phone conversation, I like it that you seem fair—willing to try to understand what's going on from both of our sides."
>
> "Good," I responded, "Did you two talk about it together?"
>
> "Just a little after the initial session—in the car, actually, going home from your office," Ken said.

"What reservations about my approach or me did either of you hear from or sense in the other," I asked.

"I don't think we had any," Marj said, and then turned to Ken and said, "Did you have reservations I didn't pick up on?"

"No," Ken responded.

"There are several reasons for my questions," I said. "First, fit is really important and sometimes, often intuitively, one can feel that there's something about a person one doesn't resonate with. Second, I believe I'm the third couples' therapist you've seen—and something didn't go right the first two times. Can you help me understand that better?"

They were silent for a few moments and then Ken asked Marj for her ideas. "I told Doctor Lewis when I called him that we both liked systematic approaches, and that he seemed fair. As you noted, we both like order—you perhaps more than I—and this seemed orderly."

Next, Ken added, "Both of the other therapists were young women—associates of Marj's therapist—and, I guess, maybe I wasn't sure they knew what they were doing."

"Help me understand that better," I requested.

"Well," Ken responded, "I'm not sure I can. Marj has said that I have trouble giving women their due. There may be some truth in that. In my family, the women were raised to be pretty helpless. I don't know the connections, though, if there are any."

"What bothered you the most about the women therapists?" I asked.

"Well, over and beyond my not feeling comfortable that they knew what they were doing, they seemed to take Marj's side—saw me as the problem," Ken added.

"So, feeling that you're being blamed for the problems in the relationship is a piece of it?" I asked.

"Yeah—I think so," Ken said.

"Let me ask you, then—both of you—to talk about that feeling if you feel it with me. It is very important that we be able to talk about feelings that come up—whether it's a feeling of being blamed or some other feeling. Not addressing it openly can really sink our effort. Can we agree on that type of openness in here?"

They both nodded and, after a short silence, I said, "There are four or five areas that I need to explore with you. Let's get started."

These early minutes of the second session were important in that I indicated how crucial their openness was to be, especially openness about me and what was going on in their sessions. I also scratched the surface of their prior experiences in couples' therapy and discovered that Ken may have difficulty seeing women as competent, and accepting help from them. This belief may have started in his family of origin and may be one part of his contribution to the marital distress. Further, however, Ken noted that he felt blamed by the prior therapists, and it was this feeling that may have led to the breaking off of couples therapy.

I knew, of course, that the issue of feeling blamed can have a number of possible roots. First of all, Ken could feel blamed for the marital problems and, in that, could be responding to the charge of being the aggressor and victimizing Marj. Whether that root would prove to be a part of it and have understandable antecedents, only time would tell.

Another possibility is that Ken's feeling blamed may be connected with underlying shame about some very real deficiencies he has in relating to women. His feeling blamed might then lead to a projection of the responsibility and protect Ken from his shame over real deficits. Again, time would tell.

A third possibility involves Marj as an active participant in entering into a coalition with the therapist that excludes Ken by making him not just the outsider, but the "bad" outsider. Ken's sense of being blamed in this scenario could be an accurate appraisal of the social reality within those therapists' offices. If there is validity to this view, I will be especially interested in family-of-origin triangles in which both Marj and Ken were caught up—perhaps even triangles in which Marj was an insider and Ken an outsider. Once again, time would tell.

Beyond my understanding of important individual and dyadic dynamics, however, I have begun the process of clarifying what I needed to be particularly watchful about. Marj had talked about fairness and Ken about feeling blamed. I needed to be on my toes about those dynamics coming into play with me and possibly defeating my efforts to be helpful.

In that which follows, I will discuss each section of my assessment process and will refer briefly to the research and clinical observations that appear particularly relevant.

DEFINITIONS OF THE PROBLEM

In the initial interview, the use of exploratory techniques led to the construction of a narrative—the jointly constructed story of Marj and Ken's current dilemma. The major themes of that narrative were loss and the fear that, in the very near future, their relationship would be called upon to provide for both of them the sense of closeness and meaning each had previously found elsewhere. Both feared that the relationship would be unable to provide enough to sustain them and the relationship.

In this section, I take a different approach and ask each spouse to identify three or more changes they believe are necessary for the relationship to not only survive but to provide what is needed. Here the emphasis changes from obtaining a coherent narrative to identifying as clearly as possible those elements each feels lacking in the relationship.

It is at this stage, following the initial session, that I begin taking notes. After the initial session, I outline on paper what I believe to be the essential features of that session and also note questions that I need to ask.

Most often, each spouse responds by discussing changes the other should make. "I want Ken to talk more about his feelings" or "I'd like Marj to be more disciplined with money" are examples. I attempt to explore each change and, in the doing, continue the emphases begun in the initial session. Using reflexive questions ("Are there times when, in particular, you wish Ken would discuss his feelings?" "Are there certain feelings that you'd like Ken to be more open about?"), I hope to move the focus away from understandings based on trait to understandings based on context. This approach may also begin to move the focus in the direction of circular causality. ("Is it, then, in the months that you make quarterly tax payments, that you are most apt to react angrily to Marj's spending by cutting back on your deposits to the joint account—which, in turn, angers Marj who then may spend more?")

It is in this initial part of the structured inquiry that the therapist may begin to observe the intensity of the couple's projective processes. Several clues suggest a strong and entrenched projective system. One is the absolute, black-or-white nature of what each spouse ascribes to the other. A second is the intensity of the affect accompanying the request for change. A third clue is the presence of pervasive pessimism about the other making any changes. Another clue is the impermeability of one or both spouses to my efforts to reframe the statement from character to context or to raise the possibility of circular causality. These clues suggest a deeply entrenched projective process that may prove to be so important for each spouse's basic sense of self that modifying it may be difficult or impossible.

Frequently, a spouse may start to interfere and rebut his or her partner's identification of needed changes. I interrupt such interruptions and may say something like, "Hold off, there. You'll get your chance to talk, but for now listen to what she (he) is saying. Often, each of us is more able to see what the other contributes to the problems than what we contribute." If the interrupting spouse continues to interrupt despite my intervention, I will often turn to him (or her) and attempt to explore why he (or she) seems unable to listen as requested. "Help me to understand what it is you're feeling as your partner describes changes he (or she) wants you to make. What thoughts or memories does it bring to mind?" These and other questions attempt to provide insight into the individual's repeated intrusive responses.

At the same time, I continue to model careful listening, a frequent focus on affect, and a variety of empathic processes. Once again, I am clear in my expectations that their subjective realities will differ and that understanding what each other thinks and feels is usually far more important than truth and certainty.

When the topic of what each would like to see change in order to improve the relationship is reasonably exhausted, I turn to the next section of my structured inquiry.

HISTORY OF THE RELATIONSHIP

"Out of all the millions of people how did you come to marry your spouse?"

I usually start with this question because it is so open-ended, and responses often provide a beginning orientation to some of the forces that were involved in their mutual attraction. The responses are almost always interesting and at times provide a starting point for an exploration of where in life each spouse was at the time of their initial meeting.

I do not think that responses to this question are necessarily factual. There are reported data, for example, that suggest that present dissatisfaction with a relationship results in more negative earlier memories of that relationship than were reported before the relationship soured

(Gottman & Levenson, 1984). Whatever the responses may reflect of past and present, they lead into a careful exploration of the circumstances that drew the spouses together.

Circumstances of First Meeting

I try to obtain a thorough understanding of where each person was in life when they met. Had either recently ended another relationship or been left by another person? What was each person's job or school situation? What was the status of each spouse's relationship with his or her family of origin? Had there been any recent losses?

It is also important to inquire about triangles. Were either or both persons also seriously involved with a third person at the time this relationship commenced? If so, how long did the triangle continue?

The affective quality of the very early stages of the relationship may provide important information. Some couples report an intense initial affective response—a powerful, love-at-first-sight experience. Often, such accounts may reflect a shared, underlying neediness and at the same time may serve as a preview of a relationship filled with passion, conflict, and remarkable reunions. Other relationships begin with great caution. There is no throwing one's self into the storm, but rather a quiet friendship that only slowly builds in romantic intensity. For some, there was no affective intensity—from the start the relationship was built about avoidance of feelings. Some couples tell of conflict from the start. Almost always, the conflict can be understood as the underlying failure to agree on the definition of the relationship.

The affective quality of the early relationship provides information about the sought-for levels of connectedness and separateness. Intense affectivity may signify intense needs for either separateness or connectedness, depending on the affects that predominate.

Some relationships are sexual from the very beginning. In others, the erotic component is slow to develop. I try to understand whether both participants were equally involved in establishing the pattern of eroticism or whether one was more active than the other.

It is also possible to see the overall pursuer-pursued relationship pattern commence at the very beginning of the relationship. One person is much more active than the other in trying to establish the relationship. For some couples, the pursuer and pursued roles are interchangeable. When the pursuer "catches" the pursued, he or she then runs from the connection and is pursued by the new pursuer. Once again, such patterns may provide initial insights into wishes for and fears of closeness or intimacy.

The Courtship

At some point, the relationship becomes serious in the sense that both participants begin to consider the possibility of spending their lives together. I often ask, "When and how did your relationship come to be serious?" Although I am interested in what each spouse remembers, I am even more interested in whether they construct a joint narrative about the change from a casual to a serious relationship:

"He knew—almost from the first date—that he wanted to marry me, but I had been burned a couple of times and was much more cautious."

"Yeah," he responded. "I thought she'd never come around. Even took her home three times before she really began to believe me. I just knew from the first time I saw her—something went click."

This interchange is important at several levels, but my emphasis here is on the couple's agreement about the story of the transition to a serious relationship and the fact that the story is jointly constructed.

I also want to know if this transition involved an explicit discussion of new rules for the relationship. Were they to stop dating others? What, if anything, were they going to tell their families? Did the change in the relationship include changes in their sexual relationship? Did they discuss living together? Throughout this exploration, I am as interested in how the rules came to be as I am in what the rules were. It is with the transition to a serious relationship that important work must be done by the couple on how they are to make decisions, how disagreements are to be resolved, and whether or not they can learn to negotiate solutions. The issue of power—and whether it is shared—comes to the surface with the advent of seriousness. There is no one "big" discussion about the global issue of the definition of the relationship, but rather a series of exchanges around everyday issues: sexuality, money, time together and apart, relationships with friends, holidays with families of origin, and scores of other issues that are the manifest content of the crucial negotiation about the definition of the relationship.

In addition, I am interested in whether they can recapture for a few moments any shared pleasure—even if it only involves memories of what used to be.

The Decision to Marry

I ask couples how they had decided to get married. For some, the answer is an unplanned pregnancy; others recall the decision as a spur-of-the-moment type of thing or as a labored, lengthy process filled with ambivalence. For some, a circumstance was involved—an impending job transfer to another city is not uncommon.

It is important to know whether either participant was under unusual stress when he or she participated in the decision. The recent death of a parent, the loss of a job, or other losses may play a role. In retrospect, one sometimes wonders if the decision had more to do with the loss than with the persona of the partner.

I ask whom they told first after making the decision. The responses of family members are explored. It is interesting to know who was most pleased by the decision and who was least pleased. The reasons for a family member's pleasure or displeasure are asked about. In some circumstances, it is clear that the choice of a mate involved either the attempt to please or the attempt to separate from a parent.

When there are obvious differences in social class, ethnicity, or religious background, they should be explored. I ask the couple how they felt about the differences at the time and how they feel about them now. Their parents' responses to such differences are also explored. Finally, it is important to know whether the spouses believe those differences are important aspects of their currently troubled relationship.

The Wedding

The wedding often presents the therapist with clues about those factors that shape the early relationship. At one extreme are those weddings that are collaboratively planned by bride and groom. At the other extreme are those situations in which the wedding becomes the property of someone else—often the mother of the bride. How much the bride and groom shape the wedding in terms of their preferences and how much they abdicate this responsibility provides an insight into transgenerational politics. To be married in the church of one's parents with a ceremony selected because of its relationship to prior family weddings is a strong statement of values. It emphasizes family, tradition, and, perhaps, other conservative values and may minimize the importance of here-and-now choices by the bride and groom.

Weddings can also emphasize differences. The Jewish woman and Italian-American man may be forced to face differing ethnic traditions as they plan their wedding. Once again, the issue of the definition of the relationship is paramount. Whose religious practices and family traditions are to prevail? How are important decisions to be made? Is there a powerful member of either family whose wishes shape the decision?

I try to obtain a detailed description of the wedding. In particular, I inquire about those moments that are perfused with specialness and those aspects of the ceremony that did not go well. I recall, for example, a young woman of Episcopal tradition whose marriage to a Jewish physician was flawed by his friends carrying her about in a chair on their shoulders at the reception. Her response to this ritual was that she was a piece of meat paraded in front of his family and friends. This interpretation of one part of her wedding both dominated her recall and provided me with the opportunity to explore with them deeper implications of their religious differences.

There are many tragic stories of mothers too drunk to walk down the aisle, of two families brought together for the ceremony who refuse to speak, and of other serious glitches that are either painful memories for both spouses or experiences that the couple wryly share in ways that augment their sense of connection.

The Honeymoon

The honeymoon does not often have the same sexual implications in these days of changed sexual practices as it did a generation or two ago. Asking each spouse to talk about the one memory that comes to mind about their honeymoon, however, may lead to responses that inform the clinician. One woman's honeymoon memory was of the tiny lizards on the ceiling of the Hawaiian beach cottage's bedroom. Another woman recalled her new husband's insensitivity to her gastrointestinal distress. A man remembered most his premature ejaculations, a dilemma he had not experienced during the courtship. Several men recalled their wives' menstrual periods as casting a pall on their honeymoons.

Honeymoon memories (like other memories) can be understood both as reports of more-or-less real occurrences and as organizing metaphors that speak to something about the person or the relationship that transcends the historical event. It is well to explore such memories with each spouse. Often, I will then turn to the other spouse and ask, "How is it for you to hear that? What does it bring to your mind?" It is surprising how often these probes result in one or both spouses expressing surprise and indicating that he or she had not known before of those thoughts or feelings.

The Early Years

Under fortunate circumstances, the couple has enough time before a child is born to complete much of the necessary negotiation about the definition of their relationship. For many couples, that may take a year or two; for a few, the relationship's definition was fairly complete before the wedding; and for others, the inability to agree on the structure of their relationship comes to characterize their life together.

Often, there are unanticipated circumstances that influence the early years. Some of these are health related, still others involve changes in work situations.

In these days in which both spouses working is the norm, there is much of day-to-day life that must be worked out. How cooking, house cleaning, grocery shopping, yard work, and all the other essentials are to be shared is even more urgent because both spouses are gone all day. A husband's failure to do his part—particularly of those tasks formerly thought of as women's work—can be a source of tension both about the tasks themselves and about the failure to negotiate a definition of the relationship that seems equitable to both partners.

Another basic relationship issue that needs to be settled during these early months and years involves the boundaries the couple wish to establish around their relationship. This process includes how the couple is to relate to their families of origin, old friends, and people at work. One index of a couple's boundaries is whether relations and friends can come by without telephoning in advance. There is no right or wrong answer—the issue is whether the spouses agree and, if so, whether they let relations and friends know of their preference.

Life Dreams

Young adulthood is considered the time in which the individual's life dream should be formulated (Levinson, 1978). For some, the dream is elaborate and detailed, but for others it is a relatively sparse thought or two. During courtship, many couples discuss their individual life dreams and begin the process of exploring whether their dreams are compatible. During the early years of the marriage, more work usually is required in the attempt to establish a shared life dream.

Life dreams are about hope and the future. They speak to the couple's ability to share a vision of where they would like their life together to be in 10, 20, or 40 years. For some, the absence of a shared life dream may reflect an underlying lack of hope for the future of the relationship. For others, it seems to be related to the failure to communicate at the level of personal hopes. For a few, it reflects their shared failure to construct individual life dreams during young adulthood.

It is not uncommon to see couples who have not begun to deal with the need for a shared life dream. They look surprised when the therapist brings it up. They may not have discussed openly their individual life dreams and, in a few instances, may deny having individual life dreams.

Life dreams are often the stimulus for effective exploration that may lead to important new learning for the couple. At the minimum, they provide the therapist with important information about the couple.

Parenthood

There are now a small number of systematic research projects that examine early parenthood, including a project from the Timberlawn Research Foundation (Lewis, 1989). It now seems clear that a number of variables acting in concert determine whether this crucial family transition goes well or poorly. The nature of the couple's relationship before a child is born is a powerful influence. Parental personality factors play a role. Family-of-origin relationships can also be influential. Attachment researchers point out that a history of secure attachment to her own mother in the mother's history predicts a secure infant-mother attachment. Infant temperament plays a role, and some data supports a "goodness of fit" model as the strongest predictor of secure attachment.

The couples therapist needs to be conversant with the empirical literature, all the while maintaining a primary focus on the ways in which the couple deal with pregnancy, delivery, and the first years of parenting. How much the couple seems together in these important life experiences and how much the experiences are characterized by strife and conflict need to be understood.

For most couples, parenthood is an important developmental challenge; for some, it represents the beginning of trouble within the relationship. Incorporating the child into the family occurs for many without excessive strain, but for some the dyad does not become a cohesive triad.

Later parenting experiences also need to be explored. I ask about the birth of subsequent children, the children's early school experiences, any problems dealing with adolescent children, and the impact of the children leaving for college, job, and marriage. Throughout these discussions, I pay particular attention to evidence that one parent has entered a special coalition with a child, a relationship that may compensate for something missing in the marriage.

There are other issues about which I inquire. One is how the children came to be given their names. There is also the issue of whether a child is identified with a particular relative from the viewpoint of appearance or personality. I am also interested in special problems posed by some children and how they are dealt with. In those instances in which the couple must deal with a seriously defective child, it is important to know whether this psychological injury is dealt with together or whether it plays a divisive role.

OTHER DEVELOPMENTAL STAGES

The couples therapist needs to be aware of the literature on marital and family developmental stages. It is important to explore the numerous issues, including retirement and the experience of aging, along with others that depend on where the couple are in their own development. In all of these developmental experiences, it is important for the therapist to think in terms of the challenges each phase presents to the couple and how the couple have dealt with them.

Many middle-aged couples, for example, seek couples therapy because the children leaving for other attachments produces too large a hole in their lives. Perceived deficiencies in the marital relationship may become more painful when the more actively involved stage of parenting is over. Other couples seek help around issues of retirement and the increase in time spent together. Some older couples come for help to deal with regrets. A few are alienated from a grown child and may wish to explore any remedial actions they can consider, but often they come to explore the regret and, perhaps, to stop blaming each other for the alienation.

FAMILY-OF-ORIGIN HISTORIES

There is probably no clearer indication of how a marital or family therapist thinks and works than the attention he or she pays to family-of-origin material. Those systems therapists who deal only with the here-and-now of the couple's interaction in the office pay scant attention to the distant past. For those therapists whose roots reach back to psychoanalytic theory and, in particular, the concept of transference, understanding each spouse's experiences as a child in the family of origin is an essential part of treatment. Whether the past is thought of in terms of internal object representations, inner working models, or assumptive sets, the implication is that earlier and now internalized relationships with parent figures play important roles in here-and-now marital relationships. Said another way, there are always other people in the room.

Because my intellectual roots go back to psychoanalytic metapsychology and because I believe transference phenomena to be ubiquitous, I pay much attention to family-of-origin histories.

I take a detailed family-of-origin history from each spouse and ask each to serve as consultant about his or her spouse's family of origin. "Listen to what your partner tells me about his (or her) family. I will want to know whether you agree or if you think your spouse is minimizing something. You need to help balance your spouse's subtle distortions about his (or her) childhood experiences—distortions in which we all get caught up. Then again, it might be a clear difference of opinion about a family member or family experience. Whatever it is, please listen closely and be ready to make comments at the end of the exploration."

Parents' Personalities and Relationship

It is important to obtain as thorough a description of each parent's personality as possible. This psychological profile should be placed in the overall context of the patient's life and any transgenerational themes noted. It is also relevant to ask about the presence of psychiatric disorders, their treatment, and outcome in order to begin thinking about hereditary tendencies.

Of equal importance is the issue of the nature of the parents' relationship. I wish to know the structure of their relationship (egalitarian, dominant-submissive, chronically conflicted, alienated, or chaotic). How openly affectionate the parents were, who was in charge of what, and how effective they were at home and on the job are useful data. Whether alcohol abuse, substance abuse, violence, and lengthy separations occurred is also important. Any chronic illness in a parent should be noted.

If the parents separated or divorced, or if one parent died, I want to know how the family dealt with the loss. In particular I explore the informant's recalled childhood feelings and current feelings about the loss.

Relationship with Each Parent

After asking the informant to describe in his or her own words the relationship with each parent, I ask focused questions about being a parent's favorite, involvement in a special coalition with a parent, being a confidant of one or both parents, and the presence of sexual and physical abuse at the hands of a parent.

Siblings and Their Life Outcomes

I ask for a description of each of the partners' siblings and something of how their lives have turned out. The informant's childhood relationship with each sibling is explored, as are current relationships. The therapist should listen for the presence of unusually intense sibling relationships. The intensity may be competitive, supportive, or erotic and may have played an important role in the informant's childhood. Once again, the therapist should inquire about the presence of psychiatric disorders in siblings, their treatment, and the outcome.

This is a good occasion to inquire about gender roles in the family and, in particular, how narrowly they may have been formulated.

I do not hesitate to address incongruities in the family history. Reflections such as, "Help me understand something. You describe your parents and their marriage in glowing terms and yet you and your siblings have each had some combination of depression, alcohol abuse, and severe marital problems. The four of you have had seven divorces. How do you understand that four children growing up in the atmosphere of loving parents with a wonderful marriage can have so many problems?"

Structure of the Family

I now have considerable information about the informant's family of origin. Often, I summarize what I have learned and then ask for additional information about the emphases given to separateness, autonomy, and successful competition as contrasted with connectedness, closeness, and intimacy. I inquire about social class, ethnic, and subcultural influences. Stressful events are explored, as are losses and whether or not there was a shared mourning. I try to be particularly sensitive to the possibility of unmourned losses.

It is useful to also explore whether the informant participated in any family triangles. The triangles might be competitive, oppositional, or split object, so that their nature as well as presence needs clarification.

Family Roles

"What was your special role in the family?" This question often leads to fruitful exploration. Common roles are 'the good child,' 'the bad seed,' 'the rebel,' 'the caretaker,' 'the go-between,' 'the sick child,' and the 'prince' or 'princess.' It is also helpful to inquire about any special roles the siblings may have been assigned and accepted.

Special roles are thought of as resulting from parental projections of either unwanted aspects of themselves or of unfulfilled aspirations. Children are understood as semivolunteering for such roles in part because they may have specialness associated with them or, on other occasions, because the child may sense something of the family's need for a child with a certain identification.

Although I know of no systematic data on the adult consequences of special childhood roles, many therapists believe they usually have negative consequences. This belief is based on two components of special roles. For one, they are almost always constricting in that they take from the developing child the opportunity to develop along natural lines, to experience the richness of incongruities, paradoxes, and ambivalence.

In addition, some special roles include strong negative implications and these are seen as almost always destructive to the child who may internalize and carry the negative projections throughout life.

Early Memories and Dreams

It is useful to ask for the earliest memory and, in addition, for the earliest memory of mother, of father, of being soothed, held, or rocked, of being alone, and of being frightened. It is also usually productive to ask about childhood dreams and nightmares. Early memories and dreams may provide insight into important processes that more focused questions sometimes fail to reach.

The Central Problematic Relationship of Childhood

In many ways, formulating and explicating the informant's central problematic relationship of childhood is the most important result of the detailed family history. As outlined in Chapter 5, this relationship is considered a powerful unconscious force in selecting a mate and negotiating the definition of the relationship.

After this relationship is clearly identified, I then ask a short series of questions about the relationship:

1. What is it that you needed and didn't get, or didn't need and got, from that relationship?
2. When you asked for what you wanted or tried to avoid what you didn't want, how did he (she) respond?
3. When he (she) responded in that way, how did you respond?

Through these questions, I attempt to document the interactional structure of the most problematic childhood relationship. This approach mirrors the work of Luborsky (1977) and his colleagues. In studying psychotherapeutic process, they have identified a central, reoccurring relationship pattern in the experiences of patients in individual psychotherapy.

It is useful for the therapist to spell out this three-part interaction in the central problematic relationship both to be sure that he or she understands the pattern and to reinforce the informant's awareness. A simple formulation might go something like this: "Let me see if I have it. Your relationship with your mother was the most problematic relationship during childhood. You wanted more affection, more obvious signs of her love. When you let her know you needed this from her, she responded by turning away or looking scornful. When this happened, you tried even harder to be a good boy. You made even better grades and tried even harder to be perfect. Do I have it right?"

Often, the individual will indicate that going over it that way with you makes it clearer than before. Occasionally, one will say that he or she now sees for the first time the ways in which the relationship with the spouse is similar to the central problematic relationship of childhood.

DEVELOPMENTAL EXPERIENCES OUTSIDE THE FAMILY

Relationships and experiences outside the family can play important roles and often compensate in part for pathological family situations. Therapists often hear about special relationships with a teacher, a coach, a friend's parents, or other adult who offers the child valuable sources of security, affection, and self-esteem.

Experiences in groups can also play a compensatory role. Church-related groups and athletic teams are occasionally noted as helpful identifications by adults who report a pathological family life. Elder (1974) reports from the Berkely Guidance Study that very young boys whose fathers lost their jobs in the Great Depression and became ineffective at home showed greater than average adolescent problems. At 40, they seemed back on track and many reported, when asked about the change, that they benefitted by being away from home in the armed forces.

Because relationships and experiences outside the family can make a crucial difference in the development of some persons it is wise to ask about them.

THE DISCUSSION OF IMPORTANT RELATIONSHIP VARIABLES

As described in Chapter 4, the research at Timberlawn Research Foundation suggests that five relationship variables are particularly important in understanding the balance of separateness-autonomy and connectedness-intimacy within the relationship. The five variables (closeness, commitment, intimacy, separateness, and power) were defined in that chapter. In this section of the assessment, I ask the spouses to discuss how they experience their relationship from the perspective of these five variables. After defining the variable, I indicate that I plan only to listen to their discussion.

Although some couples who have come for the assessment agree on each of the five variables, it is much more common for there to be considerable disagreement. Regardless, there is much to be learned from observing and listening to their interchange. For example, how clear is each spouse in his or her appraisal of how much closeness characterizes their relationship? How attentively does each spouse listen to the other? How do the couple deal with differences in their opinions, and do such differences become charged with affect and lead to blaming each other?

The therapist does not attempt to intervene, but only watches and listens. It is usually possible to both observe what may prove to be the couple's characteristic communication pattern and obtain useful information on how each spouse experiences the relationship.

At the end of their discussion of the five variables, I often offer them a summary of both what each has reported, and the process of their interchange. An example might go something like this:

> "It seems clear that the two of you differ in the way you see your relationship. Marj, you apparently feel there is very little closeness and no intimacy. Commitment, however, is strong. You see yourself and Ken as always having had a high level of separateness—at least until he retired. You also see Ken as far more powerful than you. Your statement, "I've never been able to get him to do one thing he didn't want to do," reflects your sense of powerlessness.
>
> Ken, you agree with Marj about the strong commitment each of you has to the relationship and about the absence of intimacy. However, you believe there's more closeness than Marj describes. You also feel the separateness is only moderate. You believe that Marj has more power—because she's in control of what goes on in the relationship.
>
> I also observed how difficult it is for each of you to listen carefully to the other. It also seems clear that neither of you is all that respectful of the other's way of seeing the relationship. Both of you tend to interrupt the other and, once or

twice, it appeared to me that your shared anger was going to escalate into a blaming session.

Does that seem to capture the essence? What changes do either of you have to offer?"

Once again, I try to reflect each spouse's subjective reality and remain nonjudgemental. I offer the summary both because I wish to model careful description of their interchange and because I want them to begin to develop the ability to observe themselves in action—to step back from their conversation and ask, "What is going on here? How can I best describe this interchange?" This ability to step back and both observe and describe is, of course, standard fare for most psychotherapists during therapy sessions. Some high functioning marital couples have developed this ability on their own. Few couples with troubled relationships—not excluding competent psychotherapists and their spouses—demonstrate this ability. "I know I do it in the office," a psychotherapist patient of mine noted, "but when I get here with Sybil I act like I don't know how."

SPECIAL AREAS

Rituals

Ever since reading the work of Reiss, Steinglass, and their associates about the importance of rituals in families, I have included this focus in my assessment (Reiss, 1981; Steinglass, Bennett, Wolin & Reiss, 1987).* I describe their three categories of rituals: *cultural* (Christmas, Passover, etc.), *family* (birthdays, anniversaries, etc.), and *daily routines* (meals, bedtime, etc.). Next, I ask the couple to describe the rituals they have constructed in each category. I also ask where the ritual originated—in one of their families of origin, with friends, or as their own creation.

---

* See my reviews of Reiss (1981), *The Family's Construction of Reality*, and Steinglass and colleagues (1987), *The Alcoholic Family*, in the Reading Notes on pages 252–253 and 256, respectively.

It is also important to ask how children are involved in the rituals. Rituals that are restricted to the marital couple are also important to note.

In accord with Reiss and Steinglass, I believe that rituals are living symbols of a shared life. They express something fundamental about one's connection with others. The survival of such rituals throughout stressful times not only is an index of their importance, but acts to preserve the integrity of the marriage or family.

Religion

Survey information indicates that a large majority of Americans believe in God and rank their relationship with God as the most important aspect of their lives. Fewer psychotherapists believe the same way and, perhaps partly as a result, religious issues may be relatively unattended in psychotherapy. I believe this is a mistake for a number of reasons, including the fact that it is important for the therapist to understand the patient's, couple's, or family's basic world view. For many people seen in therapy, this is most apt to be a world view structured around religious beliefs.

Thus, it is important to know each spouse's religious belief system and religious practices and whether or not the couple have a shared religious orientation. I ask about belief in God, image of God, and belief in life after death. I also inquire about prayer and its role in each of their lives.

I also inquire about church or synagogue attendance and, where relevant, participation in the sacraments of the church.

It is also useful to know whether the couple have a personal relationship with their minister, rabbi, or priest and whether that person is aware of their troubles.

Money

The ways in which a couple deals with money often reflect some of the underlying issues around power in the definition of the relationship. A couple must come to some sort of decision about how they are going to deal with money. First, there is the issue of whether they are going to have a shared philosophy about the role money is to play in their life together. Included in this philosophy is the issue of how money is to be related to security (saving for tough times) and pleasure (you can't take it with you). Second is the issue of how decisions about money are made. Here, it is instructive to know about large purchases like automobiles; how large a check either spouse can write without discussing it ahead of time; who does the bill paying and why; whether both spouses have a clear vision of their net worth; whether they use a budget; and how many bank accounts there are.

Third, it is important to know something of any enduring conflicts that surface around money.

As can be noted, I ask a good many questions about money and its role in the couple's relationship. I also indicate that I reduce my fees under certain circumstances and that, if they request a reduced fee, they should be prepared to bring fairly complete financial data (income, savings, large debts, special circumstances, etc.) and then to suggest what fee they believe they can manage. Occasionally, one or both spouses may be in individual therapy with other therapists. I generally refuse to accept a lower fee than they are paying individual therapists and have on occasion suggested that they discuss renegotiating their individual therapy fees in order to manage both individual and couples therapy.

Sexuality

A couple's sexual relationship may be at the center of their relationship or it may be more peripheral. When a relationship begins to sour, sexuality is often one of the first casualties. I want to know how important sexuality has been in the relationship and what, if any, changes have occurred. I ask about the frequency of sexual intercourse and the satisfaction each experiences sexually. It is useful to know if there are conflicts about sexuality, such as conflicts about frequency and/or conflicts about sexual practices.

It is important to inquire about common symptoms of sexual dysfunction, including those that are most common (impotence, premature ejaculation, and failure to achieve orgasm). Occasionally, referral to a urologist, gynecologist, or sex therapist should be considered.

For most of the couples I see, there has been a marked reduction in sexual activity—often over a period of months or even years. Sometimes, this proves to be associated with active extramarital affairs, but often it is not. When I ask how the absence of sexuality is experienced by each spouse, a wide range of responses can be noted. These range from relief to despair. Often, one spouse has unilaterally ended the sexual activity. In some situations, he or she is open about the reasons. "I'm not going to have intercourse until he (she) treats me with greater consideration and respect" is not uncommon. It is clear that this spouse has withdrawn sexually as part of the larger effort to redefine the relationship in a more general sense.

These special areas (rituals, God, money, and sex) are important in themselves, but they also are important because they may be the battlefield on which one or both spouses are trying to redefine the relationship. It is, therefore, important for the couples therapist to understand their importance both in themselves and as tactics in the struggle to define what the relationship is to be.

COALITIONS AND TRIANGLES

It is important for the therapist to know if either or both spouses are involved in intense coalitions with others or whether they have triangulated a third party into their relationship. The four most common coalitions involve a spouse's relationship with a member of his or her family of origin, with a child who serves as ally and confidant, with a close friend, or with a lover.

I ask about "other important relationships" at this point in the assessment. It is also useful to ask each spouse if any relationship his or her spouse has with another person is troubling. I explore the same area in the individual interviews and, on some occasions, learn for the first time of an extramarital affair.

This is perhaps a reasonable time to step aside and discuss briefly how I manage this information. First, if I am asked in advance by one spouse to keep information confidential from the other, I decline. I indicate that although I suspect I know what he or she wishes to share, I cannot promise confidentiality. The best I can do is to treat any confidence with respect and to use my very best judgement as to how to deal with the information.

I also am clear that I will not attempt couples therapy while either spouse is involved in an active extramarital affair. What I require is that the spouse agree to suspend the affair for a trial of couples therapy. By suspend, I mean no contact—not just the cessation of sexuality. Thus, I try to place the burden of responsibility for making an honest effort to salvage the marriage where it should be—on the shoulders of both spouses.

If a spouse says privately that he or she is unwilling to give up his or her lover, I suggest several options. One is to bail out of the assessment, giving the spouse whatever reason he or she wishes. The second option is to discuss the affair with his or her spouse, either by themselves or with me present. A third option is to enter individual therapy and try to explore how it is that he or she wants both the spouse and the lover.

Although extramarital affairs must be dealt with in a clear fashion, other coalitions must be approached with equal clarity. A spouse's special relationship with a parent or sibling may have been subtly negotiated as part of a trade-off in which the other spouse received something in exchange. Marj's very special relationship with her twin was part of an unspoken contract with Ken that legitimized his preoccupation with work and emotional unavailability.

A child triangulated into the parental relationship needs to be extricated from the entanglement because it is bad for his or her emotional health. The way to get the child out of this predicament is to help the couple improve their relationship and no longer need the child between them.

CURRENT DEVELOPMENTAL STATE AND EXTERNAL STRESS

As described in Chapter 5, human systems are understood as going through a series of developmental stages, each of which has one or several specific challenges to be faced. These periods of challenge are often thought to require some change within the system. It is also thought that if the system has difficulty mastering the challenge, the system will show evidence of dysfunction. This may take one of two forms—either increased conflict and disorganization in the system or the development of symptoms by a member of the system.

There are also data to suggest that any system has its limits insofar as the amount of external stress it can manage without developing signs of stress or leading to symptoms in a member of the system.

Thus, it is important for the couples therapist to inquire about the context in which the marriage is embedded. Is there a particular developmental challenge that is proving difficult? Is there a source of external stress that is readily identifiable? It also seems increasingly apparent that chronic, severe stress is a particularly difficult challenge for most systems. Chronic illness and chronic unemployment are examples.

There are multiple reasons for the therapist to identify a developmental impasse or the presence of severe external stress. Perhaps the most important reason is that without such awareness the therapist may underestimate the strengths of the marriage or family.

I ask a series of questions about the couple's current circumstances. These questions concern the extended family, health issues, recent losses, and job-related problems. It did not take any probing, for example, to recognize that Marj and Ken's dilemma occurred in the context of his retirement and the last child leaving home. It was the challenge of these developmental processes that played one role in their decision to seek help.

SPECIAL PROCEDURES

There are a small number of special procedures that I use when they seem indicated. One is a routine part of my assessment; the other two are used when I think they will prove helpful.

The Rokeach Value Survey

I ask each spouse to complete this value survey privately and bring it to the office. The survey is a forced ranking of two lists of 18 values. The first list is comprised of terminal values—ranging from family security to inner harmony to salvation. The second list presents 18 instrumental values—ranging from ambitious to logical to loving. Both lists must be rank ordered—that is, one value must be ranked highest in importance, another value second highest, and so on until the 18th (or lowest) value is ranked.

Although there are national norms, I am most interested in the ways in which the spouses differ in their value rankings. I report significant differences to the couple at the time I go over my formulation with them.

Conflict Resolution Task

I often select a disagreement that is clearly obvious (usually from the initial interview) and ask the couple to discuss and try to resolve the disagreement at home, while they are audiotaping their conversation.

They are to bring the tape to me and we are very likely to listen to it together as a part of the assessment procedure. Whether we listen or not at the time, the tape provides a baseline to refer back to after we have worked together on improving their communication skills.

Psychotherapy Function Task

As was explicated in Chapter 5, I emphasize that marriage is a search for healing from childhood trauma. I usually say to the couple that under the best of circumstances each spouse finds the other to be a therapist of sorts in that without deliberate effort they help each other work through some of the residua of adverse childhood experiences.

I may suggest to them that I videotape several brief conversations in my office. In each conversation, I ask that one spouse help the other explore a problem from earlier life. Their task is to facilitate exploration in the hope that out of such a conversation new meanings may evolve. I select the problem that is to be the focus of the exploration. I might, for example, say, "Marj, I don't believe that Ken has ever dealt with his father's disappearance from his life when he was seven years old. I wish you would try to help him explore that situation and its effect on him." When this three-to-five-minute exploration is completed, I then ask Ken to help Marj explore a problem from her childhood.

These explorations usually do not turn out well. The spouses seem to have little idea of how one helps another explore a problem. Rather, they interrupt, act judgementally, and suggest remedial actions. Seeing themselves on videotape and sensing their ineptness at exploration can have a remarkable impact. It has proven especially helpful with physicians, lawyers, and clergy, most of whom believe they know how to counsel people.

Once again, the tape is saved to refer back to after each spouse has gained considerable skill in helping the other to explore a problem.

INDIVIDUAL INTERVIEWS

At an early stage in the development of marital and family therapies, many thought a therapist should not meet privately with a spouse or family member. I believe the consensus has changed about this issue.

Regardless, I routinely have one or possibly two individual interviews with each spouse. I do so for several reasons.

First, I ask if there is something I need to know about him or her or about the relationship that has been difficult to discuss in front of the other spouse.

Second, I inquire about extramarital affairs, as discussed in an earlier section.

Third, I try to assess the level of motivation the spouse has to salvage, repair, and improve the marriage. Some individuals come for couples therapy only to go through some final motions or to placate a desperate spouse. They have no real wish to remain in the marriage. If I learn this from one of the spouses, I am reluctant to offer couples therapy. There has to be some level of motivation or the therapy is apt to be doomed from the start. If the lack of motivation is openly confirmed by a spouse in an individual interview, I then ask that spouse what he or she would like to do about it. Most often that spouse and I decide that the issue should be openly discussed in a couples interview. We may then decide to have a series of interviews around ending the relationship, developing a parenting alliance if there are children still at home, or helping the other spouse to deal with the loss. The latter may require individual therapy for that spouse and, if I feel certain the marriage is over, I may agree to become the individual therapist.

After I have systematically collected a great amount of data, the question remains as to what to do with it. I suggest three things: Study it, integrate it, and share it with the couple.

THE DYADIC FORMULATION

One of the more pervasive resistances manifested by individual therapists is delaying the act of formulating their understanding of patients' psychopathology. I routinely insist that, after several or more exploratory interviews, therapists I am supervising commit to paper a formal formulation. Through the years, I have evolved an outline of a clinical formulation that I believe reflects a biopsychosocial model of psychopathology and I give each supervisee a copy of the outline. I do not ask them to use it other than as a general guide to the breadth of thinking required about the multiple variables involved in individual psychopathology. My supervisees do what I ask—but, persuading them is often like pulling teeth.

There are two issues that I emphasize. One is that if one does not get into the habit of routinely formulating patients' psychopathology, the unfettered operation of the therapist's underlying value judgements and biases may be facilitated. Almost as bad, the therapist's model will oversimplify complex processes and he or she will settle for some narrow construct, like co-dependency, as a complete understanding of a complex phenomenon.

The second issue is that once a therapist does formulate the patient's psychopathology, he or she must avoid falling in love with his or her creation. Clinical formulations are temporary constructions that inevitably change as more is learned about the patient. It is the failure to change one's formulation that I refer to as falling in love with it. It is a sign that the therapist is not listening, processing, and asking, "How does this change my understanding of the patient's dilemma?"

There is no reason to believe the problem is anything but worse in couples therapy. How often does one hear about a couples formulation or see suggested outlines for such formulations? Only occasionally, I believe. Some years ago, as head of a psychiatric hospital, I attended three or four staffings each week. The marital-family data were presented by the social worker-family therapist assigned to the patient. I knew each of these professionals to be very competent marital-family therapists; yet, their attempt to report concise, clear, and useful understandings of the patients' marriages or families were, with rare exception, less than adequate. It was clear that they had no model of formulating a marriage or family and approached each situation idiosyncratically. Questions like, "What do you see going on in this family that may interfere with the patient's treatment?" or "What strengths in this family can we build on?" were not often answered adequately.

In Chapter 3, I discussed the challenge to an empirical approach to marriage and the family posed by constructivism. That challenge has, I believe, been a positive force within the field. A downside of that challenge, however, is that it is interpreted by some to stand for an attitude of "each family is unique and the therapist must respect that uniqueness by not looking at what the family has in common with other troubled families." This can be extrapolated to the position of treating each session as a totally independent, hopefully unique conversation that sets the stage for families to change. In other words, the constructivists' approach to marital-family therapy can be distorted by some to be a license to not think systematically about the marital-family system.

The approach I encourage is quite the opposite; it mandates considerable thought about the couple and their dilemma. I note on my schedule, for example, that the next interview with a couple will include a reporting element. I then find the time to go over my notes, the Rokeach Value Survey, and other special procedures, and write a formulation in outline form. The outline for a dyadic formulation is presented in Exhibit 7.1.

EXHIBIT 7.1
The Dyadic Formulation

I. The interactional structure
   A. Marital type
      1. Healthy
      2. Competent but pained
      3. Dominant-submissive
      4. Conflicted
      5. Severely dysfunctional
   B. Presence and intensity of covert and overt conflict
   C. Evidence of developmental impasse or stress-induced change
   D. Evidence of important triangles or other structural alignments

II. Family-of-origin memories for each participant
   A. Family-of-origin structure, level of cohesiveness, and individuation encouraged
   B. Central problematic relationship: reworking the past
   C. Unmourned losses
   D. Family role assignments
   E. Participation in family-of-origin triangles

III. Ways in which mate selection and construction of relationship are related to experiences in family of origin for both spouses
   A. Primary hope of what spouse was to heal
   B. Ways in which one's behavior impedes healing process

IV. Shared or conflicted value orientations
   A. Value orientations brought to marriage by each spouse—for example, regarding time, interpersonal space, gender roles, authority, tradition, generational continuity, freedom and individuality, mastery of world, or basic nature of human condition.

> **EXHIBIT 7.1** *(continued)*
>
>   B. Whose family-of-origin values prevailed? Are there serious value conflicts?
>   C. Rituals as an expression of core values
>   1. Cultural celebrations (Christmas, Passover)
>   2. Family celebrations (birthdays, anniversaries)
>   3. Ritualized routines (dinnertime, bedtime)
>
> V. Characteristic interactional processes
>   A. Rigidity or flexibility of communication patterns
>   B. Distance-producing and closeness-producing techniques of each spouse and their interrelationships. Both verbal and nonverbal signals should be noted.
>   C. Affective issues
>   1. Evidence of warmth
>   2. Conflict
>   a. Escalation processes
>   b. De-escalation processes such as humor, process comments, periods of retreat and cooling off
>   D. Power and authority
>   1. Gross maneuvers such as directives, total withdrawal, physical threats, threats of abandonment
>   2. Subtle maneuvers such as interrogatives, interruptions, topic changes
>   E. Presence of negotiation skills
>   F. Respect for subjective reality
>   G. Major circular hypotheses
>
> VI. Transference and countertransference possibilities
>
> VII. Strengths of the dyadic system

I wish to emphasize, however, that the reader should consider the outline as an evolving and not final form. Each time I prepare for a presentation and construct handouts I note changes that need to be made. Nevertheless, the outline can help both by encouraging the therapist to think about what has been learned about the couple and as a way of organizing the clinical data.

I share much or all of my formulation with the couple, emphasizing from the start that this is but one way of looking at their situation. Further, the formulation will change if I get to know them better. In going over my formulation, I emphasize that each spouse shares equal responsibility for the quality of their relationship—that the failure to heal is a collaborative effort.*

I ask each spouse to respond to the formulation, to agree or disagree with my view of their situation. I want it to be a focus of discussion and it usually is.

I present my formulation to the couple partly, I suspect, because I come from a medical tradition in which doctors tell patients what they believe the problems are. More than that, however, I want to give the couple a cognitive framework, a new way of looking at themselves and their dilemma. Finally, I want them to know how seriously I consider their situation and that I am thoughtful and systematic in my approach.

In actual practice, I outline and diagram my formulation and use these notes as I go over the formulation with the couple. For illustration purposes here, however, I present a more formal written account of my formulation of Marj and Ken's relationship disturbance.

> Ken and Marj appear to have had a competent but pained relationship that has regressed to a conflicted relationship under the stress of Ken's retirement, their last child leaving home, and the anticipated loss of Marj's confidant, her twin, Marie. The data suggest that Marj has been involved in important triangles with her recently married daughter and, centrally, with her twin. Ken's major focus has been on his work and that has allowed him, until recently, to find much self-esteem. An important loss Ken and Marj face is their shared dream of power and influence as president and first lady of a Fortune 500 company. Thus, multiple stressors combine to disturb a marital system that was heavily skewed toward separateness and lacked intimacy.
>
> Ken was a little boy when his alcoholic father deserted the family. Ken, an only child, became his mother's "little man" and during adolescence needed to rebel more than usual in

---

* If there has been physical violence, I am clear that the violent spouse is individually responsible for that violence, and that it must stop. At times, a violent spouse needs referral to a specific treatment program or therapist for violent spouses.

order to break out of the enmeshed relationship with his mother. Although acknowledging pain about the loss of his father, Ken believes his most problematic relationship was with his mother. He believes that he needed more encouragement to separate and find his own way and that his mother was unable or unwilling to encourage his autonomy. As a consequence, he rebelled through a variety of acting-out behaviors that brought his mother much distress.

Marj came from an intact family in which she was the more passive twin and the most compliant of four children. She believes her most problematic relationship was with her twin, Marie, because the relationship did not encourage her to become more assertive and autonomous.

It appears that Ken's underlying attraction to Marj involved the opportunity to heal himself by having a relationship with Marj that would not be enmeshed and would emphasize his capacity for separateness and autonomy. Marj was attracted to Ken for much the same reasons. She hoped to find with him a greater level of autonomy and the ability to separate from her dependent relationship with her twin.

Neither spouse found the relationship to be a healing experience. Ken did not learn to have a close, intimate relationship with a woman; his fears of enmeshment were a part of this failure. Marj did not separate from Marie; rather, she used that relationship to compensate for the distance in her relationship with Ken. Her underlying fears are understood to involve feeling separate, alone, and without sufficient support.

Despite the failure of the relationship to be healing for either spouse, it "worked" in the sense that it maintained each partner's psychological status quo. Only the developmental challenges of retirement and their last child leaving home, coupled with Marie's inoperable cancer, have combined to upset the relationship's equilibrium.

Ken and Marj are much alike in value orientations; they endorse mainstream, middle class values. Their problems do not seem to flow from significant value differences.

Their rituals all come from Marj's family, and most celebrations (Christmas, birthdays, etc.) have been jointly held with Marie and her family.

Under the current stresses, Marj has become depressed and, in her relationship with Ken, much more demanding, sarcastic, and angry. Ken is also struggling with depressive themes, particularly around the loss of his dream. As a consequence, there is less predictability to their relationship now than in the past.

Ken is more the distancer and until recently Marj has had Marie to compensate. With that anticipated loss and Ken's forced retirement, they will have to find closeness and meaning with each other. Both partners are in touch with the belief that they are going to need much more from each other than ever before and each in his or her own way is frightened about the future of the relationship.

There is some warmth in the relationship and, although now there is more open conflict than before, the conflict does not usually escalate because one or both retreat. They show only moderate capacity for negotiating differences and little respect for each other's subjective reality.

Couples therapy seems clearly indicated, with a major focus on helping them achieve greater closeness and intimacy. I suspect that we will be able to move rather quickly to the psychoeducational phase of treatment in which the emphasis will be on exercises designed to augment their listening skills, exploratory techniques, attention to affect, and empathic processes. Through these processes, it is hoped that they can achieve new levels of conversational intimacy and a relationship that will nurture each of them through the losses they face.

Although I must pay attention to their understandable needs to be treated fairly by me, I do not anticipate major transference or countertransference difficulties. I find them likeable and believe they have considerable strengths upon which to draw. The prognosis for the survival and enhancement of their relationship appears good.

TREATMENT PLANNING

In constructing my formulation of the couple's dilemma, I wish to think about as many treatment options as possible. I present these options to the couple and want them to be involved in a collaborative decision about which option or options to pursue.

Many of the couples I see are referred by other therapists. Sometimes, that therapist may be the individual therapist of one of the spouses. The referral is specifically for couples therapy. In my initial interview with the couple, I acknowledge the specificity of the referral and my respect for the referring therapist, but indicate that I wish to go ahead with my assessment both because of the need to feel certain of that direction and also as a way of understanding their relationship problem. Under these circumstances, it is rare not to come to the conclusion that couples therapy is indicated. On those infrequent occasions where I do not believe couples therapy is indicated—usually thinking one or both first should be in individual therapy—I call the referring therapist to discuss the situation and get his or her input.

What is common in some situations is to present the couple with my opinion that both couples therapy and individual therapy for one spouse are indicated. I indicate that I could be either the individual therapist or the couples therapist, but not both. They should decide how they would like to use me—and I can suggest other therapists for the other role.

If the couple question why I won't be both individual and marital therapist, I indicate that I have no problem seeing a spouse for several individual interviews, but it is done in the context of my primary loyalty and commitment to the relationship. If I am to be an individual therapist, my wish is to be, in part, the individual's advocate in the sense of seeing the world through his or her eyes.

If one of the options is couples therapy I almost always suggest 6 or 8 double sessions (90 minutes) and then a clear evaluation of whether progress is being made.

As will become apparent in the chapters to follow, I think of my approach to couples therapy as occurring in three phases: (1) the therapeutic impact of the assessment process, (2) stabilizing the couple's relationship, and (3) a structured approach to teaching communication skills. It is clear that different couples respond differently to each of these phases. For a few, the assessment process puts into motion a process of change and is all that is required. For others, the attempt to stabilize the relationship (involving centrally the attempt to deal with projective processes) takes many interviews. If the treatment fails, it usually fails because I am unable to moderate their shared projection system. Other couples move quickly to communication training and after 6 to 10 sessions are ready to terminate.

During the assessment procedure, I am often able to identify the couples for whom treatment will be difficult or will fail. These couples often seem unable, during the various explorations, to set aside their projections. They persist in blaming each other. Other couples seem deeply immersed in destructive interlocking roles such as hyperadequate-inadequate, well-sick, and parent-child.

Suspecting in advance that there will be more problems than usual is helpful in several ways. First, it is a safeguard against my getting discouraged or caught up in the couple's stalemate. Second, it stimulates me to think of new interventions to deal with the resistance to change.

IMPEDING CIRCUMSTANCES

The lengthy and formal phase of assessment of a dyadic system I have described will doubtlessly be seen by some as inappropriate to the current status of health care funding. This assessment takes from 6 to 8 hours; managed health care reviewers probably would not look kindly on funding such an assessment. Unfortunately, most indemnity insurance contracts exclude coverage for couples therapy. In light of the current strictures on funding couples therapy, the reader may ask how I can justify my kind of assessment.

Although it is clear that much of what I call assessment actually involves a number of discrete treatment interventions that are all that is required for some couples, I would not want to justify a lengthy assessment on the grounds of disguised treatment. Rather, I base my claim for justification on both philosophical and strategic positions.

From a philosophical perspective, this is a time for all mental health disciplines to examine carefully the issues we face. From a strategic viewpoint, actions should be planned based on the best possible understanding of those issues. The key issues for me include the alarming growth of reviewers telling therapists how they should treat patients, couples, and families in order to be reimbursed for their professional efforts. The reviewers are in the service of the new profit centers in health care and they wish to minimize any approach to comprehensive care. If, in order to be reimbursed, we do only the brief and often oversimplified treatment approaches, we will come to know well only those forms of treatment that are reimbursed. Soon we will cut back on our attempts to educate future therapists in anything but brief therapies. More comprehensive formulations based on systematic and theory-driven assessments leading to more thorough approaches to treatment will be forgotten.

This sequence is well underway in my parent discipline, psychiatry, where teaching psychotherapy has all but disappeared from some training programs. Indeed, the crunch of managed health care has been augmented immeasurably by the brain disease model of psychopathology. From the brain disease perspective, psychosocial variables are mostly epiphenomenal and, as a consequence, the psychotherapies are all too often seen as tangential, at best. Psychiatric residents are taught only a brain disease model, a DSM-IV directive inquiry, and descriptive diagnoses. Fewer and fewer know anything of exploratory interviews, chains of associations, major recurring themes in patients' narratives, and the importance of affect, defense mechanisms, and transference-countertransference. On audiotapes or from behind one-way mirrors, some of them behave like census takers.

Marital-family therapies have traditionally had only a tenuous foothold in most residency programs. The power of the human systems in which the patient's life is embedded to make crucial differences in treatment outcome is a neglected theme. For most residency programs, three or four didactic lectures is about all students get on marriage and the family.

All of this is by way of defining the crucial issues. At the heart of it, the issues are: How can we survive economically as therapists and, at the same time, preserve all that we have learned and pass it on to future generations?

Strategically, we need to have some of our most skilled clinicians working within managed care structures—developing new models of brief marital-family therapies and, most importantly, finding ways to identify when and how such newer and briefer therapies work. I am convinced that many of our best minds need to be in the forefront of that activity.

Others need to remain deeply involved in the comprehensive assessment and therapy of human systems and to make every effort to see that what is learned is not lost from the curricula of mental health training programs. I see what I do as in this tradition, and I do not shirk from presenting my approaches to colleagues and students.

At the same time, it is important that the two groups of therapists talk with and listen to each other. Furthermore, it is my long-term bet that managed health care will fail and the major battle of the future will be to insure that marital-family therapies are included as standard components of a centrally funded health care delivery system.

I also believe that some of what I do in assessment and therapy can be useful to other therapists using brief formats. Indeed, I have borrowed much from them in evolving this approach.

Finally, I like what I do. It suits me. It is extremely fortunate that what I do is seen by referring sources (colleagues, students, couples, families, and former patients) as valuable. I also like being in charge of my own fee structure and, in that way, having a rich variety of persons turn to me for help in sorting something out, changing a system, or facing existential issues.

8

Marital Therapy: Initial Considerations

My approach to marital therapy involves three overlapping stages: the assessment procedures, stabilizing or perturbing the system, and structured communication exercises. Before describing these stages of treatment, it seems necessary to address several general considerations about the therapist, including the person of the therapist, how he or she thinks about systems, and how therapeutic interventions are to be considered and implemented.

PERSONAL EXPERIENCES OF THE THERAPIST

Under the best of circumstances, a couples therapist should have considerable personal experience in relationships, at least some that have worked well. In the best of all worlds, the couples therapist would also have had the opportunity to get to know well some couples who do not come for treatment. Interviewing nonclinical samples of couples provides an opportunity for the therapist to expand his or her range of observations about system functioning. I found, for example, that interviewing or watching hundreds of hours of videotaped couple discussion tasks from three very different samples of research volunteer families exposed me to a subset of well-functioning couples. These couples taught me much about what is possible in relationships and also helped me to better understand the differences between well-functioning couples and dysfunctional couples.

I have noted earlier that most mental health professionals come to know personally only a small number of families. The marriage or marriages of one's parents, perhaps the marriages of truly close friends, and one's own marriage or marriages constitute a very small sample. If this personal sample has been skewed towards system dysfunction, and one's career involves days filled with couples whose relationships are not working, it is, perhaps, easy to develop pervasive pessimism about what is possible in important relationships.

THE THERAPIST'S VALUES

All psychotherapists need to be in touch with their values. It has always surprised me how little is done in most training programs to introduce students to the exploration of their own values. In a psychiatric residency program that I directed for many years, each beginning student of psychotherapy filled out the Rokeach Value Survey, and we discovered the ways in which he or she was similar to or different from both representative samples and colleagues (Rokeach & Ball-Rokeach, 1989). Students of couples therapy are also introduced to my modification (see Chapter 7) of Spiegel's extension of the Kluckhohns' work on values (Spiegel, 1971, 1982). This format, with its roots in existential issues, facilitates the student of couples therapy in examining his or her value orientation from a perspective quite different from and, in some ways, complementary to the Rokeach perspective.

Some years ago, Eisenberg (1972) published a seminal essay that pointed out that what the clinician believes about the nature of humankind strongly influences how he or she treats patients. If, for example, one believes that the individual cannot escape a core loneliness, that even under the best of circumstances human connections are but a weak balm for this loneliness, he or she may not be as creative as possible in trying to help alienated couples connect better.

TRANSFERENCE AND COUNTERTRANSFERENCE

Another crucial issue is how well the couples therapist comes to understand both his or her potential for evoking particular transferences and those relationship issues that provoke his or her countertransference. Both forms of transference are ubiquitous and a couples therapist's awareness of personal propensities provides the possibility of an important source of information and intervention. Each therapist needs to be aware of the subjective experiences that signal either too much distance from the patient's or couple's experience or too much identification with it. In an early paper (Lewis, 1979), I have suggested ways of self-monitoring such countertransference signals.

There are a number of ways to develop increasing awareness of one's transference-countertransference propensities. Personal psychotherapy and psychoanalysis are the most traditional approaches, but supervision (particularly, I believe, that involving audio- and videotapes of couples therapy) and group supervision with one's peers can also be helpful. Seeking consultation from an experienced colleague can often not only resolve treatment impasses but also illuminate the frequent role of transference-countertransference issues in such impasses.

THE THERAPIST'S CENTRAL RELATIONSHIP

The ongoing presence of a central relationship in the life of the therapist is important for many reasons. This is particularly so if that relationship provides the therapist with intimacy. Under these circumstances, there is less likelihood that the therapist's work will be used to provide self-esteem, closeness, and intimacy. All training directors have noted the trainee who seems to never leave the clinic or hospital, whose whole life seems to rotate about relationships with patients. Usually, such trainees have either no emotionally important central relationship or one that is unsatisfactory.

THE THERAPIST'S VIEW OF HUMAN SYSTEMS

Another important area involves how the therapist thinks about human systems. Although I believe their numbers are not great, there are couples therapists whose orientation is at the level of the individual. They describe their work with couples almost entirely in the language of personality traits, individual syndromes, or individual psychodynamics. One distinguished psychoanalyst who treats couples (as well as analysands) suggested to me that, in his opinion, couples therapy was the treatment of choice for individuals with severe personality disorders. "Having each spouse there is important in confronting and working through the patient's defenses," he explained. Contrary to the usual focus on the couple's interactions, his focus was on doing individual work with each partner with the assistance of the other partner.

In Chapter 3, I outlined the current dialectic between empiricism and constructivism as it applies to how one thinks about human systems. Although I find the constructivists' challenge to the empirical perspective on human systems valuable because of the importance of the issues they emphasize, I spelled out my belief in the empirical tradition. Human systems have an "out there" reality that exists independent of the act of observation. Further, despite the need to attend closely the context in which a particular marriage or family is embedded, it is possible to assess the overall adaptive competence of the system.

Central to this approach, however, is the need to spell out the values underlying the definition of competence. If one is clear about the underlying values, others may agree or disagree that such values are a reasonable foundation for a definition of system competence. If, for example, the values underlying family competence are defined as facilitating the continuing maturation of the adults' personalities and raising children who can both function autonomously and relate intimately, others can decide whether they agree with such a value-based definition.

I believe there is more agreement among couples therapists about the essential characteristics of human systems than there is about the idea of overall adaptive competence. Whether or not the therapist accepts the usual list of system characteristics (e.g., boundaries, power, affective expressiveness, problem-solving efficiency, etc.), he or she may often come to emphasize a particular characteristic or two. Thus, some couples therapists focus heavily on the transmission of generational themes; others focus on power distribution within the system or on boundary permeability with the outside world. It is important for the clinician to know that his or her emphasis on particular system characteristics differs from those of other therapists and may lead to ways of understanding the system and intervening in it that are somewhat idiosyncratic.

THE THERAPIST'S APPROACH TO INTERVENTIONS

A major area that couples therapists have to decide about concerns approaches to intervention—the pragmatics of couples therapy. There are a number of issues that must be faced. Perhaps the first issue is the extent to which the treatment plan and the interventions flowing from it is to be specific for each couple. There are some therapists who have a more-or-less set routine and use it with all of those who come for help. I recall some years ago, for example, when after a presentation at a psychiatric society meeting I was asked what I thought about transactional analysis. I responded by asking the clinician why he asked. He responded by saying that he used it with his patients. "Which of your patients?" I then asked. "All of them," was his response.

My position is that, insofar as possible, each couple's treatment needs to be individualized. In that process the overall organizational structure of the relationship system should guide the therapist. Couples with severely conflicted or chaotic relationships will need different approaches than those couples with more functional relationships who are dealing with acute stress or here-and-now developmental challenges.

Initial decisions involve how to define the problem and in Chapter 1 an example was offered that illustrates some of the complexity that can ensue. How much to accept the patient's or couple's definition of the problem and how active the therapist is to be in the process of definition are important concerns. In psychiatry, for example, the current emphasis is on descriptive diagnoses, and the process of diagnosing is something the clinician does to (or for) the patient. Many couples therapists want the process of problem-definition to be collaborative; yet, there are situations in which the couple's definition allows serious system pathology to go unattended. The couple with a chronically conflicted relationship and severe alcohol abuse who initially define their problem as their child's behavior disorder is an all too common example.

THE THERAPIST'S POSITION ON THE USE OF POWER

The stance taken about the definition of the problem is a reflection of a central issue each couples therapist must face. The issue is how the therapist is to use his or her power. In both Chapter 1 and Chapter 6

I have suggested some of the issues involved and my attempts to resolve them in a way that works for me and seems helpful to those coming to me for help. I am, however, unable to know with certainty how much of my approach to the use of power is related, in part, to the nature of my practice. Many of the people who seek my help have achieved considerable social power. As I write, for example, physicians, lawyers, successful business men and women, and other therapists constitute 90 percent of my practice. For the most part, these are conventionally successful persons whose achievements have come despite clear deficits in their marital relationships. How I might use power in the treatment situation might be quite different if, as early in my career, my context was public psychiatry and my patients, socially disadvantaged and with little power.

The issue is complex. Most clinicians value collaborative processes, the avoidance of heavy-handed uses of power, and sensitivity to the patient's or couple's subjective reality. Although there is a growing body of research that attempts to define the nature of the psychotherapeutic alliance associated with successful outcome in individual psychodynamic psychotherapy, there remains much that we need to learn. Perhaps we need to do more thinking about the kinds of questions that need to be asked. One such question is, "What are the types of situations in which the couples therapist may need to use all the power he or she can muster?" Spousal and child abuse come quickly to mind. From the opposite perspective, "In what clinical situations should the couples therapist attempt to minimize his or her power?" An example is the couple openly grieving for the first time the loss of their only child. The therapist may need only to "be there" and, in that sense, help the couple to hold the grief.

There are other issues around the thoughtful use of power by the couples therapist. One is suggested above and involves the decision as to when to just "be there" and help with the holding function, and when to be more active in using a range of interventions. I raise the question of how holding or actively interventional a couples therapist chooses to be for particular couples, despite my awareness that many therapists develop a style that usually prevails more generally for all couples. I find that I am more actively interventional in couples therapy than in individual psychotherapy. I like the balance of providing mostly quiet listening, with occasional reflections and interpretations, with individuals, and the more active structuring and, in many ways, educational aspects of couples therapy.

THE THERAPIST'S USE OF DISTANCE

Another important dimension of couples therapy about which the therapist must come to some decision is how close to or distant from the couple's subjective reality he or she wishes to work. There are those therapists who remain mostly outside the couple's or family's experience, preferring a position of detached authority. The late Murray Bowen appeared to have preferred this stance. Others eschew such distance with its objectivity and authority and call for what sometimes seems to be a radical form of empathy—such as the existentially oriented therapist's mandate of "being" and "staying." The Relationship Enhancement Therapy of Guerney (1994) and the feminist-constructivist approach of Weingarten (1992) are contemporary examples of working close to the subjective experience of each partner.

Once again the issue, perhaps, is whether it is possible to decide how close to or far from the couple's experience is apt to be most helpful for particular couples with specific characteristics. It seems to me that in regard to this aspect of couples therapy we might think of the expert as one who can modify his or her approach to best fit each couple. The issue then becomes whether it is possible to come to know the optimal working distances for a broad range of couples.

TREATMENT GOALS

Another related issue is how treatment goals are to be established. To what extent does the couples therapist have in mind the kinds of changes that must be made for the treatment to be considered successful? If there is evidence from research that suggests that highly competent marriages (see Chapter 4) have certain characteristics, should such characteristics influence the goals of treatment for some, most, or all couples?

It appears that there is a broad range of therapists' opinions about this. Some propose that couples should set their own treatment goals and the therapist should restrict treatment to the pursuit of those goals; when such goals are achieved, treatment should be terminated. Others believe that the therapist cannot avoid having opinions about functional, competent, or highly satisfying relationships and that such opinions will inevitably influence his or her treatment efforts. Some of these therapists believe that the best approach is to use research findings regarding well-functioning systems and be clear in working with couples about what is known about such systems.

There is no right or wrong way in so much of this; rather, one hopes that these and other decisions about one's clinical approach are thoroughly considered and thoughtfully chosen, rather than letting oneself drift into first one approach then another.

SOURCES OF MY APPROACH

In the following pages, it will be clear that I use interventions from a number of schools of marital therapy. Much of the theory that guides my work is based on a psychoanalytic object relations perspective. My use of interpretations comes from my long-term interest in practicing, teaching, and supervising individual psychoanalytically oriented psychotherapy.

My focus on distance regulation as a powerful perspective from which to consider interventions has multiple roots, including family therapy, attachment theory, and psychoanalysis. My emphasis on subjective experience, affect, and empathic processes also has multiple roots, including self-psychology and psychoanalysis. I also use interventions such as trade-offs that are clearly behavioral. My emphasis on communication skills and my efforts to teach them is also derived from multiple roots.

Thus, in addition to the 15 theoretical premises outlined in Chapter 5, my work borrows much from a broad range of perspectives. I do, however, vary my approach with couples of differing levels of dysfunction. Those couples, for example, with the more severe levels of dysfunction (chaotic, severely alienated, and/or those intensely invested in mutual projections) require different and, in some ways, more active interventions than do many couples with lesser levels of dysfunction.

Some of these general considerations about couples therapy and the couples therapist can be illustrated with the following clinical vignette.

> They were referred to me by his psychotherapist, the third he had seen in the past 18 months. The current therapist described him as in the midst of an atypical depression with

paranoid trends and periods of cognitive disorganization. He was a trial lawyer but had been unable to practice for six weeks. She was a radiologist and described by his therapist as very rational, intellectual, and somewhat remote.

His symptoms had begun after their youngest child, a daughter, had married. There was a history of one prior episode of a similar syndrome during his first year of college and at that time he dropped out of school and returned to his parents' home. "I saw my rabbi every week for several months and learned that I have difficulty with separations. My mother is a very dominant and overwhelming person and much as I wished to avoid her, I had trouble leaving her," he said.

His wife nodded in agreement and said, "I try not to be too forceful with Hal because I know how it reminds him of his mother. She is a holy terror and we avoid her whenever possible. I'm a convert to Judaism and a second class citizen in her eyes. The problems I have with Hal, though, are that I'm naturally pretty direct—I'm Chief of Radiology, and running a radiology department at a large private hospital requires a lot of administrative decisions. Hal, himself, is forceful and a crackerjack trial lawyer—except when he's like he has been for the past year or so. Then he acts so helpless that someone has to take over and make decisions."

Hal sighed often and said little spontaneously during the initial interview. At one point I asked him what was involved in his having seen three therapists since he had been feeling so bad. He responded by saying, "I don't know. None of the medications prescribed have helped and the doctors seemed to get discouraged. The first two therapists each suggested a consultation and I ended up staying with the consultant."

"It sounds like you've really tried to get some help," I responded, "but nothing has been helpful."

"Yeah," he said, "I'm very discouraged. Living this way is simply not worth it—I'd rather be dead."

"Thought about suicide?" I asked. At this point she intervened. "Doctor, I don't believe it's best to talk about suicide.

I won't let Hal discuss it—the more you talk and think about it the more you may be tempted!"

I turned to her and said, "I know how anxious Hal's depression and the thought of losing him must make you—"

She interrupted, "Doctor, I've been through it once—with my brother—and I'll not tolerate it again. It damned near did me in."

"There's perhaps nothing worse than to have someone you truly care about kill himself or herself—it always leaves so many unanswered questions—," I reflected.

She looked away with obvious sadness. I turned back to Hal and raised my eyebrows. He stared at me and, finally, I said, "And so, Hal?"

He shook his head from side to side and said, "I don't know what to do. Nothing helps, I'm feeling more hopeless and helpless each day, and Jane can't stand it. I think there is—I don't know—"

"You were about to say?"

"Well—Jane can't stand helplessness. I think I could beat her, have an affair, and she'd tolerate it—but my feeling the way I do is absolutely intolerable for her."

As is often the case, I was fascinated by this interchange. It brought up a variety of issues that I find of central importance for the practice of couples therapy. Perhaps the first issue is how to think about what one has observed and heard from Hal and Jane.

One group of such issues centers about the interpersonal perspective on psychopathology in general and depressive syndromes in particular. In Chapter 3, I reviewed briefly some of the relevant literature and my current position about these issues. Hal and Jane's initial interview brings several of them to the forefront.

First, the therapist needs to understand the role of loss as a precipitant of Hal's syndrome. Why was their youngest child's marriage defined as the point of origin of Hal's syndrome? He suggests that he is unusually vulnerable to separations and losses dating back to his attempts to separate from his dominant and controlling mother.

In addition to whatever sensitivity to loss he may have, what does the role of the loss of this daughter to marriage say about Hal and

Jane's relationship? Was this child somehow necessary to the maintenance of their relationship? Was she involved in regulating their balance of separateness-autonomy and connectedness-intimacy? Or did she provide either Hal or Jane with something missing in their relationship? Couples therapists often see middle-aged couples after the last child leaves and the spouses must face whether their relationship is enough. Such questions only scratch the surface of what the couples therapist needs to understand about the role or roles that the daughter's separation from them may play.

A second issue that needs to be understood is the relationship of Hal and Jane's marital system to Hal's depressive syndrome. The position taken here includes several key points. The first point is that symptoms inevitably come to have communicative significance in the patient's immediate context. When one spouse develops depressive symptoms, those symptoms are understood to express underlying messages to the spouse and others in the marital-family system.

Although the messages expressed by the depressive symptoms can be idiosyncratic, several are common. The first is the implicit request for help. "Make me feel better," "Reassure me that I'm worthwhile," or "Tell me you love me," are examples of the unspoken request for help. A second message often involves the theme of the other's failure to help. "Nothing you say or do makes any difference" is the common unspoken second-level message. Thirdly, the depressive symptoms may carry an angry message of revenge. "Because you don't give me what would help, you, too, should hurt" is the essence of this level of what depressive symptoms may communicate.

It is rare that these messages are consciously considered by the depressed person. Sometimes, however, they come to be experienced by the recipient in a conscious way. This is particularly apt to be so in chronic depressive syndromes and in relationships that have greater than usual conflicts around dependency, closeness, and intimacy. Often, the spouse with the depressive syndrome has lesser power in the relationship and the syndrome can be understood from this perspective as an attempt to redefine the relationship in the direction of reducing the perceived power of the more dominant spouse.

Another aspect of the ways in which a person's depressive symptoms and his or her marital system are connected is their circularity. It is important for the couples therapist to understand that depressive syndromes inevitably have multiple causes, some of which involve hereditary tendencies, and others which involve developmental experiences during childhood. Certain individual personality structures also appear to increase the probability of depression.

Often, the influence of marital conflict, skewed power relationships, and the absence of closeness and intimacy are best understood as crucial determinants of the course of the depressive syndrome. It is important to keep in mind that depression in a spouse, particularly if chronic, can injure even a good marriage over time. On the other hand, the more dysfunctional the marriage, the greater probability of the development of a depressive syndrome (or other symptomatic state) in one of the participants.

For these reasons, it is my belief that a marital consultation is indicated in all depressive syndromes that do not respond to individual psychotherapy and antidepressive medications. Put simply, the resistance to improvement or cure may be more in the system than in the depressed person.

It seems clear that Hal's chronic depression and Hal and Jane's marriage have something to do with each other. Using only the data presented in the brief segment of the initial interview, one should entertain a number of possibilities. The first is that Hal's chronic symptoms—particularly his helplessness—have great impact on Jane. A forceful, direct person in her own right, Jane has difficulty tolerating Hal's helplessness and the helpless position in which she is placed. She is unable to find ways to help Hal and it appears that his death wishes and, perhaps, suicidal ruminations take Jane back to her brother's suicide and how helpless she may have felt in preventing that tragedy. Certainly, she attempted to avoid the intensity of Hal's suicidal intent by indicating that she prohibited such discussions. I suspected that this very powerful intervention on her part is a clear reflection of how frightened she is to once again feel helpless about a loved one's depression.

The brief segment does not tell us very much about the usual state of their relationship; rather, what they say suggests some of the directions that future explorations should take. Jane seems very powerful during the first interview and describes her job as one requiring comfort with decision-making that influences the lives of many in her department. At the same time, her response to my question about suicidal thoughts suggests that beneath the surface is much fear—fear that may have to do with feeling helpless. There is much I need to know about Jane, her childhood experiences, and the unconscious needs that influenced her selection of Hal as a spouse.

Jane describes Hal as forceful when not depressed and his choice of litigation as a legal specialty can be understood as attracting and requiring high levels of forcefulness. Hal may have learned that to be forceful allowed him to avoid facing underlying dependency needs; that learning may have started early in life in his relationship with his mother.

There is also the issue of his counselling with his rabbi during his earlier depression when he attempted to leave his mother to go to college. Did the rabbi help him understand better the issues involved in his depression and to form a clearer sense of his own identity? Was Hal helped to separate from his powerful mother? These questions suggest some of what the therapist needs to know.

In addition, however, it will be helpful to develop understanding of what Hal's inner hopes were in selecting Jane as a life partner. Did he select someone who had some of his mother's power and hope that he could work through his fears of women? Or did he unconsciously realize that Jane wouldn't push for too much closeness?

I also wish to understand better the structure of their relationship before Hal's depression. As noted above, why did their last child leaving home seem to precipitate Hal's depression? Did it reawaken his failed effort to leave his mother? Did it remove some important influence on Hal and Jane's marriage?

More than the role of this loss, however, what kind of marriage had Hal and Jane constructed? Was it characterized mostly by high levels of separateness-autonomy with little closeness and no intimacy? Or was there considerable underlying conflict about the definition of the relationship? How can I better understand the hints that the themes of dependency, power, and helplessness may have particular significance in Hal and Jane's relationship?

These questions do not begin to exhaust the possibilities. I offer them here to illustrate something of the cognitive challenge faced by the therapist as he or she begins to try to understand a complex clinical dilemma.

At a different level, however, there are other important issues. These involve the transference-countertransference clues that are suggested during the initial encounter with Hal and Jane.

After the first interview, I wondered about Hal and, in particular, his having seen three individual psychotherapists in the past 18 months. This pattern raises the possibility that there is something about Hal's current relationship tendencies that turn off psychotherapists. They

Sources of My Approach

may be relieved to request consultation and then encourage the consultant to become the primary clinician. If there is any truth in such a speculation, I suspect that it is Hal's helplessness, failure to improve, and suicidal rumination that may threaten a psychotherapist.

The implications of this line of thought have much relevance for me. This is because I have struggled since childhood to avoid any sense of helplessness. The inevitable moments of helplessness involved in raising four children—particularly through the flower child and drug-oriented 60s and 70s—and, more recently, the confrontation with helplessness involved in life-threatening surgery have helped me to come to be somewhat less anxious about helplessness. In looking back to the days of my residency and early individual psychotherapeutic practice, I recall how badly I managed patients with pervasive helplessness.

All of this should alert me to be particularly watchful for evidence of my wishing to, in some way, distance myself from Hal.

I must also be sensitive to Jane and her potential for evoking a destructive countertransference. Although she may welcome my involvement with her and Hal, there is the possibility that she may attempt to draw me into a competitive struggle about Hal and the management of his depression. I need to keep in mind that there is likely much fear behind her forcefulness and not allow her aggressive exterior to threaten my sense of competence.

Another issue is my belief that Hal should continue to see the referring psychotherapist if that therapist is willing. With Hal and Jane's permission, I need at some early point to talk with her about the situation.

There are other issues that come out of the initial encounter, certainly including those that are concerned with how the problem gets defined. This aspect of the early interviews was the focus of Chapter 1, and I will not repeat those observations. Rather, Chapter 9 addresses the therapeutic efforts of the structured assessment procedure and what I have learned about stabilizing the marital system in preparation for the effort to teach couples communication skills that characterize intimate, healing relationships.

9

Marital Therapy: Therapeutic Effects of the Assessment and Stabilizing the System

It is clear that there is much that can be therapeutic about the assessment procedure for some couples. Although my initial verbal contract with the couple is for an assessment only, I believe there are several ways in which what goes on between therapist and couple may prove beneficial.

THE HOLDING FUNCTION

First, the structure of the assessment and its deliberateness provide some relief from what has all too often been a strife-torn and increasingly chaotic situation. This "slowing things down" acts to contain the pain in the relationship and, as such, has a holding function.

There are some occasions when one or both spouses struggle against the imposed structure. Most often, one spouse leads the battle by insisting on discussing his or her agenda over and over again. I deal with this by paying attention to what this spouse wants to talk about, but return again and again to the assessment format. On rare occasions, I have said directly something like, "It seems that there is a tension here about what we're going to talk about during these initial sessions. Can one of you help me understand what this is about?"

The Holding Function

On other occasions the resistance to the structure of the assessment is less direct. One such example is the couple who do relatively well in the interval between appointments only to have a serious crisis the night before or the morning of the next interview. The crisis occupies our attention and diverts from the assessment structure. Although many couples can have occasional crises between sessions, it is when a pattern develops that the therapist should consider addressing the pattern. Perhaps something like this can be said. "I've noticed that in the 12 to 24 hours before each of our last sessions you two have managed to have a really bitter argument. Do either of you have any thoughts about what that's all about?"

Most often, the couple will minimize the temporal correlation, but sometimes very productive discussions ensue. Several themes have emerged. One involves the idea that it's safer to argue knowing that within hours they will be back in the therapist's office. Another theme involves shared anxiety about the assessment process. No one has ever spontaneously said, "We don't like having someone impose his or her structure on us so we're attempting to control what we talk about," or "Neither of us has an easy time with authority figures." I will, however, sometimes bring up the resistance theme with statements like, "I do understand that it can be scary to put yourself in the hands of someone you hardly know, and I wonder if your arguments before our sessions might not also reflect some understandable caution you have about letting someone temporarily take over?"

It does seem apparent that the assessment procedure and its imposition is a powerful act and that for some couples it evokes a host of feelings that need to be dealt with as openly as possible. In this regard, my ideas about the use of power in therapeutic relationships are relatively simple. The therapist should use all the power he or she needs to in order to reduce the intensity of the presenting problems and stabilize the system.

When that is accomplished, the therapist should immediately begin processes aimed to minimize his or her power and to move the relationship to a more collaborative status. To the extent that the therapeutic relationship is experienced by the patient(s) as collaborative, the more likely he, she, or they, will experience positive changes as their own. Under the best of circumstances, the individual or couple who have done a good piece of work will feel that, although the therapist helped facilitate change, the positive outcome came mostly out of their joint effort.

On several occasions in the last five years, a couple have not returned for a second appointment. Because they only called and left the message, I have no way of knowing to what they were reacting, but my guess is that the issues of power, the imposition of the assessment procedure, or something else about my approach or me may have been involved.

THE INTRODUCTION OF COMMUNICATION SKILLS

During the assessment procedure, I make a deliberate effort to model basic psychotherapy skills in my explorations with the couple. I listen with a high level of attention and do not often interrupt, use judgemental statements, or change the subject until the spouse or spouses have said what they wish to say. I also focus on the affective component of most communications and make every effort to put myself in the experiential position of the other. This modeling of several empathic processes communicates a respect for each participant's subjective reality. When what one spouse says contradicts what the other has said, I try to be clear that I anticipate each will experience a shared situation differently, and that my primary interest is not "the truth" but to understand how each experienced the situation.

I use reflexive or circular questions in the effort to emphasize context. "Although you say he never pays any attention to your feelings, can you remember any times when he seemed to be more interested?" "What was there about that situation that was associated with his appearing interested?" "Are there times when you can be certain he won't be interested in your feelings and other times when you're less certain?" These reflexive questions are meant to emphasize the context and diminish the emphasis on character traits.

A number of spouses have commented on these aspects of the assessment process. Often, the comments focus on fairness—how I seem equally interested in both of their inner experiences. As will be discussed in a later section about my approach to communication skills training, it has been my experience, however, that for partners to learn to listen, focus on affect, make empathic reflections, and develop respect for each other's subjective reality requires repetitive and focused efforts.

THE INTRODUCTION OF A NEW COGNITIVE SET

The systematic approach to data collection almost always introduces a new assumptive set to the couple on both the nature of marital problems and how one goes about studying a marriage. The perspective introduced in my approach to assessment has several basic features. One is that the characteristics of a marriage are understandable. This construct implies directly that the universe of marriage has but a small group of important variables that, in concert, determine the ultimate nature of the relationship.

The second feature is that it is possible to step back and study a human system with a considerable degree of "objectivity." Although I present myself as an expert (informed uncertainty), the procedure also suggests that the spouses can become experts about their relationship. Thus, the assessment procedure introduces the couple to a scientific world view. If they are thorough enough and use a "scientific" approach to data collection, it is possible to better understand and change their relationship.

A third feature is complexity. The model of important relationships introduced during the assessment procedure is one of multiple interacting variables. It is not because one's spouse is withholding or undisciplined that the marriage is in trouble; rather, many previously unrecognized factors are involved. The relationship is more complex than ever before realized. Further, so many factors appear to be involved that simple and certain explanations seem inappropriate.

Another feature of this approach is the deliberate introduction of a new model of what marriages are about. When one begins the process of presenting a new cognitive map of marriage, several important constructs are introduced. One is that "almost everyone"* has problems left over from childhood relationships and that these problems can be reasonably reduced to a central problematic relationship from childhood. Furthermore, problematic relationships can be identified with a three-part interactional format involving: (1) a wish, (2) response of other, and (3) response of self.

---

* "Almost everyone" is almost certainly an exaggeration. We do not know how many persons from a truly representative sample describe problems in their childhood families. It is also clear that current life circumstances influence how early memories are recalled (Lewis & Owen, 1996).

Further, marriage often involves the search for an experience that "heals" the problematic relationship, now internalized as one part of the sense of self. In the unconscious wish for healing, the definition of what the relationship is to be like is paramount. In that definition, a critical element lies in the decisions regarding how much of what kinds of closeness and separateness are to characterize the relationship.

In this model, the emphasis is on the greater importance of context (circumstances) over character (enduring individual traits). Further, whenever possible, the therapist emphasizes circular causality rather than linear causality. Cause and effect can be arbitrary definitions dependent upon how complex interactions between the spouses are punctuated.

All of this is meant to introduce complexity, increase doubt, and reduce certainty. Specifically, it intends to question the simple characterizations of self and other as victim or aggressor, adequate or inadequate, well or sick. It is meant to "boggle the mind" of both spouses.

SUGGESTIONS ABOUT THE THERAPIST

As indicated in Chapter 6, the patient or couple are also assessing the therapist. All of the therapist's assessment procedures (or their absence) speak directly to important characteristics of the therapist. Most directly, they are a window into his or her way of thinking about behavior, relationships, and what is possible in a shared life. Assessment procedures, however, tell patients more about the therapist than his or her cognitive style. They speak directly to the issues of power and authority. They reflect on the level of planfulness and the seriousness of the therapist's intent. The therapist's capacity for fairness and his or her ability to hold opposite views of the same situation in mind without taking sides are important. The assessment procedure also reflects how interested and curious the therapist is.

My sense of the conclusions couples often come to about me through these initial appointments and the specific data gathering that makes up the assessment procedure are based on what I am told. The comments of present and past patients, however, almost always have multiple roots and I do not assume they are *all* that couples conclude about me. Another source of information comes from the comments new referrals may report from couples seen earlier. Almost always, new patients say that the former patients told them their impressions of me and how I work. Another factor is that many have seen other couples therapists and talk about the ways in which my structured assessment differs.

The fact that my initial contract is for an assessment only is important to some. Second, it is reassuring to many that I appear to know what it is that I need to know about them. Third, most of the couples either know beforehand or soon learn that I have been interested in, studied, and written about what works in marriage and the family and this seems important to many. Fourth, many of the people whom I see express positive reactions to the structure of the assessment itself. "Does your actual therapy also have some sort of structured approach?" is not an infrequent question.

Finally, the idea that I will discuss with them my observations and early formulation and suggest options is almost always commented upon favorably. Most couples appear to like the idea that I will suggest options to them and ask them to think about the options individually, after which I suggest they set aside an hour or so to explore and jointly decide which direction they prefer. For some couples, this approach augments the sense that they must ultimately be in control of their future.

I believe that for all but a few couples the messages the assessment procedure gives about who I am and how I work is therapeutic in the sense that it facilitates an initial working alliance, suggests an ambiance of safety, introduces a new cognitive set, and restores some degree of hope.

STABILIZING OR UPSETTING THE SYSTEM

During the assessment procedure, the therapist should be able to develop an initial formulation of each spouse's central problematic relationship of childhood and its core dynamics. This leads to the early tentative formulation of each spouse's key dynamics that play a role in his or her search for a healing relationship and, if healing does not occur, are reenacted within the marital relationship.

The therapist should also be able to develop insight into the couple's interactional distance regulation dynamics through observing their discussions of the levels of closeness, commitment, intimacy, separateness, and power. Additional understanding of the interactional dynamics is often obtained by observing their discussions of differences of opinion about religion, sexuality, money, life dreams, and rituals. If a taped conflict-resolution task has been asked for, it, too, will provide important interactional data. Thus, the therapist should have three brief formulations in view—one of each spouse's individual central dynamics and the couple's mutual interactional dynamics.

What is needed is a concept that helps to tie together these individual and interactional formulations. The concept often emphasized by those who link individual object relations constructs and dyadic distance regulation interactions is that of projection and projective identification.

Projection, Projective Identification, and Distance Regulation

There are two different ways to understand the conflicts couples present to the therapist. One perspective is that each partner has unconsciously selected the other because the partner actually resembles in important ways, psychologically, the internalized fragments of the parent involved in the most problematic relationship of childhood. Thus, a man who fears closeness based on his early relationship with a harsh, intrusive, and domineering father has selected a wife who has some of those characteristics. When she signals a need for closeness—most often presented as the need to be understood—his unconscious fears of being invaded and dominated are activated and he retreats. The retreat may take different forms: physically leaving the scene, changing the subject, making judgemental statements, or provoking conflict. Often, these responses activate her underlying fears—frequently centering on abandonment—and she responds with anger. Escalation may then follow.

This type of formulation is based on the therapist's ability to recognize the characteristics of the partner that are feared by the other. In my work, these characteristics are obvious either on direct observation or in listening with the couple to audiotaped homework assignments.

> A middle-aged attorney described a period of conflict between appointments. He said it started when he came home from work to find a doctor's bill that he had paid

months earlier but continued to be billed for. His response was an angry outburst: "Damn, why don't they get it straight! I've called his office twice and both times they said they'd take care of it. Now, this dammed bill."

His wife, whom he experienced much like his controlling mother, responded, "What you ought to do is just forget the whole thing—why can't you handle it that way?"

At this point he turned on her and a verbal, escalating conflict ensued. This was followed by several days of angry alienation.

In the office, I asked her how she experienced his description of the situation. She responded by saying it was accurate—that's what she had thought and said. I asked her how she might reflect what he was experiencing if she could put herself in his position. She responded by saying that he was always concerned about paying bills on time; she felt it had to do with his sense of honor and fairness.

I asked, "What might you have said to reflect your understanding?" She responded, "I know how important it is for you to not owe anybody—and I can understand your anger." Turning to him, I asked how he might have responded to that statement and he replied that he thought it would have lessened his anger.

She then said to me, "You know we've had this same kind of situation on several of our tapes—and my tendency to tell him what to do is a big part of the problem. I must learn to put myself in his shoes and let him know it."

In the next several sessions she continued to avoid the empathic position by telling him what to do, thus suggesting that her distancing of his feelings served a defensive function for her. Later, it was possible for her to begin to face the underlying fears of the closeness and intimacy she wanted so much. For his part, the husband was encouraged to be in touch with and express more directly the concerns that provoked his anger.

There are other occasions, however, in which the partner appears not to share very many, if any, of the characteristics of the internalized object. In most situations, the partner does not appear to be controlling, rejecting, or whatever it is that is feared. But in certain situations, however, this same partner behaves differently and more like the internalized object. In such situations the therapist needs to understand marital projective systems and projective identification.

There is growing appreciation that marital projection systems and projective identification occur not only in pathological situations but across a wide range of relationships. These processes are considered to be mechanisms that are central to the regulatory functions of relationships and, within certain limits, can be considered normal processes.

Partners in an emotionally important relationship help each other to regulate self-esteem, difficult affects, impulsive behaviors, and, perhaps, certain physiologic functions. It is also apparent that individual ego boundaries must be considered to function as more than only a barrier. Polster (1983) has suggested that ego boundaries also involve reaching out, making contact, and entering into the experience of another. From this perspective, it is easier to understand that the "position" taken regarding one's subjective experience by an important other can regulate the way the self is experienced.

Projective identification involves the partner's accepting the projection and dealing with it in a way that is helpful to the projector, who then identifies with the partner's management of the projection. I suggest that this process can be considered pathological only when the projection is primitive and the recipient is "forced" to hold the projection so constantly that it is incorporated into the recipient's basic sense of self. Under more usual circumstances, the recipient's acceptance of the projection is a short-lived process and it does not become a part of the recipient's basic sense of self.

For the purposes of this chapter a detailed history of the development of the construct of projective identification is not possible. Those psychoanalysts and psychotherapists who have led the way in describing the importance of projective identification for understanding marital dynamics need mentioning. Those whose writings have been particularly helpful to me include the early contributions of Dicks (1963), Main (1966), Zinner and Shapiro (1972), Wynne (1986), Skynner (1976), and Meissner (1978).

More recently, Catherall (1992) has described the ways in which projective identifications can lead to marital conflict. He suggests that it is when the recipient is either unable to identify with the projection or unable to contain the projection that the projection is acted out and conflict occurs. If the recipient is able to identify with and contain the projection, he or she appears understanding and tolerant. Catherall suggests that, although the goals of individual therapy may include helping the patient to project less, in marital therapy the goals may include helping the spouse to better contain projections.

The reader may wonder whether in understanding a conflictual marital interaction it is important to know whether the partner appears to resemble the internalized object or appears to have responded as if a projective identification has occurred. My response is tentative because there are couples for whom I am not clear about which of the two perspectives is more helpful. Secondly, in many couples there seems to be a mixture of both "reality" and projection. Finally, I am most certain of the operation of projective identification in those more disturbed relationships in which the projections both have a primitive quality (e.g., all good versus all bad, or well versus sick) and have been accepted to a significant extent by both partners.

My approach to intervening in conflictual interactions depends to a considerable extent on whether I have been able to moderate the blaming process during the assessment procedures.

Intervening in Conflict

The three most common presentations seen in my office are the conflicted couple, the devitalized or apathetic couple, and the couple with one spouse the clearly identified patient. The conflicted couple is far more common in my practice and I shall describe intervening in that circumstance first.

Most of my attempts to intervene in a couple's conflict involve everyday vignettes the couple reports from the interval between appointments. Often, one spouse reports that everything went well for a period (usually hours or days) following the preceding appointment and, then, he (or she) either did (or did not) do something that upset the reporting spouse. The spouse's response to the other's behavior is usually described as "hurt" by the reporting spouse, but the other spouse describes it as sarcasm, hostility, or rage—"totally out of proportion to the circumstances."

> "It was our anniversary and I was pleasantly surprised when he asked me to go out to dinner. On that afternoon, he

even sent flowers. Then he called early in the evening and said he was delayed by a client's problem and would I meet him at the restaurant? I said sure. He was 30 minutes late and brought the client with him! They had both had several drinks...."

"You're not telling the whole story," he responded. Why don't you tell it all?"

She stared at him for several seconds before responding, "The *whole* story is nothing more than your lies—you've always got some excuse."

He looked at me, sighed, and said, "When I called her to tell her I was running late, I told her this client had just found out that his wife has cancer and he was upset—needed to talk about it."

"It's always someone else who needs to be listened to. How long is it since you've given me the time of day?" she said with considerable venom.

He snorted, "You're always so damn angry; all you want to do is bitch and that gets very old. You were a first-class bitch at dinner. The poor guy was sinking and you wouldn't give him the time of day."

These increasingly angry interchanges continued for several more sequences before I interrupted. The pattern of their shared avoidance of closeness seemed clear. The basic issue seemed to be her wish for signs of his love and her hurt and anger when he allowed outside circumstances to interfere with her expectations. He had a history of overinvolvement in his consulting practice that represented to her, in part, his fear of and avoidance of intimacy. Over time, she had become bitter, hardened, and easily provoked. She was more the pursuer and he the pursued. The more he failed to meet her needs, the more angry she became. Her anger then led to his spending more time with clients and being less available to her.

The responsibility for their failure to have a special anniversary experience was shared. Each had the opportunity to avoid the disastrous experience. He might have called and explained the difficult situation he was in, telling her he didn't feel he could walk away from it, and asked her to decide whether to join him for dinner with the client or postpone the anniversary dinner until the next night. She could have asked him which of those or other options he felt was preferable. Neither appeared to have made much of an effort to avoid the conflict, and my belief was that both participated in setting up a distance-producing conflict. Although she was more often the pursuer and he the distancer, I believed both had underlying fears of closeness and intimacy.

It is often helpful to explore with the couple the 24 hours or so preceding the onset of the conflict in order to search for a period of unusual closeness or intimacy. In this couple, there was such an experience that involved a long walk the evening before and for the first time a serious discussion about building a new home. Each spouse felt closer than usual to the other and their discussion of building a home together was a statement about their hopes for a shared future.

It was this brief period of shared closeness that I first explored with them. I indicated that conflicts were often preceded by such periods of intimacy. As with other couples who demonstrate a fear-driven pattern of conflict following an experience of closeness, I suggested they monitor this pattern on their own. Following any conflict between appointments, they were to take the time to examine whether the conflict followed a period of shared closeness. To do the monitoring together is preferable, but if such a collaborative effort is not possible, I ask each spouse to take turns in acting as the monitor.

The basic approach to intervening in conflictual interactions involves the following steps:

1. Observe, then interrupt the pattern.

2. Explore the context in which the reported conflict was experienced.

3. Go back to the conflict experience and explore each partner's underlying affects.

4. Summarize what has been learned about the interplay of underlying affects, emphasizing both the family-of-origin roots and the distance-regulation perspective.

5. Reconstruct the conflictual situation along with instruction as to alternate ways of dealing with it that emphasize empathic processes and the importance of subjective reality.

6. Clarify the new understanding, emphasizing joint responsibility for its implementation.

These six steps are not often as separate in practice; much overlapping is the rule. Very similar approaches have been described by Jacobson (1989), Catherall (1992), and Lansky (1991). In the following pages, each of these steps is discussed in more detail.

1. Observe, then interrupt the pattern.

In Chapter 7, the problems associated with couples who persist in their shared blaming activities were noted. Although many couples respond to simple requests, others do not. In these instances, it may be necessary for me to take a strongly directive stance. I do so despite awareness that for some such couples the entrenched marital projection system may be understood as defending against primitive underlying fears and precarious individual ego boundaries. The justification for a more powerful intervention is simply that treatment is impossible unless the blaming process can be controlled during the treatment sessions. Those couples who are unable or unwilling to desist in their attacks on each other are quite likely not candidates for marital therapy and may need parallel individual therapies.

2. Explore the context in which the reported conflict was experienced.

As noted earlier, one reason for such an exploration is to determine whether the conflict can be understood as a fear-driven response to a period of closeness or intimacy. Conflict in such a situation is understood as alleviating the fears aroused by the closeness through the mechanism of producing a period of safe distance.

There are, however, other interactions that may produce conflict and can be ascertained by careful exploration. One involves the failure of one partner to contain the projections of the other partner. Most commonly, this involves one partner experiencing distress that the other partner dismisses or minimizes. The distressed partner then turns angrily on the dismissive partner. These episodes can be understood as failures to contain a projection or, more commonly, as empathic failures. An example of this common dynamic is the attorney noted in the clinical vignette earlier in this chapter who, enraged by the failure of the physician's office to credit his account, turned the rage toward his wife when she failed to respond empathically.

There is a range of situations involving what I have elsewhere called synchrony (Lewis, 1989). In this situation, two partners, often with a mutually acceptable balance of separateness-autonomy and connectedness-intimacy, have an experience in which one partner has intensified needs for either separateness or connectedness and his or her partner has the opposite need. This can result in disappointment and anger leading to an increased distance that allows for both a cooling off and a reassessment of the experience. In better functioning couples, these periods of disengagement are usually brief—lasting minutes or several hours, but not days or weeks.

Another dynamic that can be understood through exploration of the circumstances of the conflict involves the failure of the partner to be clear about his or her needs, the use of idiosyncratic distance-regulation signals, or the failure of the partner to read and respond accurately to the signals of the partner. Over time, it is reasonable to expect that partners will come to understand each other's signals, even those that differ from cultural norms.

3. Go back to the conflict experience and explore each partner's underlying affects.

This is a pivotal stage in the intervention. I ask one partner to sit quietly and observe my exploration. He or she is asked to refrain from interrupting, contradicting, or rebutting and is told that his or her time is coming. I have no fixed rule about which partner to involve first, preferring to start with the partner who appears more accessible. Catherall (1992) prefers to start with the "recipient" partner's experience. Lansky (1991) suggests that the therapist start with the more intellectualizing, withdrawing spouse.

The primary intent of the exploration is to move beyond the anger to those affects that are masked by the anger. Most commonly, anger is a response to being hurt, ashamed, or afraid and, from this perspective, can be considered a secondary affect. Most commonly, the masked affect or affects can be uncovered without much difficulty. "So although you responded with an angry attack, what you felt and didn't share was how afraid you were that she would not understand," is the kind of summarizing statement I usually use toward the end of the exploration. It is then helpful to turn to the other partner and ask, "How would it have been for you if he had expressed this fear rather than his anger? What might you have said in response to the fear?"

The emphasis here is on modeling careful attention, responding particularly to the affective component of the individual's experience, and remaining nonjudgemental about that experience. Doing so encourages the couple to be in better touch with underlying affects and to be clear and open in expressing them. It encourages the partners to listen attentively and to better hear affective communications. They then begin to learn something of the processes of empathy.

Encouraging each partner to develop exploratory methods of addressing each other's emotional experiences is a formidable task that I will address later when I discuss my use of structured, audiotaped homework assignments. For present purposes, however, I wish to emphasize that with couples, as with beginning students of psychotherapy, giving up very directive ways of conversing with others is a difficult task.

Although my major focus during the exploration with each partner is on the individual's affective experiences, I am also interested in helping to clarify the relational theme in which the affects are embedded. It is important for the psychotherapist to keep in mind each partner's most problematic relationship of childhood (Chapter 7) to see whether the current marital experience is similar to the three-part dynamics—(1) wish, (2) response of other, and (3) response of self—that constitute the most problematic relationship of childhood. Calling attention to such similarities can provide helpful insights to both the individual and his or her partner.

> "Okay—now let's summarize to see if we have it. When she said that she needed more space, more time alone, you responded with angry withdrawal. Beneath that, however, you were afraid that she was going to leave you. You wanted some sort of reassurance from her but didn't ask for it."
>
> "Yes—that's really it—that's exactly where I was."
>
> "Okay. What does that experience bring to mind?"
>
> "What do you mean?"
>
> "Being afraid of being left and retreating into sort of a sullen position."
>
> "Well—I guess it's just like my mother and all her hospitalizations for depression when I was a little kid. I was afraid she'd never return and I couldn't talk to anyone about it. I was both afraid and angry with her."

"Yeah, it does seem to be a good deal like those early experiences. Can you (*turning to the partner*) see the parallels, too?"

My focus on teaching exploratory skills with a major focus on the affective experiences of the other is molded by over 30 years of teaching basic psychotherapy skills to beginning psychotherapy students (Lewis, 1974, 1978b, 1991a, 1991b). I was challenged to develop teaching modules that involved students doing what experienced psychotherapists actually do in psychotherapy. In particular, my initial teaching efforts focused on the development of affect sensitivity and empathic processes. The use of both audiotaped and videotaped material proved to be helpful to those beginning students and, in a similar fashion, has proven helpful in couples therapy. I will describe these techniques in the next chapter.

My focus on the centrality of affect in couples therapy has been informed by the writings of several serious students of the topic. Although I will not undertake a thorough review of their work, there are several whose ideas have been so helpful that they must be noted.

There has been no more careful student of the role of affect in marital interactions than Gottman and his colleagues (Gottman, 1980, 1994; Gottman & Katz, 1989; Gottman, Markman & Notarius, 1977; Gottman & Krokoff, 1989; Gottman & Levenson, 1984). Their work has been particularly instructive because it includes physiologic measurements. A few highly selected findings follow to give the reader something of the flavor of this body of research.

Sixty percent of the variance in marital satisfaction could be accounted for by using physiologic measures of affect. The simultaneous measurement of spouses' heart rates, skin conductances, pulse transmission times, and other somatic activities revealed that dissatisfied couples during a high-conflict interaction showed greater physiologic linkage than did satisfied couples.

Satisfied and dissatisfied couples are more readily discriminated by their ability to deescalate conflict than by their exchange of positive affects. Affective exchanges were also more predictable (structured) in dissatisfied couples. In particular, this was true regarding the exchange of various forms of hostility. If one partner expresses hostility (in dissatisfied couples), there is a higher likelihood the other partner will respond in kind. Further, Gottman and Levenson (1984) report that closeness is maintained by low-intensity exchanges of feelings as occurs in sharing the events of the day.

Gottman (1994) proposes that the four most disastrous ways of interacting involve criticism, contempt, defensiveness, and stonewalling (withdrawing). Men are more easily overwhelmed physiologically by marital conflict and, thus, may be protecting themselves from excesses of pulse rate and blood pressure by retreating. Their stonewalling, however, produces dramatic increases in their wives' pulse rates.

Gottman also proposes that nothing foretells the future of a marriage as well as how the couple retells the story of their earlier relationship. The more negative the current retelling of the past, the greater the probability of the dissolution of the relationship.

Gottman's findings emphasize the need to monitor carefully the affective experiences of the partners and to allow "time outs" when there is evidence that a spouse is overwhelmed physiologically (flooded) by his or her affects. This and others of his research findings emphasize the importance of the affective interchange in predicting the course of a marriage and, as well, its centrality for effective couples therapy.

During the past decade the field of couples therapy, with a central emphasis on affect, has been significantly molded by the contributions of Greenberg and Johnson (Johnson & Greenberg, 1985, 1994; Greenberg & Johnson, 1986a, 1986b).* In a series of publications, these authors have outlined what they call Emotionally Focused Therapy (EFT). Based primarily on attachment theory and its implications for adult love relationships, EFT focuses on affective interchanges between partners as the essential signals of either successful or unsuccessful attachment.

A basic tenet of EFT holds that each partner needs contact, security, and protection from the other. When these needs are clearly expressed and appropriately responded to, the partners feel secure, close, and safe. When, however, the attachment needs are not clearly expressed or met by the other, fear results. The fear concerns rejection, abandonment, and loss. Rather than directly expressing such fears, the individual in a dysfunctional (insecurely attached) relationship responds with anger. The anger results in a stereotyped and often escalating angry interaction. Thus, for Greenberg and Johnson, affect is the organizing force of attachment behaviors and, in particular, fear, shame and anger are centrally involved.

---

* See my review of Johnson and Greenberg (1994), *The Heart of the Matter : Perspectives of Emotion in Marital Therapy*, in the Reading Notes on p. 250

In another publication (Greenberg & Johnson, 1986a), these writers have summarized the principles that direct an affect-focused couples therapy. They are:

- Emotional experience and expression is a powerful tool to use in reorganizing interactional positions.

- Accessing emotion in marital therapy provides partners with new information that can be used adaptively.

- Psychological intimacy is created by emotional experience and expression.

- Previously unavailable feelings need to be experienced and expressed to produce change.

- Reworking the emotional bonds is the central concern of couples therapy.

- The central concern of the therapist in each session is best directed at evoking emotions and facilitating their reprocessing.

- Changing the way the self is experienced in relation to the partner is a central part of couples therapy.

- Emotional contact is the foundation of intimate relationships.

- Emotion must be clearly defined in order to be used helpfully in couples therapy.

- Interventions at the affective level assist in creating bridges between a wide variety of etiological vectors.

Growing out of these interventional principles, Greenberg and Johnson strive to change the interactional patterns of couples by helping them to interact directly with each other, with a particular emphasis on the disclosure of and response to underlying feelings that emerge during each session. Thus, in EFT, the therapist actively assists each partner to become both more expressive and more responsive. The disclosure of vulnerability (fears and shame) is essential because without such disclosure the exchange of vulnerabilities with its capacity to evoke closeness and protection is impossible.

What is particularly compelling about the work of these writers and their colleagues is that they have moved beyond description to test the effectiveness of their form of couples therapy (Greenberg & Johnson, 1986b; Dandeneau & Johnson, 1994).

Weingarten (1992) writes from a feminist-constructivist perspective about the importance of intimate interactions between the therapist and clients. She believes that such interactions are often therapeutic and that non-intimate therapist-client interactions are rarely so. Common ways for a therapist to participate in non-intimate interactions include: (1) the failure to acknowledge being a part of the system by presuming objectivity, (2) arriving at premature understandings, (3) imposing new meanings, and (4) constructing for clients new narratives that come primarily from the therapist's life.

Finally, in view of the emphasis given to affect and intimacy as growth-fostering in relationships, it is useful to ask just how such experiences facilitate growth for both partners. Miller (1994) is one of few writers to discuss this intriguing issue.

Miller (1994) suggests that when empathy is reciprocal both persons grow in five important ways. First, the sense of initial connection gives each a sense of increased energy. Second, both are able to be active participants and the resulting sense of empowerment extends to other relationships. Third, each person better understands himself or herself and this provides a more knowledgeable base for actions. Fourth, each person feels an increased sense of self-worth and, fifth, both desire more connection.

Miller describes the failure of this process as a disconnection that may lead to a terrifying isolation in which one may feel powerless and blame herself or himself. Over time and many such experiences, the individual may come to disconfirm his or her true self, a step toward the development of various psychopathologies, including, especially for women, depression, phobias, and eating disorders.

4. Summarize what has been learned.

It is important that the therapist emphasize the dynamics that have been uncovered in the exploration with each partner. If possible, the following should be highlighted:

a. The feeling masked by the anger, usually fear, shame, or some other type of hurt.

b. The relationship of the underlying feeling to the central problematic relationship of childhood.

c. The effects of the expression of anger rather than the masked feeling. Here the emphasis is on distance regulation—and its consequences. The consequences may be protective or self-defeating.

Thus, summary statements may take the following form:

> "Although you expressed anger at her for being late, you were, first of all, afraid—afraid that she might not show up at all. Although all of us fear abandonment to one degree or another, it appears that your mother's death when you were a little boy has made you particularly sensitive to any hint of being left. Your anger, though, led to her walking out of the restaurant. It produced the very thing—being left—that you fear the most."

There are clear oversimplifications in such summaries, but they are meant to provide new and relatively simple cognitive structures that emphasize the individual's own role and responsibility in the interaction with the partner.

It is also important to explore briefly with the partner what he or she has learned about the dynamics of the other. Often, this results in an expression of surprise: "I had no idea that fears of being left were involved in his preoccupation with my always being on time or early. I have always seen it as only a perverse controllingness—his fear puts it in a different light."

5. Reconstruct the conflictual situation along with instruction as to alternate ways of dealing with it.

I ask the couple to go back to the conflictual situation and explore different ways of dealing with it, in particular, emphasizing empathic processes and respect for subjective reality. The start of such reconstructions begins with one partner expressing his or her fear, shame, or other emotion associated with a sense of vulnerability rather than responding with anger. This is the most difficult part of the reconstruction and I actively help with it. One way is to introduce them to the use of qualifying phrases such as, "As strange as it seems—" or "This sounds sort of crazy, even to me, but . . . ." Often this makes it easier for the individual to say something like, "When you're late, it stirs up some fears in me that you won't come back."

I introduce the couple to basic empathic skills, focusing on the affective component of the reconstructed statement and reflecting that back to the speaker. The need to remain nonjudgemental about the feelings of the other and to avoid suggesting solutions or changing the subject is emphasized. On many occasions, couples report that they had never responded to each other in this way.

I also introduce them to what are called "general encouragers"—statements or requests that encourage the other to talk more about his or her subjective reality. "Help me to understand that better" or "How interesting—can you tell me more about it," are examples.

Throughout all of this, I emphasize the importance of understanding and respecting each other's subjective reality. I say things like, "The truth is only rarely more important than subjective reality—maybe, for example, the truth is more important if your car is stalled on the railroad tracks. You need to know the truth about when the next train is coming. Far more often, however, knowing and respecting what one another is *experiencing* is more important."

I may also share some results from our studies of well-functioning marriages, indicating that interest in and respect for each other's subjective reality is a frequent finding in couples with high levels of shared marital satisfaction.

6. Clarify the new understanding, emphasizing joint responsibility for its implementation.

I ask couples to try to deal with the everyday conflicts that will arise in the intervals between appointments, using the new format. They are told that this will require a new level of collaboration between them and that they will have to work hard to interrupt the old, self-defeating patterns.

Almost always, couples fail to accomplish this change easily. The old ways are too ingrained; the distance that conflict produces is, however unpleasant, too safe to give up readily. Another factor, however, is that couples need more intense and structured instruction. My approach to this third phase of treatment will be described in Chapter 10.

COUPLES WHO PRESENT WITHOUT PROMINENT CONFLICT

A minority of the couples referred to me do not present with prominent conflict. Several of the situations of this type are: the couple referred with a symptomatic child, the couple presenting with one partner as patient and the other partner as healthy, and the apathetic, devitalized couple.

1. The Couple with a Symptomatic Child

In these situations, most commonly there is clear evidence of underlying, but rarely expressed, marital conflict. The focus is almost entirely upon the symptomatic child, whose symptoms are understood as diverting attention away from the marital conflict and, in the extreme situation, preserving the marriage.

The management of these couples is to facilitate their dealing more openly with their conflict. If such is accomplished, the symptomatic child may show significant improvement. Once the conflict is out in the open, it is dealt with in the way described for couples who present with open conflict.

On other occasions one sees couples with a symptomatic child who appear to have an effective relationship but are having to struggle with the chronic stress of an ill child. Usually, the child has become very powerful and, often, the whole family needs to be in family therapy.

2. The Couple Presenting with One Partner as Patient and the Other as Healthy

This situation can be a difficult treatment challenge, particularly if there is no apparent conflict. Most often, however, there *is* conflict and the "patient" feels that he or she has been chronically mistreated or devalued, or, in some other way, has not had a relatively equal role in the partnership. The symptoms (see case vignette in Chapter 8) are understood to have multiple roots and purposes. From the interpersonal perspective, the most common purposes of the symptoms include achieving power, expressing rage, and asking for help.

The couples therapist must also keep in mind that most psychiatric syndromes need to be understood from a biopsychosocial perspective and that genetic and early developmental influences may play decisive roles. Indeed, one important perspective is that marital and family system factors are often more influential in determining the course of the syndrome than they are as primary causes.

Regardless, it is the presence of underlying conflict that makes the treatment prognosis better. Those couples for which the sick and well roles have been accepted without either conflict or complaint may be difficult, if not impossible, to engage in treatment.

3. The Apathetic or Devitalized Couple

Most often, these distant, arid relationships present around an affair one partner is involved in, considerations of divorce ("There must be more to life than this"), or some developmental crisis of one partner (e.g., last child leaving home, retirement). Some of these relationships have been basically pleasant even though they have been without passion from the start. Other couples describe early years of excitement and passion that have gradually disappeared.

Sometimes, a shared tragedy may, in retrospect, have been the starting point for the process of devitalization and distancing. The couple described in Chapter 1 had lost a daughter and had been unable to be together in their grief. This failure was an important part of their growing apart.

After the assessment procedure, I attempt to explore empathically with each partner the losses, loneliness, or emptiness experienced in the relationship. If there is evidence that both partners want to try to improve their relationship, I move directly to the structured exercises that are designed to increase closeness and intimacy in the relationship (see Chapter 10). It is often surprising how much difference a relatively small change in the balance of separateness and connectedness can make in the level of shared satisfaction.

Finally, there are a small number of couples who come during a crisis and appear to need only several supportive exploratory sessions. Often, they appear to have had a relationship with many strengths and high levels of satisfaction prior to the crisis.

10

Marital Therapy: Teaching Relationship Skills

Over 35 years ago, when I came to the conclusion that psychotherapeutic skills needed to be taught in a structured way to beginning students, it seemed clear to me that affect, affect sensitivity, and empathy were where to start (Lewis, 1974, 1978b, 1991a, 1991b). After some initial experimentation with experiential methods, I came across the work of Carkhuff (1969) and Truax and Carkhuff (1969). Using Rogerian theory, they had developed a systematic approach to teaching empathic processes. Delighted with this discovery, I quickly incorporated much of their work into my seminars for beginning psychotherapists.

Later in my career, it seemed wise to develop a systematic approach to teaching intimate communication for couples. Since I believe that marriage is, in part, an unconscious search for healing and that, under the best of circumstances, each partner provides a therapeutic experience for the other, it seemed natural for me to look to my seminar for beginning psychotherapists for some of the teaching methods.

This I have done and, although I continue to experiment with new techniques, it was not until the writing of this book that I began to explore what others have written about communication training as an approach to couples therapy. A paper by Pierce (1973) provided a historical overview of the use of communication training in marital therapy. I should not have been surprised to learn that Pierce believed that this approach with couples sprang from the work of Carkhuff and his colleagues. Thus, from Pierce's perspective about the roots of communication training in marital therapy, I had unknowingly followed the same path as others in the search for methods.

HOMEWORK ASSIGNMENTS

Once the intensity of the marital conflict has been moderated (see Chapter 9), I indicate to the couple that I want them to do some homework assignments. First of all, they will need a good audiotape recorder. They will need to experiment with it in order to be certain that the resulting audiotapes can be easily heard. I indicate to them that what appears to be a relatively simple process—tape recording conversations—actually turns out to be very complex for many couples. More specifically, they may find that their approach to this task is curiously ineffective. Some couples, for example, forget to do the assignment. Others believe they are doing their first taping but forget to turn on the tape recorder. Others fail to complete the assignment by quarreling about when or where to do the taping. There is, in short, much evidence that, despite endorsing this approach when they first hear about it, many couples appear resistant to doing it.

I suggest that part of the resistance may be that most persons consider themselves experts at communication. Many doctors, lawyers, and other professionals *know* they communicate well. Business executives believe success strongly reflects good leadership skills—and leadership is based on effective communication. The psychotherapists seen in marital therapy consider effective communication the heart of their craft. All of this is by way of suggesting that some of the resistance to taping may be within the individual and reflect self-esteem or other personal issues. It is a mistake, however, to consider the resistance to taping to be primarily an individual matter. There is often clear evidence that the partners collude in avoiding the task.

The couple's collusive resistance may reflect several themes. First, there is the issue of oppositionalism, particularly to tasks imposed by an authority figure. Another theme can involve a marital structure so chaotic that the minimal executive skills necessary to plan and execute a task are not present.

I am most impressed, however, with the resistance springing from the partners' underlying shared fears of closeness and intimacy. As will be discussed below, the first assigned task involves sharing and exploring experiences of vulnerability. Since the definition of intimacy used here is the reciprocal sharing of vulnerabilities, and a major function of marital conflict is considered as maintaining or increasing the distance in the relationship in order to avoid vulnerability, this initial task can be understood as directly confronting their shared fears. It is no wonder that many couples forget to turn the tape recorder on or fail to tape because of arguments of when and where to tape!

I explore with those couples who fail to accomplish the assignment their awareness of the feelings involved. Although this sometimes uncovers the nature of the resistances, most often it does not. It is generally after several failures that couples begin to acknowledge that "something must be going on" and make more genuine attempts to explore the resistance. If, however, we are unable either to resolve the resistance or the couple continue not to produce tapes, I suggest that the assignments be done in my office.

The reasons I do not routinely have them do these assignments in the office involve my wish to have them find the time and privacy to accomplish the assignment twice each week. I want them to plan on sitting together and talking with each other 15 to 30 minutes twice a week. In other words, I want them to begin doing what many couples with high levels of marital satisfaction do routinely.

There is also something serious and potentially important about taping marital conversations, bringing them to one's therapist's office, and listening to one's efforts with one's spouse and a therapist (who must believe in their importance in order to take the time to listen). I deliberately emphasize this belief with statements like, "The only way I know that people can change a relationship is by changing the way they talk to each other" or "It is through how we talk with each other that we determine how disconnected and alone or connected and safe we feel together."

INSTRUCTIONS

In the instructions, I give the couple certain topics and offer guidelines. The following represents a typical set of instructions:

> Much of the time when we talk with someone important, we want, most of all, to be heard and understood. If we want advice or a judgement, it is important to make that clear or clarify it at the beginning of the conversation.

We've learned some things about being heard and understood from both the study of psychotherapy—how therapists listen to patients—and from studying the communication that often goes on in couples with highly satisfactory relationships. What has been discovered sounds simple, but if you haven't discovered it on your own, it can take real time and effort to master.

The rules are:

1. *Listen Intensely:* Most of us only listen halfway to those we love. Our minds are on the business deal, the six o'clock news, or the letter from a child at school or camp. To really listen to each other requires effort and a real interest in what the other is feeling and thinking.

2. *Explore Rather Than Direct:* Even those who are interested and take the time to listen are apt to be very directive in their responses. One directs the flow of the conversation by asking a lot of "who," "what," and "when" questions that indicate to the other what the *questioner* thinks is important. When one does so, the partner's narrative is shaped or constrained. Try not to ask those kind of questions. Rather, think about how to encourage your partner's telling his or her story as freely as possible.

One can encourage such free, open-ended conversation in a number of ways. First, focusing on the feelings their partner expresses encourages many to explore more deeply what is on their minds. Simple statements like, "That really hurt your feelings," or "No wonder you felt angry," can lead the other to both feel understood and to explore further.

Often what you might call "general encouragers" facilitate more exploration. "Go on," "Tell me more," or "Help me to understand that better," all express interest without suggesting that it is some specific aspect of the story that is most important.

If you use questions, try to use those that open up a discussion rather than narrow it down. "Are there times that hearing that sort of criticism seems less offensive?" or "Are there some people with whom it is particularly painful to hear that from?" can be understood as inquiries that invite both a widening of the focus and a consideration of the role of context.

Most of all, people shut down in their efforts to share with each other when the listener appears disinterested, sleepy, or preoccupied. Perhaps nothing, however, shuts down an exploration as quickly as criticism. "Oh, you didn't say *that*," said with raised eyebrows and the hint of contempt, can shut anyone down.

Another important part of exploratory conversations is the focus on feelings. There are three parts of many communications—the content, the feelings, and the message that attempts to define the relationship. Most of the time it is important to respond to the feeling component of the statement. Let me illustrate:

"I just don't know what to do about my relationship with my daughter. I suspect she is on drugs—her grades have fallen and she's often out all night. I'm terribly upset."

It is possible to hear three different parts of that statement. The content involves the speaker's relationship with her daughter and the daughter's changed behavior. The feeling message needs to be clarified, but the starting point should take into consideration the speaker's expression of being "upset" and her confusion about what to do. The relationship-defining message is suggested by "I just don't know what to do," and may reflect the speaker's underlying wish to be told how to manage the situation.

These three perspectives—content, feelings, and relationship-definition—are not inscribed in stone, but rather are starting points. All three are important and may need to be explored. There is evidence, however, that responding to the feeling message is very apt to lead many speakers to increased self-exploration.

3. *Respect the Other's Subjective Reality:* There is no greater gift to give than respect for another's subjective reality. Respect goes farther than being interested, although it must start with interest. To respect how an important other is experiencing a situation puts aside issues of right or wrong, the truth, and one's own perspective. It acknowledges uniqueness, differences, and idiosyncrasy. It facilitates the speaker's moving on to explore previously untapped feelings, thoughts, memories, fears, and hopes.

Respect for another's subjective reality is thus a part of the process of equalizing the power distribution in the relationship. It connotes that one's own view is neither better nor worse—only different, that we are all searchers hoping to find order and meaning in our lives.

These instructions sounded longer and more stilted than when I relay them to couples. In part, I suspect, that is so because they write like a speech, whereas in reality the couple interrupts, questions, and asks for clarification. As a consequence, there is a greater give-and-take feel to them. I have been asked why I don't write them out and give them to each couple. My answer is that I like the verbal give-and-take component and, in addition, it is helpful to note how well the instructions are remembered. Some couples recall them in detail; others remember little. Often, after reviewing their initial tapes, couples will ask me to repeat the instructions while they take notes.

THE INITIAL ASSIGNMENT

The initial assignment is as follows:

> I would like each of you to describe a situation in which you felt vulnerable. The situation can be recent or a memory from childhood, but should not involve each other. In other words, the situation involving vulnerability should have occurred outside of the relationship. If at all possible, the situation should be one that the listener has not known of beforehand.
>
> The listener should try to facilitate the speaker's story in the ways we have discussed. This may lead to the speaker both feeling deeply understood and developing new understandings. The listener-facilitator frequently learns something important about the speaker.
>
> Although there are no time limits for the discussions, most couples take somewhere between 10 and 20 minutes for each discussion.

This task can be seen as a direct challenge to the lack of psychological intimacy in the relationship. The immediate responses to hearing about the assignment fall into several categories. One is interest and excitement. Another is characterized by open anxiety expressed by one or both partners. A third is understood as defensive. For example: "Gee, that sounds hard—but very interesting. Thinking of actually talking about feeling vulnerable to anyone makes me very upset. I doubt I can do it." Or, "I don't know about vulnerability. Maybe I've never had such experiences."

Although many couples do not produce a tape for the next meeting, ultimately almost all couples bring in the tapes of their vulnerability discussions. As with all homework assignments, I do not begin the session with a focus on the tapes. Rather, I usually begin with what has become a standard opening: "Well, how have things been between the two of you since we last talked?"

Often, couples will then discuss a conflict they have experienced in the interval between appointments. I respond in one of several ways. If the couple is at the beginning of marital therapy, I may take the lead in exploring the context in which the conflict occurred and attempt to explore the underlying affects (see Chapter 9). If, however, the couple is well into treatment, I may suggest that they "replay" the conflict, this time trying to get beyond the conflict on the surface to the deeper feelings that are involved.

Although most often I work with couples in double sessions (90 minutes), the conflict exploration may take up the entire time. More frequently, however, the conflict exploration takes part or all of the first half of the session, and I next direct our attention to the audiotape containing both of their explorations. I ask each to describe first what the experience of taping was like. Most often, they describe considerable procrastination—waiting, for example, until the night before to find the time to actually tape. Sometimes, each partner describes amazement about what has been learned regarding the other.

We play the tape and listen to it with the understanding that any of the three of us can stop the tape to make a comment or ask a question. Often, there has been significant distortion of the task. This may take the form of talking about feeling vulnerable within the relationship or failing to discuss experiences in which there was any sense of vulnerability.

For the most part, I take the lead in doing a careful dissection of the conversation—all the time raising questions like: "What do you hear him saying?" "What feelings are being expressed?" "What did you find yourself thinking as you heard him describe the vulnerable situation?" "What might you have said differently to let him know you really understood?" "Do you notice how many tightly focused questions you're asking?" "Does it seem to you that you're trying to move her description in a certain direction rather than following where she seems to be going?"

After many of these questions, I will ask, "What can you think of here and now that might have been more helpful? Can you say it now?"

Most of these initial attempts at a more affect-centered, exploratory conversation (being heard and understood) do not go well. For some couples, it seems clear that one or both partners do not listen well. Many use very focused "how," "when," and "why" questions that both move the conversation away from affect and point it in the direction the listener appears to favor. Other listeners are openly disrespectful and may change the subject or decide unilaterally and prematurely that the conversation is completed. A few are patently judgemental about what they are hearing.

I sometimes interpret these responses as resulting in distancing one's self from the subjective experience of the other. When I do so, I emphasize the impact of such responses rather than their intent. I often attempt to soften the experience of ineptness with statements like the following:

> Look, I know how it is to feel incompetent when you just try something new. Think about it as you might taking lessons to improve your tennis or golf swing. First, you have to stop doing what you have always done—what seems natural. Then you have to try a new swing—and it seems unnatural as can be. Once you get the hang of it, however, and use it repetitively, it becomes yours—not mine—and will come to feel more natural.

I may also make comments designed to soften the challenge to their competence. The following is an example:

> You know this business is complex. First of all, how sensitive one is to the feelings of an important other probably has

some biologic roots. Newer studies suggest that certain portions of the brain may be better developed in some than others—and those differences probably have a hereditary component.

We also know that the sensitivity our primary caretaker showed to our feelings during the early years of life can really spur the early development of our own sensitivity. (Here I may use personal information from the assessment, such as pointing out that if one's mother was very depressed throughout one's childhood, she may have been relatively preoccupied and insensitive.)

It also is clear that some of us grow up in families in which the expression of feelings either was not encouraged or, when expressed, was criticized. The deal of the cards—the qualities of the family in which we were raised—can also influence how our own sensitivity to feelings develop. (Here again I may point out the less than helpful family characteristics reported in the assessment process.)

Although I believe it's even more complicated than this brief description, the optimistic thing is that I've seen individuals and couples learn how to be more sensitive to each other, with very powerful impact on the relationship. Don't, however, expect too much too soon. Don't be too hard on yourselves.

The following is an example of the type of interaction that occurs when the first tape is listened to:

> They were in their mid-forties and had been married 20 years. As their children moved into adolescence, Jill became more involved in the community and ultimately accepted a job with a public relations firm where she was highly valued. Dan's law practice was very successful and together they accumulated many of life's luxuries.
>
> Jill was bright, articulate, and very intellectual in her interests. Dan was more easygoing and more openly warm and caring. They came to see me after several years of escalating conflict. Dan was more dissatisfied than Jill. His complaints were that Jill was increasingly unavailable to him. With her new and successful career, she was with him only on the

weekends. More importantly for Dan, Jill seemed more and more remote emotionally. "I think we were close early in our relationship—but maybe that's my imagination. At any rate, I think it's an empty relationship now—superficial at best. Jill is so analytic—and hard to get close to."

Jill's position was that Dan was in some sort of midlife crisis and that the marriage was basically sound, at least for her.

After the assessment interviews and an agreement on a contract for 10 more sessions, we spent several interviews dealing with episodes of conflict, as described in Chapter 9. They were both responsive to these early attempts to focus on the feelings behind the anger, and I next asked them to do a vulnerability tape. They brought one in for the next appointment and the following are several fragments from that session.

Jill described to Dan an experience in the sixth grade when, without warning, she had her first period and the menstrual flow stained her dress. She described feeling humiliated and believed that other students were laughing at her.

Dan's initial efforts at facilitating exploration were inept. Rather than reflecting on Jill's feelings of humiliation, he began with a series of directive questions.

DAN: Hadn't your mother warned you about your periods?

JILL: I don't think so—I can't remember any talks about it. She was sort of prudish. I know she never talked with me about sex.

DAN: What do you think her hangups were all about?

JILL: I'm not sure. Her father was a fundamentalist preacher—all hell and damnation. Her mother was subservient and not at all educated. My guess is that Mother never got that kind of everyday sensitivity from her mother. She didn't know how to talk about sex and menstruation.

DR. LEWIS: Let's stop the tape now. Jill, what's your reaction to this first part?

JILL: Well, I think it's going fairly well. Dan seems interested and all that.

DR. LEWIS: Dan, what's your reaction?

The Initial Assignment

DAN: most of all—as I think about your instructions—it is clear that I'm asking really focused questions.

DR. LEWIS: Yes, it's as if your questions are really directing the conversation.

DAN: Yeah—I pointed it to her mother right from the start. I didn't respond to her feelings at all.

DR. LEWIS: If you had responded to Jill's feelings what might you have said?

DAN: Let's see—I would say something about her embarrassment. Like "Were you embarrassed?"

DR. LEWIS: Would you have to ask?

DAN: No, not really, It was clear from her story. Maybe I could have just said something like, "You must have been really embarrassed."

DR. LEWIS: Jill, does embarrassment describe the feelings involved in that experience?

JILL: No—somehow embarrassment is not strong enough. I was *humiliated*.

DR. LEWIS: So, for Dan to be really on target, he would have to have understood it was more than embarrassment—it was a deep sense of humiliation.

JILL: Yeah (*beginning to tear up*).

DR. LEWIS: As you get back into that experience, you begin to cry. It really still hurts.

JILL: (*Nods and wipes her eyes*).

DAN: Damn. I not only took over with my questions—but given a second chance I undershot her real feelings. (*Turning to Jill*) "I'm not very good at this—I'm sorry I missed you so thoroughly. You really still have very strong feelings about that sixth grade humiliation. Wish I could have reached them."

JILL: Thanks, Dan.

DR. LEWIS: I'm encouraged with this initial effort and our discussion. Let's listen some more. Ready, Jill?

Another fragment is toward the end of this four-minute exploration. Jill has returned to the feeling of humiliation.

JILL: Feeling humiliated is for me so terrible—maybe it is for everyone—but, it's like I spend so much energy trying to avoid any possibility of feeling humiliated. I think it's part of a kind of normal state of vigilance I experience.

DAN: You think that's why your blood pressure is often elevated?

JILL: Probably—but even more than that, I'm always tense except if I'm alone and reading. I hate being so wary.

DAN: Are there other times when you're more relaxed?

DR. LEWIS: Let's stop again. Dan, what do you hear?

DAN: More of the same. My taking over and kind of forcing our conversation into a form that I select. I hate to be so inept, but hearing it on the tape is really helpful.

DR. LEWIS: You'll get better at it—both of you will. It might have been more helpful to have responded to Jill's feeling of vigilance, of the need to always be on guard in order not to feel humiliated.

JILL: I think it would have.

DAN: I want to do another tape.

This taping of the initial vulnerability assignment went well and is about as competent as can be expected. Dan came quickly to understand how he controlled the conversation with questions and failed to focus on Jill's feelings of humiliation and vigilance. Jill's attempt to facilitate Dan's exploration was also revealing. They reported that Jill put off the second taping until the night before the session. The tape revealed that Jill terminated the exploration in less than one minute.

Dan described an early experience of vulnerability involving his running away from an older bully when he was seven years old. He described the experience without obvious feelings.

JILL: So, if I understand it right, this older boy picked on you and you ran from him?

DAN: That's what happened.

JILL: Sounds like you did the right thing—you were only seven and he was older and bigger.

DAN: Uh huh.

JILL: Well, I don't know anything more to say. Let's stop (*end of recording*).

DR. LEWIS: Jill, what comes to mind as you listen?

JILL: Well, it's awfully brief.

The Initial Assignment

DR. LEWIS: Anything else?

JILL: Just that it is so short.

DR. LEWIS: Dan—what's your reaction to what you've heard?

DAN: Besides its brevity—Jill doesn't seem interested in my feelings—how scared I was.

DR. LEWIS: Yeah—you were only a little boy and this bigger kid was picking on you and you ran because you were scared.

JILL: That seems so obvious it didn't need comment.

DR. LEWIS: Dan, how did it feel to you that Jill didn't acknowledge your being afraid?

DAN: Well, it was like she wasn't really interested—she just wanted to get it over with.

DR. LEWIS: (*Turning to Jill*) That's the way it sounds to me, too. Jill, it sounds like you wanted out of there. Got any ideas of what that's all about?

JILL: No (*looks away*).

DR. LEWIS: What are you feeling now?

JILL: Nothing.

DR. LEWIS: That's not what your expression says.

JILL: Oh well—I don't like this stuff—I don't really want to do it.

DR. LEWIS: And your feelings—

JILL: Oh shit. I feel humiliated. Like I've made an ass of myself.

DR. LEWIS: Sure. How clear it is. We're beginning to learn how much your life is filled with the fear of being humiliated and your efforts to avoid it—and here the taping is rife with the opportunity to feel inept and even humiliated—and that's what happened. (*Silence for 20 seconds*) Dan, what's your reaction to this?

DAN: Really sort of confused. At first, I felt like Jill really wasn't interested in me—but listening and beginning to understand this humiliation thing puts it in a different light. (*Turning to Jill*) Do you often feel humiliated with me?

These conversations suggest some of the ways in which the vulnerability exercise can be helpful. First, the opportunity to hear one's self and, in particular, the ways in which one does not move towards the other's subjective reality is helpful to many. Dan's responses illustrate something of this type of learning. As will be discussed later, if the same sort of avoidance of the other's experience continues on subsequent tapes, my assumption is that the avoidance defends the individual against experiencing his or her own fears of closeness and intimacy.

Indeed, such was so in Dan's case. Despite his apparent understanding of what he wasn't doing correctly, he continued to control Jill's explorations through directive questioning and the failure to focus on her feelings. Thus, it appears that Dan's participation in the lack of closeness and intimacy (despite his complaints) is not solely based on not knowing how, but includes also a defensive function.

A second type of learning that may occur is illustrated by Jill's experience on the tape. Her selection of the humiliating experience of staining her clothes at the time of her first menstrual period is understood as both a "real" experience and an organizing metaphor that pervades her life. She came to understand that her intense fear of humiliation started even before the reported experience and involved her relation with her father. This relationship, and her recall of his technique of controlling her through the use of humiliating techniques, had been identified during the assessment as her central problematic relationship of childhood. This insight remained at the center of our work, while the equally important implications of her mother's failure to prepare her for womanhood, although acknowledged, remained somewhat on the periphery.

Dan, too, learned about his fears of closeness and intimacy. His memory of being afraid and running from the bully stemmed, in part, from his childhood experiences with an alcoholic and occasionally violent father. Dan's laid-back quality and ability to please others was both his attempt to placate the bullying father of childhood and a defense against his fears of getting truly close to another.

Thus, Jill and Dan began to learn something both about how one goes about intimate communication and about the origins of their fears. Taken together, these fears and inability to communicate were instrumental in producing a distant relationship. The lack of closeness and intimacy came to be painful to Dan as their children's development and psychological separation occurred, and as Dan entered a stage of his own midlife development in which a reappraisal of his life dream occurred.

A third source of learning involves a sharing of conversational ineptness and the underlying fears that often emerge in the presence of the therapist. The therapist's ability to explore and accept each partner's subjective experience and vulnerability without judgement or harshness can be crucial. To feel safe in the presence of both the therapist and the spouse can be the beginning of the process of working through the fears and the defensive distancing.

I am uncertain if the problematic relationship of childhood is ever completely resolved. Luborsky and his colleagues (1989) suggest that core conflictual relationship patterns are not completely resolved in successful individual psychotherapy. Rather, the individual comes to feel a significant measure of control over the extent to which the relationship pattern affects contemporary life. My observations from both individual and couples therapy are in accord with those conclusions.

I am, however, much impressed that however incompletely the fears are worked through, many of the couples seen in my practice are able to learn something of empathic processes and move their relationship towards greater closeness.

On some occasions I fail to respond empathically and one of the spouses feels injured by the explorations of the tapes. It is very important that these empathic failures be acknowledged and explored. It is frequently helpful at the end of such an exploration to summarize with statements like the following: "I can readily understand how you experienced me as detached and uncaring—the very situation that has been so painful much of your life. I do hope that you'll continue to try to trust and that my errors will be very infrequent."

SUBSEQUENT ASSIGNMENTS

Under most circumstances, sessions focusing on the initial vulnerability exercises involve considerable learning and I assign the same exercise over and over again. Sometimes, couples will be requested to talk about experiences involving vulnerability on four or five separate occasions. I want them to have as much practice as possible in talking with each other about feeling vulnerable before attempting topics that do not focus explicitly on vulnerability.

Sometimes, however, the couple's responses to the initial vulnerability assignment are so fragmented and chaotic or suggest in other ways that the task is currently too threatening, that I back away and ask them to explore other and, hopefully, less threatening experiences. Asking them, for example, to share with each other and explore the happiest experience recalled about childhood or experiences in which they felt competent may lead to a less distressed taping experience.

Listening Exercise

There are other occasions in which the level of inattention to each other's experiences is so blatant that I prescribe a different exercise that emphasizes attentive listening to the content of the partner's experience. The exercise I use is introduced with the following instructions:

> I'd like you to try a different sort of assignment. I want each of you to describe another experience of vulnerability, but the listener is asked only to listen carefully and then report what he or she has heard. The emphasis here is not so much on the feelings of the other as it is on hearing and summarizing everything you've heard.
> "Then, I'd like the partner to tell the listener what, if anything, he or she did not hear or report about the vulnerability experience. The listener then should include this overlooked information and summarize again.

I believe this task calls for a more distant, "objective" stance on the part of the listener and not only emphasizes attentive listening but provides relief from the underlying fears of closeness and intimacy.

We listen to these tapes as we do the affect-focused explorations of vulnerability experiences. On some occasions, there may be evidence of collusive avoidance. Most often, this involves a secondary theme embedded in the experience. An example is the man who described his profound reaction to his mother's sudden death when he was 13 years old. The listening wife accurately summarized this major theme and he agreed she had it all. On our listening to it together, however, it became clear that he had also briefly alluded to how alone he was with his pain—that his father had been so overwhelmed that he wasn't there for him. The wife did not include this secondary theme in her summary; nevertheless, he had agreed she had summarized completely. I understand such collusive omissions as the shared avoidance of painful themes. He could report his loss and suggest how alone he was. She could summarize what he reported about the loss, but together they avoided the aloneness.

Affect-Focused Processes

Another situation involves the persistent inattention to the feelings of the speaker. If one or both partners continue to avoid responding to each other's feelings, I introduce a new exercise to be done with me in the office. The exercise involves listening to audiotapes in which either I or a woman colleague have described some made-up experiences as if one were talking to a therapist. Each segment involves an interpersonal experience with an associated affect. An example is a taped segment in which I am clearly depressed in responding to my youngest daughter leaving for college. I also say that my wife left me for another man several years ago. The brief description is one of loss and the associated affect is sadness. Other segments deal with a wide range of interpersonal experiences and affects. I ask each partner to listen closely and identify both the major interpersonal theme and the predominant affect. If the specific affect is not clear, I suggest the use of general descriptors like "upset," "troubled," or "pained," but if the nature of the affect is clear I emphasize that the general descriptors not be used and that the specific affect be correctly identified.

There are often several affects in the same segment and the partners are encouraged to correctly identify each affect.

Another issue that occasionally needs addressing is one or both partners describing vulnerability experiences without reference to any feelings. An approach to this avoidance of communicating affect involves a different kind of homework assignment. I ask that each partner tape their brief descriptions of several experiences involving different affects. Often, I will start by asking them each to tape their experiences in which anger predominated. The next time I may ask for experiences involving fear, loneliness, or shame.

These tapes are brought to the office and the three of us listen to them. Frequently, the requested affect is described but in a manner devoid of the affect. I may ask that the individual describe the experience to express the affect as he or she is describing it. It is also helpful to involve the listening spouse in this exercise. Most often, I do so by asking for his or her feelings and thoughts. "Where were you when Jim was describing this situation and the shame he felt?" Most often, the partner may begin by expressing how amazed he or she is to be hearing all of this and how much is being learned about his or her spouse.

Although these assignments are responsive to inadequate listening and the failure to either express feelings or respond to the feelings of the partner, the major thrust of my effort is to assist in the development of an exploratory, affect-focused conversational process. This emphasis flows from the observation that the majority of the couples I work with need to redefine their relationship to include more closeness and intimacy. The exploratory, affect-focused conversational process is understood as a process leading to closeness and intimacy.

Other Topics for Exploration

At some point for each couple, the emphasis on the experiencing of vulnerability appears to have accomplished the goal of greater sharing of such experiences, and I introduce new assignments. The sharing of early memories that have not previously been shared is often helpful. I ask them to share and explore the earliest memory of mother and the earliest memory of father. The assignment asking them to share and explore the earliest memory of feeling nurtured, soothed, or safe often leads to both longings for and fears of connections to others. In a similar way, the couple are asked to share and explore the earliest memories of feeling alone, afraid, or in danger. This task may lead to explorations concerning separateness and separation anxiety.

It is also sometimes helpful to focus on the future. One task that can be used is to ask the couple to share with each other their visions of where each would like their relationship to be in 5 or 10 years, or after the children have left, or one or both have retired.

All of these assignments have the dual purpose of increasing the amount of sharing of relatively private feelings and thoughts and teaching the couple the process of attentive listening, exploratory conversations, and affect-focused responsiveness. The assignments have centrally to do with the importance of subjective reality and of each partner developing respect for the other's subjective reality.

At a later point in the treatment effort, I suggest that a couple select their own topics for exploration, emphasizing that, if possible, the specific topic be one that has not been previously shared. Couples have selected topics as diverse as Christmas memories, life after death, and oral sex. Almost always there is some new learning about each other because of their willingness to share and explore previously taboo subjects.

For some couples, the ultimate sharing is the explorations involving the relationship itself. Because most or all of these couples have been unable to explore disappointments and hurts about the relationship without anger and blaming, this task requires great effort. At least some of the time, most couples return temporarily to the old pattern of denial and projection. It is important for the therapist to comment on those tapes in ways that accept the inevitability of such "misses" even in relationships of high levels of satisfaction. For example: "Feeling blamed and defending ourselves is a part of life. What we hope to do is to replace it with sharing and exploring vulnerabilities some of the time. None of us should be too critical of ourselves or of our partners when we occasionally fail."

It is also helpful to suggest that when the old denial-projection process gets started it is sometimes possible to interrupt it if one or both partners recognize the beginning of the pattern. Metacomments like, "I'm afraid we're off in the wrong direction—let's start over again" or "I find myself getting defensive and lashing out—let's hold off for a few moments" can be effective.

Comments that focus on the other, like, "*You're* back in the old pattern of blaming again" are clearly destructive because they *are* the old pattern.

What one hopes for is that the taping experiences, the couple's review with the therapist, and practicing the more productive approach to problem solving will generalize to everyday life. The important steps include: (1) expressing the fear, shame, or other hurt rather than the secondary anger; (2) responding to the fear, shame, or other hurt in an exploratory, empathic way; and (3) acceptance of the often wide variance in each other's subjective reality. Those responses to be avoided are blaming, criticism or contempt, any judgemental statements, and all dismissive comments.

It has been my experience that a sizeable number of couples make significant improvement in their relationships without getting to the stage of treatment in which they tape explorations of their own relationship difficulties. Those that do, however, have accomplished a direct experimentation with intimacy which, I believe, serves them very well. A much abbreviated example follows;

> Harold was a creative business man who started one business after another, seeding each with the central ideas, the initial structure, and capable associates. At age 46, he was wealthy but increasingly unhappy with his wife, Alice. He focused on what he called her inefficiency in dealing with time, space, and money, saying, "I've lost all respect for you."
> Alice, a non-practicing physician while her children were still young, agreed that she was different from Harold about time, space, and money. She focused, however, on his emotional remoteness and harsh judgmentalness.
> They moved quickly to taping vulnerable experiences. Once Harold "caught on" to the idea of subjective reality, he saw himself as much of the problem. Late in what was a relatively brief treatment (assessment plus five 90-minute treatment sessions), they taped vulnerabilities experienced within the relationship. Harold described the following experience:
> HAROLD: After I've sold my share of a business and begin to start on a new deal, I go through a period of weeks—maybe even several months—in which I am afraid. It isn't present all the time, but is most likely to occur when I come home from a trip and walk in the front door.
> ALICE: How remarkable! You experience fear when you come home! I would have never known—self-confidence has always been your middle name.
> HAROLD: Yeah—I have a lot of that—but the fear is real, too.
> ALICE: And it's mostly when you come back from a trip and walk in the house?
> HAROLD: You've got it.
> ALICE: Help me to understand better.
> HAROLD: I don't know if I can. I sort of look around—and see this wonderful house—and then the girls run and hug me. And then you come out of the kitchen or study—and I can taste the fear.

ALICE: It's like you're back to—well, everything you love—and, then, how strange—fear.

HAROLD: Well, you know each new business is a gamble and although I don't invest all our assets, I do invest a lot of them.

ALICE: And you haven't lost yet.

HAROLD: It may be that this all has something to do with losing—

ALICE: Money?

HAROLD: No, I don't think so. I know every deal can't be a winner. It may be—well, the thought occurs to me that I may be afraid of losing your approval—as strange as that seems.

ALICE: Like behind all of your real self-confidence there's still a little guy who needs approval. Golly, I had no idea.

HAROLD: As we talk I'm beginning to think of Mother, her unavailability and disapproving nature—and how hard and unsuccessfully I tried to win her approval.

ALICE: Gee, Harold, I feel like crying.

HAROLD: It is sad how long these deals last.

This taping was a pivotal experience for both partners. Harold shared both a fear and a need, and Alice's responses were most helpful. The two not only came to understand a previously unknown dynamic in their relationship, but were also able to make useful connections between present and past.

AN OVERVIEW OF TREATMENT RESULTS

Although most couples I treat show real improvement in their relationship, I have no systematic follow-up data or control groups. Thus, the emphasis should be on the tentative and impressionistic nature of my conclusions.

Fist, my practice is unusual in that it is comprised of mostly successful persons or graduate students who appear on their way to conventional success.

Second, I am able to avoid the intrusion of managed health care and can, with rare exceptions, treat people as I think best. As noted in an earlier chapter, I much prefer to reduce fees if such seems indicated rather than have someone on a phone tell me how I must treat my patients in order to be reimbursed.

Third, I see few working-class individuals or couples and do not know the extent to which my approach to assessment and treatment would succeed with such a sample. The few couples from the working class with whom I have worked appear to have improved much like the more affluent, upper middle class couples who are more numerous in my practice.

Fourth, my approach to couples therapy appears to work with gay and lesbian couples and parent-adult child relationships.

Fifth, couples appear to benefit in varying ways from my treatment approach. A small number appear to make impressive changes as the result of the assessment procedure (see Chapters 6 and 7). They may stop after the assessment or go on to do one or two vulnerability tapes and then stop. Rather than appearing to be resistant, most of these couples have had more competent relationship structures, no long history of the mutual projection of primitive parts of their selves, and no evidence of clearly diagnosable individual syndromes.

A sizeable minority of the couples I see stop treatment after a number of sessions involving the approaches to everyday conflicts outlined in Chapter 9. Although some go on for a few taping sessions, it appears that their improved relationship status results from the combination of the assessment and the new approach to conflict resolution they have learned.

Most of the couples I treat, however, are involved with multiple taping experiences (12 to 24 sessions) and much of their improvement appears to stem from the exploration of each partner's subjective reality. Often, these are couples with longstanding relationship conflicts, heavily invested mutual projection systems, or the presence of clearcut individual syndromes in one or both partners.

These are the couples who appear to confirm a system premise: Major changes in the overall functioning of the system may result from relatively modest alterations in key system interactions. I continue to be surprised that what appear to be modest gains in closeness and intimacy may result in significant decreases in conflict and major improvement in the level of shared satisfaction.

My impressions of those couples who fail to improve as a result of the treatment efforts described here encompass several groups. First, there is the small number of couples who do not return for a second appointment, usually calling to say that they have decided to pursue other options. I have speculated in Chapter 6 that most often this may reflect a negative reaction to me and/or my approach. Out of 30 to 40 new couples seen each year, only one or two couples fit this pattern.

A second group that come only for the initial appointment or, perhaps, several appointments and then decide to pursue other options may involve a spouse who appears to have already made the decision to terminate the relationship and comes only to placate either the spouse or his or her own conscience. Sometimes, in this situation it is wise to try to encourage the couple to have a brief series of appointments to facilitate the best possible ending of the relationship. If there are children, the focus of this work can be the attempt to assist in the development of a parenting alliance. On some occasions, it seems wise to suggest individual therapy for one or both spouses. A recent example involved a lawyer who declined to return for a third assessment appointment. He agreed to come for an individual session in which he told me that he had never been in love with his wife. It quickly became apparent, however, that he had never truly loved any woman. He accepted my referral to an individual therapist to explore "whether it's my marriage or my inability to love."

The situations outlined above can be considered treatment failures only by the most stringent criteria, for the couples never really were involved in a treatment process. There are, however, couples who appear to try hard to salvage and improve their relationship, appear genuinely involved in treatment, and yet fail to change a painful, unsatisfactory relationship. There are several types of relationships that are in this group.

I have referred to one group earlier as dominated by a relatively fixed shared projection system in which one partner is seen as good, well, or the victim, and the partner is seen as bad, sick, or the victimizer. These projections may be associated with conflict or accepted with relatively little conflict. I find the former situations to have a more favorable prognosis, in part because their conflict reflects some effort to resist each other's projections. Relationships with such primitive projections and little, if any, conflict are very difficult to treat. Most often, the couple are referred to me by the symptomatic spouse's individual therapist or analyst who perceives, correctly I believe, that much of the individual's resistance in individual psychotherapy is in the mutual projection system.

Another type of situation that can be difficult to treat involves couples with a symptomatic child whose disturbance diverts the focus away from any underlying and serious marital conflict. It is often necessary to include the whole family in the initial assessment procedures before making the recommendation for marital therapy. Many such couples can be treated successfully, although some prove resistant.

CONCLUDING OBSERVATIONS

At the level of clinical impressions I believe that improvement in the couples I treat almost always involves increased closeness and the development of greater capacity for intimacy. It seems apparent that change can come about in different ways for different couples. For some, insight appears to play an important role. Learning about one's central problematic relationship of childhood and its reenactment with one's partner in adult life frequently involves also learning about the ways in which one subtly recreates this dysfunctional relationship structure. This type of insight provides some with guidelines for different ways of relating.

For others, improvement appears to be closely related to experiencing new ways of dealing with conflict. This avenue of improvement relies in part on better understanding the conflict, but even more, perhaps, on learning the approaches to conflict resolution outlined in Chapter 9.

A considerable number of the couples I treat appear to improve as the result of learning new ways of communicating with each other, ways that lead to greater opportunity for closeness and intimacy. It is as if these couples need to hear over and over again the recordings that document their insensitivities and consequent failure to offer each other the empathic experiences that are emotionally supportive and possibly crucial for emotional and physical health and give life its meaning. It is as if only the raw data of their tapes viewed from the perspective of distance regulation, fears of intimacy, and empathic connections enable many to begin the change process.

For some, improvement appears to require multiple avenues of change. Insight, new methods of conflict resolution, and experimentation with revealing vulnerability seem to act in concert to bring about greater closeness, intimacy, and enhanced satisfaction.

Finally, the treatment approach I have outlined also has significant effects on the therapist. Indeed, it may be difficult to know who learns the most. Although I believe this type of involvement as a couples therapist may have all sorts of impact on the therapist, it will come as no surprise that it is in the area of the therapist's capacity for intimacy that I believe the greatest effect can be experienced.

Reading Notes

It is often difficult for me to know the source of my ideas. There is a group of writers who share my interest in the psychotherapies whose writings I return to time after time and many of their ideas are similar to mine. It is likely that this correspondence reflects several themes. Almost certainly, I have appropriated some of their ideas as my own and, without intention, have come to experience them as my creations.

Another theme is the nature of the work of psychotherapy. If one spends several thousand hours each year as a therapist involved with individuals, couples, and families, certain ideas about the human condition bubble to the surface. If the therapist also teaches, supervises, or writes, these ideas may become the central issues around which these activities rotate. Unless the therapist is rigidly tied to a particular theoretical lens so that alternate understandings become unlikely, it is not surprising that many therapists arrive at broadly similar ideas. Thus, those writers whose work is important to me and I may have reached similar conclusions quite independently.

All of this is not meant, however, to in any way reduce my debt to those whose work I comment on in the following pages. It is out of the most often silent dialogues I have with them that much of my learning occurs.

I learned early in life that reading was a form of self-soothing and an escape from ongoing family tensions and conflicts. As a consequence, I have always been an addicted reader. To select a small number of writers whose work has been particularly important for me will certainly omit many others who have also been influential. Such decisions are unavoidable for many reasons so it is within that framework that I present the following notes about the work of important colleagues.

Diane Ackerman
A Natural History of Love. Vintage Books, New York, 1995.

This beautifully crafted book provides the couples therapist with an illuminating historical perspective. The author dates the outset of reciprocal love to the Middle Ages and suggests that it was considered a dangerous idea by the Church, which taught that love was one-sided and appropriate only for God. The new concept of mutual love introduced the idea of personal choice and altered radically how people defined themselves.

Ackerman emphasizes that romantic love is "a remembrance of things past, a refinding of lost happiness—one carries an old, worn family photograph in one's unconscious, and is attracted only to people who resemble that yellowing image" (p. 125).

This review of love from the history of early Egypt through Greece, Rome, the Middle Ages, and up to modern times includes interesting comments on the contributions of Plato, Stendhal, Proust, and Freud.

This is an excellent resource for the couples therapist. Ackerman's language, not surprisingly, is that of the poet.

W. Robert Beavers
Successful Marriage: A Family Systems Approach to Couples Therapy.
W. W. Norton & Company, New York, 1985.

Rereading Beavers brings back many positive memories of the eight years in which we collaborated in the study of healthy families. He, more than any other individual, introduced me to systems concepts and, along with John Gossett and others, we worked together to identify crucial variables that might be quantified by raters.

Thus, it is hardly surprising that I find so many parallels in our current perspectives. Whether it is the role of projection and transference, the pursuit of intimacy, the central importance of power, or the view of the characteristics of well-functioning relationships, Beavers and I often seem on the same track.

Beavers places greater emphasis, perhaps, on the centrality of individual ambivalence and gives somewhat less emphasis to distance regulation than I do. It is also clear that my emphasis on structured communication training is very different from his therapeutic approach.

I encourage students to read Beavers as an outstanding example of a theory-driven therapy. This book is not a "how-to-do-it" manual; rather, it states Beavers' theoretical premises and discusses at a general level the treatment implications of those premises. Whether or not one agrees with all his premises, Beavers' writings stand as an outstanding example of the translation of theory to practice. All clinicians can profit from a careful reading.

John Gottman
Why Marriages Succeed or Fail (with N. Silver). Simon & Schuster, New York, 1994.

John Gottman's research has stood as a mark of excellence for many years. Although several of his most provocative findings were reviewed in Chapter 5, I summarize here those aspects of his work that seem most relevant to couples therapists.

At the core of Gottman's findings is the conclusion that the couple's ability to resolve the inevitable conflicts is the strongest predictor of a lasting marriage. He emphasizes three adaptive approaches to conflict resolution: The calm, compromising approach; the agree-to-disagree dynamic; and the volatile, passionate conflict, followed by grand reunions. Each of the three styles of conflict resolution may characterize marriages that appear to work well.

Gottman's focus on affect and, in particular, the physiologic aspects of affect expression and reception are strong features of his work. Affects can be understood as expressed in his "Four Horsemen of the Apocalypse"—criticism, contempt, defensiveness, and stonewalling—which, if unchanged, predict the disintegration of the relationship. Under these circumstances, couples come to reconstruct their earlier experiences together in much more negative terms. This negative reconstruction predicted divorce in Gottman's volunteer couples.

The interested reader may wish to pursue Gottman's research as published in a long series of books, technical papers, and chapters. For an introduction to his work, however, *Why Marriages Succeed or Fail* is a good starting point for couples therapists who have somehow missed these important research findings.

Leston L. Havens
Approaches to the Mind: Movement of Psychiatric Schools from Sects toward Science. Little, Brown & Co., Boston, 1973.

Participant Observation. Jason Aronson, New York, 1976.

Making Contact. Harvard University Press, Cambridge, MA, 1986.

A Safe Place: Laying the Groundwork of Psychotherapy. Harvard University Press, Cambridge, MA, 1989.

There is no greater influence on my thinking as a psychotherapist than the writing of Leston Havens. From the ways in which *Approaches to the Mind* helped clarify how psychotherapies differed, to his later writing on empathic processes and the language of empathy, I can think of no one to whom I return so repetitively.

For years, I have underlined sentences, paragraphs, and pages of books that intrigued me. My secretary then types what is underlined and I have "reading notes" to which I return when needed. The length of a book's reading notes is a rough index of how important I believe the book is. My secretary has often commented, "You sure believe Havens has a lot to say," because my reading notes of his books are so long.

There are several reasons for the importance of Havens' work to me. One is his clarity about theory. Second, he demonstrates the relationship between theory and psychotherapeutic interventions. A third is that his vignettes from psychotherapy sessions often reflect either the ways in which I had handled comparable moments or, much more often, the ways I wished I had handled similar situations. Finally, Havens' emphasis on language and its implications for psychotherapeutic process is unique and, in my opinion, translates readily to teaching intimate communication to couples.

Havens is a "must" for therapists of all persuasions.

Harville Hendrix
Getting the Love You Want: A Guide for Couples. Harper & Row, New York, 1990.

Keeping the Love You Find: A Guide for Singles. Pocket Books, New York, 1992.

Hendrix's writings are directed at the general public rather than at professionals. I include them here because I believe they are the most elaborate articulation of the object relations or transference model of marriage currently in print.

Couples therapists will savor the breadth of his thinking, the essential coherence of his ideas, and the intuitive appeal of his clinical approaches.

Hendrix's suggestions regarding clinical interventions are valuable and he has the ability to provoke seasoned clinicians to thoughtful reexaminations of their approaches.

There is much of value in these books and I recommend them to both beginners and experienced clinicians. They may dispel some of the resistance to taking seriously publications aimed at nonprofessionals. I learned much from Hendrix's creative approach to thinking about marriage and marital therapy.

Susan J. Johnson and Leslie S. Greenberg (Eds.)
The Heart of the Matter: Perspectives of Emotion in Marital Therapy. Brunner/Mazel, New York, 1994.

I have a bias against edited books because of the usual unevenness of the contributions. This volume is a remarkable exception. If one believes that affect is crucial both in marital interactions and marital therapy, there is simply no better place to start than with this book.

First of all, as noted in Chapter 9, the editors, Johnson and Greenberg, are themselves outstanding contributors to the topic. Their opening chapter, "Emotions in Intimate Relationships: Theory and Implications for Therapy," is a masterpiece. Their 10 fundamentals of the use of affect in couples therapy need emphasis over and over again. They reflect so directly my thinking that I wonder how we came to such solid agreement without apparent cross-fertilization.

Although all the chapters are of value, three, in particular, have been helpful to me. Pierce's chapter on authentic emotional contact is excellent. His "ideal sequence" of "problem—feeling—deeper feeling—historical connections—new awareness about self and partner—improved cognitive structure for guiding future behavior" (p. 89) is a succinct statement of that which I described in Chapter 8 as the attempt to moderate projection and blaming in couples therapy.

Cusinato and L'Abate present a spiral model of intimacy and the therapeutic considerations that flow from it. Their sequence of interventions is much the same as mine and their reliance on structured exercises within therapy have parallels to the way I work.

Guerney's description of Relationship Enhancement Marital-Family Therapy brings to the reader a therapeutic system that the author has evolved over 20 or more years. It is built upon an almost radical form of empathy that reminds one of the existential constructs of "being" and "staying." I am much in agreement with his efforts to have each partner become the other's therapist in order to begin or complete the healing process.

D. Kantor & W. Lehr
Inside the Family. Josey-Bass, San Francisco, 1975.

This book is the first work that called attention to the centrality of distance regulation in family life. Kantor and Lehr posited that affect (intimacy and nurturance), power (the freedom to decide), and meaning (an explanation of reality and identity) were the primary goals of marital-family systems. Family members regulate each other's access to these goals through verbal and nonverbal distance-regulation signals.

Nurturance and intimacy are so important to family members that failure to negotiate levels satisfactory to all concerned results in conflict and crisis. Each marital or family system seeks to inform its members of the optimal actual and metaphorical distance in their relationships with each other and the outside world. In these transactions, family members may play one of four parts: mover, opposer, follower, or bystander. Generational influences are considered to be powerful forces in the establishment of the optimal distance and in the assignment of family roles.

Although the authors' theory of distance regulation does not specifically address dyadic relationships, the transposition from family to marital couple is easy to make. Their exploratory research and resultant theory introduced many couples therapists to the richness of the distance-regulation perspective.

Peter D. Kramer
Moments of Engagement: Intimate Psychotherapy in a Technological Age. W. W. Norton & Co., New York, 1989.

Listening to Prozac. Penguin Books, New York, 1993.

Peter Kramer's two books and monthly column in *The Psychiatric Times* have established him as an important writer. There is no voice today probing the nuances of psychotherapy in greater depth. His discussions of the impact of the use of psychotropic medications on patient, therapist, and the processes of psychotherapy are remarkably informative. Any couples therapist who emphasizes the importance of affect and empathic responsiveness needs to be familiar with Kramer's work. More than that, however, these two books should be on the required reading lists for all mental health trainees.

Augustus Y. Napier
The Fragile Bond. Harper & Row, New York, 1988.

Napier's way of thinking about the dynamics of marriage is closer to my own than almost anyone else's I have read. Undoubtedly, this is part of why I keep going back to this book over and over again. His thinking is basically derived from an object relations perspective, but he also focuses on the search for healing and the centrality of power and distance regulation. He believes that marriage in this culture may be the most popular form of psychotherapy.

We are "powerfully drawn to marrying someone who will help us recapitulate those early struggles with our parents" (p. 14). We do so in order to attempt to find those parts of ourselves that were repressed, walled off in the childhood relationship. By recapturing the original circumstances, one hopes that the outcome can be different, that one can finally be whole.

Napier believes that this form of healing is often partially successful. I would add that in many of the couples whom I treat, the partially successful healing has been more obvious for one spouse than for the other.

Napier's three important metaphors for the practice of couples therapy are equity, closeness-distance, and power and vulnerability. These themes also occupy a central position in my work. What is different, however, is that Napier works with a co-therapist (who is his wife) and I work alone.

A very special aspect of *The Fragile Bond* is the amount of Napier's self-disclosure. He uses his and his wife's search for mutual healing, and this intense personalness is, for me, a powerful stimulus to learning. I recommend this book to students and experienced couples therapists with much enthusiasm.

David Reiss
The Family's Construction of Reality. Harvard University Press, Cambridge, 1981.

Reiss and his colleagues at George Washington University have made many contributions to understanding family systems. Their empirical approach to the worlds of marriage and family is the prototype for other investigators, and to select but one of their contributions, and at that a theoretical premise, seems unfair. Nevertheless, the idea of family paradigms has been their contribution that has had the most lasting impact on me.

Family paradigms are underlying shared beliefs that shape both the framing assumptions the family has about the world and the recurrent interactional patterns manifested within the family and in the family's involvement with the surround. The family paradigms are rarely conscious, but can be inferred through recognition of the family's way of relating internally and with others.

Reiss believes that family crisis leads to disorganization. When the previously existing paradigms fail to provide stability and continuity, a new paradigm arises that deals successfully with the crisis.

As spouses-to-be come together, each brings unconscious paradigms from his and her family of origin. Although some may be attracted because of similar paradigms, others either adopt one family-of-origin set or construct new paradigms.

In my work, the attempt is made to explore each spouse's value orientation through the use of the Rokeach Value Survey (see Chapter 7). Although this provides information often useful to the process of therapy, it does not quite reflect Reiss's concept of underlying paradigms. More often, paradigms are seen to underlie the individual's distance-regulation proclivities. The extremes of separativeness and connectedness can be understood as reflections of underlying assumptions about the nature of human nature, as well as responses to traumatic childhood relationships.

Reiss's work is helpful in many ways, but most of all it speaks to important concepts that couples therapists need to have carefully considered in order to have as many potentially helpful ways as possible of framing their patients' disturbances.

C. J. Sager
Marriage Contracts and Couples Therapy. Brunner/Mazel, New York, 1976.

Twenty years ago Sager presented his work in book form and it has influenced several generations of couples therapists. His thinking is broadly based and takes from many perspectives. At the center of his work, however, are the psychoanalytic principles of the unconscious, the interpretation of defenses, dream analysis, and transference.

Perhaps most of all, however, Sager's work has endured because of the idea that couples establish contracts that give their relationships structure. He posits three levels of awareness about marital contracts: those contracts that are conscious, verbalized, and explicit; those contracts that are conscious, unverbalized, and implicit; and those contracts that are unconscious. Most chronic marital dysfunction is believed to stem from unconscious contractual disagreements at the third level.

Sager's ideas about contracts were my introduction to the reciprocal, interlocking nature of the partners' unconscious needs and fears. Although there was much recognition before Sager of the transference factors involved in marital object choice, his emphasis on their joint operation increased professionals' awareness of the processes of unconscious trade-offs. This premise is useful in my work in that it takes the couple's relationship away from individual traits and toward complex circular interactions. "I won't ever abandon you as long as you don't allow us to become too close," or "As long as you won't leave me, I'll keep refusing your demands for intimacy," both speak to how contracts arise out of unconscious agreements regarding wishes, fears, and resulting behaviors. For this contractual emphasis, we are much in debt to Sager.

David E. Scharff & Jill Savage Scharff
Object Relations Family Therapy. Jason Aronson, Northvale, N.J., 1987.

This book is the classic, "pure" translation of object relations metapsychology for couples and family therapies. It is comprehensive, coherent, and rich with clinical examples. For psychoanalysts it presents an approach to marital-family therapy that is powerfully congruent with mainstream psychoanalysis.

For others, too, the book is a resource of great value. In particular, the nonpsychoanalytic marital-family therapist can learn much about the use of interpretations and insight, holding environments, and transference-countertransference issues in working with couples.

The Scharffs' interpretations and insight are central to marital-family therapies. A basic issue is the need for the therapist to understand why the partners' internalized bad objects dominate the relationship, usually after a lengthy period in which the relationship was dominated by the good, exciting introjects. Helping both partners to understand the connections between *then* and *now* and to begin to modify the shared system of projections is paramount.

The author's descriptions of the multiple transferences (individual and shared) that the couple presents to the therapist is most helpful. The relationship between both individual and shared contextual transferences to the internalized parental relationship and its holding function provides therapists with opportunities for new ways of understanding and intervening.

A particular strength of this book is in the theoretical discussions of countertransference, as well as in the illustrations of how the therapist may use these feelings in his or her work with couples.

R. Taylor Segraves
Marital Therapy: A Combined Psychodynamic-Behavioral Approach.
Plenum, New York, 1982.

Segraves' theory and way of working with couples is much like that which I have evolved. He presents 10 hypotheses that begin with chronic marital discord as based on both spouses having cognitive schemas for each other that are markedly discrepant with the other's personality. The schemas themselves were learned with the opposite-sex parent or in later opposite-sex relationships.

Segraves posits that the failure to discriminate the partner's real self from the earlier learned cognitive schema is based on one or both spouses' deficit in the capacity for cognitive complexity. Further, the resulting distortion of the spouse is both oversimplified and of negative valence.

The theory also emphasizes the capacity of each spouse to elicit behaviors from the other that confirm the underlying schema (in other words, projective identification). This premise lays the theoretical groundwork for Segraves' belief that what appears to be the spouses' contrasting personality configurations are often found to be the result of their interactions (in other words, state rather than trait).

Conflict arises when one or both spouses deviate from the behaviors prescribed by the other's opposite-sex cognitive schema. Finally, Segraves emphasizes that transference distortions within the marriage can be modified by the spouse presenting a consistent disconfirmatory reality.

Segraves' interventions are much like mine in their reliance on new cognitive understandings, interrupting projections, and teaching new ways of responding. Once again, I am impressed that a number of us who write about couples therapy have arrived at similar interventions although starting with different theoretical orientations. Segraves' writing is clear and he reviews the empirical support for his premises. His book is an excellent starting place for those who wish to include therapy with couples in their professional work.

Peter Steinglass
The Alcoholic Family (with Linda A. Bennett, Steven J. Wolin, & David Reiss). Basic Books, New York, 1987.

Although this book is a wonderful source of information regarding alcoholism and the family, its significance for me transcends the subject of alcoholism. I use Steinglass' concepts as an orienting perspective with which to understand one aspect of the interface between human system and chronic pathology. The chronic process can be alcoholism, but it is often chronic depression, severe arthritis, or long-standing neurologic deficits. The idea of the extent to which the disease process disrupts the family (or marriage) and, in particular, its rituals has major therapeutic implications.

Most of all, however, I have been informed by Steinglass' elaboration of family rituals. Rituals are considered as regulatory behaviors that enhance affect, symbolize important characteristics of the system, and stabilize the system over time. Couples and families can differ greatly in the importance given to rituals. It is useful to think of a continuum of ritualization that ranges from high to low levels of ritualization.

Steinglass' categories of rituals (family celebrations, family traditions, and ritualized routines) have provided me with a framework to explore each couple's rituals and how they originated (see Chapter 7). They have also assisted me in thinking about the circumstances in which couples are asked to construct either a marital or a family ritual and put it into operation.

Steinglass and the other members of the George Washington University group provide therapists with important ideas from which both new understandings and new interventions evolve. Their work should be required reading for this reason, as well as for its careful empirical foundation.

George E. Vaillant
Adaptation to Life. Little, Brown, & Company, Boston, 1977.

The Wisdom of the Ego. Harvard University Press, Cambridge, 1993.

I suspect that Vaillant's contributions are not standard fare for couples therapists, but they should be. He has a deeply penetrating view of adult development based on his hands-on research experience with longitudinal samples of adult men. Vaillant's long-term preoccupation with individual defense mechanisms should not dissuade readers interested in relationship dynamics; the study of individual defenses can illuminate the interpersonal.

Vaillant's study of adult men over a 50-year span emphasizes the importance of a central relationship, for there is no stronger predictor of good individual outcome than an enduring, stable marriage. His focus on mature defenses has broadened the thinking of countless therapists about the importance of ego defenses in general.

More than any other theme, however, Vaillant's work speaks to the ongoing saga of stability and change in the adult life of individuals. In *The Wisdom of the Ego*, he emphasizes that he is writing about middle-aged men and women still learning how to love and search for meaning. Their life narratives document that the internalizations that may result in health can occur in adulthood. For Vaillant, such internalizations are marked by the waning of reliance on immature defenses—those that make others suffer—and the emergence of neurotic and mature defenses.

Vaillant's work has been on my reading list for beginning therapists not because he writes about psychotherapy per se but because he is so insightful about the individual's contributions to human systems.

Edward M. Waring
Enhancing Marital Intimacy through Facilitating Cognitive Self-disclosure. Brunner/Mazel, New York, 1988.

Waring has been studying intimacy for years and, although his definition of intimacy is much broader than mine, his work is of great value to couples therapists. In this book, he spells out his theory of marital intimacy and the therapeutic techniques flowing from that theory.

He places the quantity and quality of marital intimacy as the single greatest determinant of family functioning. Intimacy is also understood as the dimension determining the level of marital satisfaction. Waring places major emphasis on each spouse's parents' level of marital intimacy. Although each spouse may blame one parent more than the other for the lack of intimacy, Waring believes that spouses are selected because of the very traits that were seen as objectionable in the blamed parent. The spouse then attempts to change those behaviors of his or her spouse—present in both offending parent and spouse—and, thus, is labeled by Waring a "misguided marital counselor."

This theory is a variant of object relations metapsychology and Waring relies heavily on Kelly's theory of cognitive schemas.

Perhaps because of these theoretical roots, Waring emphasizes cognitive self-disclosure as the royal road to achieving increased marital intimacy. Affect, particularly negative affect, is avoided during treatment. Waring presents many fascinating ideas, a transgenerational theory, and a format for brief marital therapy that in these days of managed health care should be of interest to many couples therapists.

Irvin D. Yalom
Existential Psychotherapy. Basic Books, New York, 1980.

For those couples therapists who see couples who are in their 50s or beyond, Yalom's book helps to crystallize those existential issues that are often on or just beneath the surface of the presenting issues. It is, therefore, a rich orientation for psychotherapists of all persuasions.

Yalom introduces his perspective by pointing out that existential psychodynamics involve conflicts flowing from the individual's confrontation with the givens of existence. I would add that these givens are equally important to couples. The focus of his work is on four givens: death, freedom, existential isolation, and meaninglessness.

The inevitability of death and the wish to continue to be have particular relevance for couples because, in addition to personal death, each partner must face the inevitability of the other's death. For many, that involves both the loss of the other and the loss of meaning that the relationship often provides.

Freedom is viewed as the absence of external structure, the realization that each individual constructs his or her world, life design, and choices. When much of this is done within the relationship, anxiety may spring from the conflict between the wish for ground and structure and the realization that reality is constructed by the individual or couple.

Existential isolation, the third ultimate concern, springs from the realization that regardless of how close and intimate one is to another, there remains an essential aloneness. One dies alone, the existentialists emphasize, and, I believe, this accounts for the wish many have to die while sleeping or to die at the same time as one's loved one.

Meaninglessness involves the confrontation with randomness in the world and the struggle to assure one's self that life has meaning. Couples often construct a joint meaning system that is most often challenged when they face an unanticipated random tragedy.

These existential givens operate throughout life and may present at any time, although they surface most often with older couples. Couples therapists need to be sensitive to these givens in individuals, couples, and families, and, of course, in themselves. Yalom's writing is of much help in developing such a sensitivity.

References

Ainsworth, M. D. S. (1989). Attachments beyond infancy. *American Psychologist, 44(4)*, 709–716.
Albee, E. (1963). *Who's Afraid of Virginia Woolf?* New York: Pocket Books.
American Psychiatric Association (1994). *Diagnostic and statistical manual of mental disorders* (4th ed.) Washington, DC: Author.
Amundson, J., Stewart, K., & Valentine, L. (1993). Temptations of power and certainty. *Journal of Marital and Family Therapy, 19(2)*, 111–123.
Angier, N. (1991). A potent peptide prompts an urge to cuddle. *The New York Times*, January 22.
Anthony, E. J. & Cohler, B. J. (Eds.) (1987). *The invulnerable child*. New York: Guilford Press.
Balint, M. (1972). *The doctor, his patient, and his illness*. New York: International Universities Press.
Barnett, P. A. & Gotlib, I. H. (1988). Psychosocial functioning and depression: Distinguishing among antecedents, concomitants, and consequences. *Psychological Bulletin, 104(1)*, 97–126.
Bartholomew, K. & Horowitz, L. M. (1991). Attachment styles among young adults: A test of a four-category model. *Journal of Personality and Social Psychology, 61(2)*, 226–244.
Beahrs, J. O. (1986). *Limits of scientific psychiatry*. New York: Brunner/Mazel.
Belsky, J., Youngblade L., & Pensky, E. (1989). Childrearing history, marital quality, and maternal affect: Intergenerational transmission in a low risk sample. *Development and Psychopathology, 1*, 291–304.
Belsky, J. & Pensky, E. (1988). Developmental history, personality and family relationships: Toward an emergent family system. In Robert A. Hinde & Joan Stevenson-Hinde (Eds.), *Relationships within families: Mutual influences*. New York: Oxford University Press.
Bennett, A. (1992). *The madness of George III*. London: Faber and Faber Limited.
Berman, E. M. & Leif, H. I. (1975). Marital therapy from a psychiatric perspective: An overview. *American Journal of Psychiatry, 132(6)*, 583–592.
Bowlby, J. (1973). *Attachment and loss: Vol. 2. Separation*. New York: Basic Books.
Bowlby, J. (1980). *Attachment and loss: Vol 3. Loss, Sadness, and Depression*. New York: Basic Books.
Bowlby, J. (1982). *Attachment and loss: Vol. 1. Attachment* (2nd ed.). New York: Basic Books.
Brody, J. E. (1992). Personal health: Maintaining friendships for the sake of good health. *The New York Times*, February 5, B8.
Brothers, L. (1989). A biological perspective on empathy. *American Journal of Psychiatry, 146(1)*, 10–19.
Brown, G. W. & Harris, T. (1978). *Social origins of depression*. London: Free Press.

Broyard, A. (1990). Doctor talk to me. *New York Times Magazine*, August 26.
Bruner, J. (1986). *Actual minds, possible worlds*. Cambridge, MA: Harvard University Press.
Burman, B. & Margolin, G. (1992). Analysis of the association between marital relationships and health problems: An interactional perspective. *Psychological Bulletin, 112(1)*, 39–63.
Callenback, E. (1975). *Ecotopia*. New York: Bantam Books.
Carkhuff, R. R. (1969). *Helping and human relations: Volume I: Selection and training*. New York: Holt, Rinehart and Winston.
Carkhuff, R. R. (1969). *Helping and human relations: Volume II: Practice and research*. New York: Holt Rinehart and Winston.
Caspi, A. & Elder, G. Jr. (1988). *Relationships within families: Marital influences*. Oxford: Clarendon Press.
Casti, J. L. (1989). *Paradigms lost: Images of man in the mirror of science*. New York: William Morrow & Company.
Catherall, D. R. (1992). Working with projective identification in couples. *Family Process, 31(12)*, 355–367.
Chess, S. & Thomas, A. (1984). *Origins and evolution of behavior disorders from infancy to early adult life*. New York: Brunner/Mazel.
Chessick, R. D. (1990). Hermeneutics for psychotherapists. *American Journal of Psychotherapy, XLIV(2)*, April, 256–273.
Cicchetti, D., & Greenberg, M. T. (1991). The legacy of John Bowlby. *Development and Psychopathology, 3*, 347–350.
Cloninger, C. R., Svrakic, D. M., & Przybeck, T. R. (1993). A psychobiological model of temperament and character. *Archives of General Psychiatry, 50*, December.
Cohn, D. A., Silver, D. H., Cowan, C. P., Cowan, P. A., & Pearson, J. (1992). Working models of childhood attachment and couple relationships. *Journal of Family Issues, 13*, 432–449.
Dandeneau, M. L. & Johnson, S. M. (1994). Facilitating intimacy: Interventions and effects. *Journal of Marital and Family Therapy, 20(1)*, 17–33.
Davidson, R. J., Ekman, P., Saron, C. D., Senulis, J. A., & Friesen, W. V. (1990). Approach-withdrawal and cerebral asymmetry: Emotional expression and brain physiology I. *Journal of Personality and Social Psychology, 5(2)*, 330–341.
Dawson, G., Klinger, L. G., Panagiotides, H., Hill, D., & Spicker, S. (1992). Frontal lobe activity and affective behavior of infants of mothers with depressive symptoms. *Child Development, 63*, 725–737.
Dicks, H. V. (1963). Object relations theory and marital studies. *British Journal of Medical Psychology, 36*, 125–129.
Doane, J. A., West, K. L., Goldstein, M. J., Rodnick, E. H., & Jones, J. E. (1981). Parental communication deviance and affective style: Predictors of subsequent schizophrenia spectrum disorders in vulnerable adolescents. *Archives of General Psychiatry, 38*, 679–685.
Dyer, B. (1995). The divorce rate isn't what you think. *The Dallas Morning News*, May 6.
Egeland, B., Jacobvitz, D., & Sroufe, L. A. (1988). Breaking the cycle of abuse. *Child Development, 59*, 1080–1088.

Eisenberg, L. (1972). The human nature of human nature. *Science, 176(4031)*, April 14, 123–128.

Elder, G. H. (1974). *The children of the Great Depression*. Chicago: University of Chicago Press.

Ewart, C. K. (1993). Marital interaction—the context for psychosomatic research. *Psychosomatic Med, 55*, 410–412.

Ewart, C. K., Taylor, C. B., Kraemer, H. C., & Agras, W. S. (1991). High blood pressure and marital discord: Not being nasty matters more than being nice. *Health Psychol, 10(3)*, 155–163.

Feeney, J. A. & Noller, P. (1990). Attachment style as a predictor of adult romantic relationships. *Journal of Personality and Social Psychology, 58(2)*, 281–291.

Feldman, L. B. (1979). Marital conflict and marital intimacy: An integrative psychodynamic-behavioral-systemic model. *Family Process, 18*, March, 69–78.

Fischmann-Havstad, L. & Marston, A. R. (1984). Weight loss maintenance as an aspect of emotion and process. *British Journal of Clinical Psychology, 23*, 265–271.

Fogarty, T. F. (1976). Marital crisis. In P. J. Guerin (Ed.), *Family therapy: Theory and practice*. New York: Gardner Press.

Foucault, M. (1982). The subject and power. Afterword. In H. S. Dreyfus & P. Rabinow, *Michel Foucault: Beyond structuralism and hermeneutics* (2nd ed.). Chicago: University of Chicago Press, 208–226.

Fraenkel, P. (1995). The nomothetic-idiographic debate in family therapy. *Family Process, 34(3)*, 113–121.

Fox, N. A. (1991). If it's not left, it's right. *American Psychologist, 46(8)*, 863–872.

George, M. S., Ketter, T. A., Parekh, P. I., Horwitz, B., Herscovitch, P. & Post, R. M. (1995). Brain activity during transient sadness and happiness in healthy women. *American Journal of Psychiatry, 152(3)*, 341–351.

Gergen, K. J. (1985). The social constructionist movement in modern psychology. *American Psychologist, 40(1)*, March, 266–275.

Glenn, N. D. & Weaver, C. N. (1981). The contribution of marital happiness to global happiness. *Journal of Marriage and the Family*, February, 161–168.

Goering, P. N., Lancee, W. J. & Freeman, S. J. J. (1992). Marital support and recovery from depression. *British Journal of Psychiatry, 160*, 76–82.

Goleman, D. (1995). *Emotional Intelligence: Why it can matter more than IQ*. New York: Bantam Books.

Gottman, J. (1994). *Why marriages succeed or fail* (with N. Silver). New York: Simon & Schuster.

Gottman, J. M. (1980). Consistency of nonverbal affect and affect reciprocity in marital interaction. *Journal of Consulting and Clinical Psychology, 48(6)*, 711–717.

Gottman, J. M., Markman, H., & Notarius, C. (1977). The topography of marital conflict: A sequential analysis of verbal and nonverbal behavior. *Journal of Marriage and the Family, 39*, 461–477.

Gottman, J. M. & Katz, L. F. (1989). Effects of marital discord on young children's peer interaction and health. *Developmental Psychology, 25*, 373–381.

Gottman, J. M. & Krokoff, L. J. (1989). Marital interaction and satisfaction: A longitudinal view, *Journal of Consulting and Clinical Psychology, 57*, 47–72.

Gottman, J. M. & Levenson, R. W. (1984). Why marriages fail: Affective and physiological patterns in marital interaction. In J. C. Masters & K. Yarkin-Levin, (Eds.), *Boundary areas in social and developmental psychology*, Orlando: Academic Press, Inc.

Greenberg, L. S. & Johnson, S. M. (1986a). Affect in martial therapy. *Journal of Marital and Family Therapy, 12(1)*, 1–10.

Greenberg, L. S. & Johnson, S. M. (1986b). When to evoke emotion and why: Process diagnosis in couples therapy. *Journal of Marital and Family Therapy, 12(1)*, 19–23.

Griffith, J. L., Griffith, M. E. & Slovik, L. S. (1990). Mind-body problems in family therapy: Contrasting first- and second-order cybernetics approaches. *Family Process, 29*, March, 13–28.

Guerney, B. G., Jr. (1994). The role of emotion in relationship enhancement marital/family therapy. In S. M. Johnson & L. S. Greenberg (Eds.), *The heart of the matter: Perspectives on emotion in marital therapy*. New York: Brunner/Mazel.

Haley, J. (1980). *Leaving home: The therapy of disturbed young people*. New York: McGraw-Hill.

Haley, J. (1969). The power tactics of Jesus Christ. In *The power tactics of Jesus Christ and other essays*. New York: Grossman Publishers.

Haley, J. (1981). Development of a theory: The history of a research project. In *Reflections on therapy and other essays*. Chevy Chase, MD: Family Therapy Institute of Washington, D. C.

Hazen, C. & Shaver, P. (1987). Romantic love conceptualized as an attachment process. *Journal of Personality and Social Psychology, 52(3)*, 511–524.

Hofer, M. A. (1984). Relationships as regulators: A psychobiologic perspective on bereavement. *Psychosomatic Medicine, 46(3)*, 183–197.

Hoffman, L. (1985). Beyond power and control: Toward a "second order" family system therapy. *Family Systems Medicine, 3(4)*, Winter.

Hoffman, L. (1990). Constructing realities: An art of lenses. *Family Process, 29(1)*, March, 1–12.

Holmes, T. H., and Rahe, R. H. (1967). Life change and illness susceptibility. In B. S. Dohrenwend & B. P. Dohrenwend (Eds.), *Stressful life events: Their nature and effects*. New York: John Wiley & Sons.

Hooley, Orley, & Teasdale (1986). Levels of expressed emotion and relapse in depressed patients. *British Journal of Psychiatry, 148*, 642–647.

Jacobson, N. S. (1983). Beyond empiricism: The politics of marital therapy. *The American Journal of Family Therapy, 11(2)*, 11–24.

Jacobson, N. S. (1989). The politics of intimacy. *Behavior Therapist, 12(2)*, 29–32.

Jacobson, N. W. & Margolin, G. (1979). *Marital therapy: Strategies based on social learning and behavior exchange principles*. New York: Brunner/Mazel.

Johnson, S. J. & Greenberg, L. S. (1985). Emotionally focused couples therapy: An outcome study. *Journal of Marital and Family Therapy, 11(3)*, 313–317.

Johnson, S. J. & Greenberg, L. S. (1994). Emotion in intimate relationships: Theory and implications for therapy. In S. J. Johnson & L. S. Greenberg (Eds.), *The heart of the matter: Perspectives of emotion in marital therapy*. New York: Brunner/Mazel.

Justice, B. (1988). *Who gets sick*. Houston: Jeremy P. Tarcher.

Kagan, J., Reznick, J. S., & Snidman, N. (1987). The physiology and psychology of behavioral inhibition in children. *Child Development, 58,* 1459–1473.

Kagan, J., Reznick, J. S., Snidman, N., Gibbons, J., & Johnson, M. O. (1988). Childhood derivatives of inhibition and lack of inhibition to the unfamiliar. *Child Development, 59,* 1580–1589.

Kagan, J., Gibbons, J. L., Johnson, M. O., Reznick, J. S. & Snidman, N. (1990). A temperamental disposition to the state of uncertainty. In J. Rolf, A. S. Masten, D. Cicchetti, K. H. Nuechterlein & S. Weintraub (Eds.), *Risk and protective factors in the development of psychopathology.* New York: Cambridge University Press.

Kantor, D. & Lehr, M. (1975). *Inside the family.* San Francisco: Josey Bass.

Karen, R. (1994). *Becoming attached.* New York: Warner Books.

Kaufman, J. & Zigler, E. (1987). Do abused children become abusive parents? *American Journal of Orthopsychiatry, 57(2),* April.

Kernberg, O. F. (1991). Aggression and love in the relationship of the couple. *Journal of American Psychoanalytic Association, 39(1),* 45–70.

Kidder, T. (1993). *Old friends.* New York: Houghton Mifflin.

Kielcolt-Glaser, J., Malarkey, W. B., Chee, M. A., Newton, T., Cacioppo, J. T., Mao, H., & Glaser, R. (1993). Negative behavior during marital conflict is associated with immunological down-regulation. *Psychosomatic Medicine, 55(5),* Sept–Oct, 395–409.

King, L. L. (1985). Redneck blues. In *Warning: Writer at work.* Fort Worth: TCU Press.

Kluckhohn, C. (1951). Values and value orientations. In T. Parsons & I. Shils, *Toward a general theory of action.* Cambridge, MA: Harvard University Press.

Kluckhohn, F. R. & Strodtbeck, F. L. (1961). *Variations in value orientations.* Evanston, IL.: Row, Peterson.

Kolata, G. (1995). Man's world, woman's world? Brain studies point to differences. *The New York Times,* February 28, B5 & B8.

Lansky, M. R. (1991). Shame and fragmentation in the marital dyad. *Contemporary Family Therapy, 13(1),* February, 17–31.

Laub, J. & Sampson, R. (1994). *Crime in the making.* Cambridge, MA: Harvard University Press.

Lazarus, R. S. (1993). From psychological stress to the emotions: A history of changing outlooks. *Annual Review of Psychology, 44,* 1–21.

Levinson, D. J. (1978). *The seasons of a man's life.* New York: Ballantine Books.

Lewis, J. M. (1974). Practicum in attention to affect: A course for beginning psychotherapists. *Psychiatry,* May.

Lewis, J. M. (1978a). The adolescent and the healthy family. In S. Feinstein & P. Giovacchini (Eds.), *Adolescent psychiatry, Vol. VI.* Chicago: University of Chicago Press.

Lewis, J. M. (1978b). *To be a therapist: The teaching and learning.* New York: Brunner/Mazel.

Lewis, J. M. (1979). The inward eye: Monitoring the process of psychotherapy. *Journal of Continuing Education in Psychiatry,* July.

Lewis, J. M. (1984). Marital therapy and individual change: Implication for a theory of cure. In J. M. Myers (Ed.), *Cures by psychotherapy: What effects change?* New York: Prager Publishers.

Lewis, J. M. (1986). Family structure and stress. *Family Process, 25.*
Lewis, J. M. (1988a). The transition to parenthood: I. The rating of prenatal marital competence. *Family Process, 27,* 149–165.
Lewis, J. M. (1988b). The transition to parenthood: II. Stability and change in marital structure. *Family Process, 27,* 273–283.
Lewis, J. M. (1989). *The birth of the family: An empirical inquiry.* New York: Brunner/Mazel.
Lewis, J. M. (1991a). *Swimming upstream: Teaching psychotherapy in a biological era.* New York: Brunner/Mazel.
Lewis, J. M. (1991b). Thirty years of teaching psychotherapy skills. *International Journal of Group Psychotherapy,* October.
Lewis, J. M. (1996). Confiding, colds and cancer. In *The Monkey-Rope: A psychotherapist's reflections on relationships.* New York: Bernel Books.
Lewis, J. M., Barnhart, F. D., Howard, B. L., Carson, D. I., & Nace, E. P. (1993a). Work stress in the lives of physicians. *Texas Medicine, 89(1),* 62–67.
Lewis, J. M., Barnhart, F. D., Howard, B. L., Carson, D. I., & Nace, E. P. (1993b). Work satisfaction in the lives of physicians. *Texas Medicine, 89(2),* 54–61.
Lewis, J. M., Barnhart, F. D., Nace, E. P., Carson, D. I., & Howard, B. L. (1993). Marital satisfaction in the lives of physicians. *Bulletin of the Menninger Clinic, 57(4),* 458–465.
Lewis, J. M., Beavers, W. R., Gossett, J. T., & Phillips, V. A. (1976). *No single thread: Psychological health in family systems.* New York: Brunner/Mazel.
Lewis, J. M. & Looney, J. G. (1983). *The long struggle: Well functioning working-class black families.* New York: Brunner/Mazel.
Lewis, J. M., Nace, E. P., Barnhart, F. D., Carson, D. I. & Howard, B. L. (1994). The lives of female physicians. *Texas Medicine, 90,* March, 56–61.
Lewis, J. M. & Owen, M. T. (1996). Stability and change in family-of-origin recollections over the first four years of parenthood. *Family Process, 34,* 455–469.
Lewis, J. M., Owen, M. T. & Cox, M. J. (1988). The transition to parenthood: III. Incorporation of the child into the family. *Family Process, 27,* 411–421.
Lieberman, A. F. (1991). Attachment theory and infant-parent psychotherapy: Some conceptual, clinical and research considerations. In D. Cicchetti & S. L. Toth (Eds.), *Rochester symposium on developmental psychopathology: Vol. 3. Models and Integrations,* 261–287. Rochester, NY: University of Rochester Press.
Luborsky, L. (1977). Measuring a pervasive psychic structure in psychotherapy: The core conflictual relationship theme. In N. Freedman & S. Grand (Eds.), *Communicative structures and psychic structures,* 367–395. New York: Plenum Press.
Luborsky, L., Crits-Christoph, P., Mintz, J., & Auerbach, A. (1989). *Who will benefit from psychotherapy: Predicting therapeutic outcomes.* New York: Basic Books.
Luborsky, L., McLellan, A. T., Woody, G. E., O'Brien, C. P., & Auerbach, A. (1985). Therapist success and its determinants. *Archives of General Psychiatry, 42,* 602–611.
Lynch, J. & Cicchetti, D. (1991). Patterns of relatedness in maltreated and nonmaltreated children: Connections among multiple representational models. *Development and Psychopathology, 3,* 207–226.

Main, M. & Goldwyn, R. (1988). *Adult attachment classification system. Version 3.2.* Unpublished manuscript, University of California, Berkeley.
Main, M., Kaplan, N. & Cassidy, J. (1985). Security in infancy, childhood and adulthood: A move to the level of representation. In I. Bretherton & E. Waters (Eds.), *Growing points in attachment theory and research. Monographs of the Society for Research in Child Development. Serial No. 209, 50*(1–2), 66–104.
Main, T. F. (1966). Mutual projection in a marriage. *Comprehensive Psychiatry, 7(5),* October, 432–449.
Malan, D. H., Heath, E. S., Bacal, H. A., & Balfour, F. H. G. (1975). Psychodynamic changes in untreated neurotic patients: II. Apparently genuine improvements. *Archives of General Psychiatry, 32,* January, 110–126.
Malarkey, W. B., Kiecolt-Glaser, J. K., Pearl, D., & Glaser, N. (1994). Hostile behavior during marital conflict alters pituitary and adrenal hormones. *Psychosomatic Med, 56,* 41–51.
Mangelsdorf, S., Gunnar, M., Kestenbaum, R., Lang, S., & Andreas, D. (1990). Infant proneness-to-distress temperament, maternal personality, and mother-infant attachment: Association and goodness of fit. *Child Development, 61,* 820–831.
Marris, P. (1982). Attachment and society. In C. M. Parkes & J. Stevenson-Hinde (Eds.), *The place of attachment in human behavior.* New York: Basic Books.
Maziade, M., Caron, C., Cote, R., Merette, C., Bernier, H., Laplante, B., Boutin, P., & Thivierge, J. (1990). Psychiatric status of adolescents who had extreme temperaments at age 7. *American Journal of Psychiatry, 147(11),* 1531–1536.
McGlynn, F. (1979). Why did you marry your spouse? A nonpersonal answer may indicate marital dissatisfaction. Unpublished paper.
Mehlman, P. T., Higley, J. D., Faucher, I., Lilly, A. A., Taub, D. M., Vickers, J., Suomi, S. J., & Linnoila, M. (1995). Correlation of CSF 5-HIAA concentration with sociality and the timing of emigration in free-ranging primates. *American Journal of Psychiatry, 152(6),* 907–913.
Meissner, W. W. (1978). The conceptualization of marriage and family dynamics from a psychoanalytic perspective. In T. J. Paolino & B. X. McCrady (Eds.), *Marriage and marital therapy: Psychoanalytic, behavioral, and systems theory perspectives.* New York: Brunner/Mazel.
Meissner, W. W. (1981). The schizophrenic and the paranoid process. *Schizophrenic Bulletin, 7(4),* 611–631.
Meissner, W. W. (1993). The family and cancer. *Psychiatric Annals, 23(9).*
Miklowitz, D. J., Goldstein, M. J., Nuechterlein, K. H., Snyder, K. S., & Mintz, J. (1988). Family factors and the course of bipolar affective disorder. *Archives of General Psychiatry, 45,* 225–231.
Miller, J. B. (1994). Women's psychological development. In M. M. Bergen (Ed.), *Women beyond Freud.* New York: Brunner/Mazel.
Minuchin, S. (1974). *Families and family therapy.* Cambridge, MA: Harvard University Press.
Minuchin, S. (1992). The restoried history of family therapy. In Jeffrey K. Zieg (Ed.), *The evolution of psychotherapy: The second conference.* New York: Brunner/Mazel.

Napier, A. Y. (1988). *The Fragile Bond*. New York: Harper & Row.
Paris, J. & Braverman, S. (1995). Successful and unsuccessful marriages in borderline patients. *Journal of American Academy of Psychoanalysis, 23(1)*, 153–166.
Parker, G. & Hadzi-Pavlovic, D. (1984). Modification of levels of depression in mother-bereaved women by parental and marital relationships. *Psychol Med, 14*, 125–135.
Paterson, R. J. & Moran, G. (1988). Attachment theory, personality development, and psychotherapy. *Clinical Psychology Review, 8*, 611–636.
Pearson, J. L., Cohn, D. A., Cowan, P. A., & Cowan, C. P. (1994). Earned- and continuous-security in adult attachment: Relation to depressive symptomatology and parenting style. *Development and Psychopathology, 6*, 359–373,
Pennebaker, S. W., Kiecolt-Glaser, J. K., and Glaser, R. (1988). Disclosure of traumas and immune function: Health implications for psychotherapy, *J of Consult and Clin Psychol, 56*, 239–245.
Pierce, R. M. (1973). Training in interpersonal skills with the partners of deteriorated marriages. *The Family Coordinator*, April, 223–227.
Polster, S. (1983). Ego boundary as process: A systemic-contextual approach. *Psychiatry, 46(8)*, 247–258.
Quinton, D., Rutter, M., & Liddle, C. (1984). Institutional rearing, parenting difficulties and marital support. *Psychological Medicine, 14*, 107–124.
Rapaport, D. (1967). The points of view and assumptions of metapsychology (with Merton M. Gill). In M. M. Gill (Ed.), *The collected papers of David Rapaport*. New York: Basic Books. (Original work published 1959.)
Rausch, H. L., Barry, W. A., Hertel, R. K., & Swain, M. A. (1974). *Communication, conflict, and marriage*. San Francisco: Josey Bass.
Reiss, D. (1981). *The family's construction of reality*. Cambridge, MA: Harvard University Press.
Reiss, D., Gonzalez, S., & Kramer, N. S. (1986). Family process, chronic illness and death. *Archives of General Psychiatry, 43*, 795–804.
Rogers, C. R. (1942). *Client-centered therapy*. Boston: Houghton Mifflin.
Rokeach, M. & Ball-Rokeach, S. J. (1989). Stability and change in American value priorities, 1968–1981. *American Psychologist*, May, 775–784.
Rose, P. (1983). *Parallel Lives*. New York: Vintage Books.
Ross, E. D. (1981). The aprosodias: Functional-anatomic organization of the affective components of language in the right hemisphere. *Archives of Neurology, 38*, 561–569.
Roy, A. (1981). Vulnerability factors and depression in men. *British Journal of Psychiatry, 138*, 75–77.
Rutter, M. (1988). Function and consequences of relationships: Some psychopathological considerations. In R. A. Hinde & J. Stevenson-Hinde (Eds.), *Relationships within families: Mutual influences*. New York: Oxford University Press.
Searles, H. F. (1975). The patient as therapist to his analyst. In P. Giovacchini (Ed.), *Tactic and techniques in psychoanalytic therapy, Vol. II: Countertransference*. New York: Jason Aronson.

Silverman, L. H., Lachmann, F. M., & Milich, R. H. (1982). *The search for oneness*. New York: International Universities Press, Inc.

Skynner, R. (1976). *Systems of marital and family therapy*. New York: Brunner/Mazel.

Smith, T. (1993). Survey on adultery: 'I do' means 'I don't.' *The New York Times*, October 19.

Spiegel, J. (1971). *Transactions: The interplay between individual, family and society*. J. Papajohn (Ed.). New York: Science House.

Spiegel, J. (1982). An ecological model of ethnic families. In M. McGoldrick, J. K. Pearce & J. Giordano (Eds.), *Ethnicity and family therapy*. New York: Guilford Press.

Steidl, J. H., Findelstein, F. O., Wexler, J. P., Feigenbaum, H., Kitsen, J., Kliger, A. S. & Quinlan, D. M. (1980). Medical condition, adherence to treatment regimens, and family functioning. *Archives of General Psychiatry, 37*, 1025–1027.

Stein, M. Miller, A. H., & Trestman, R. L. (1991). Depression, the immune system, and health and illness. *Archives of General Psychiatry, 48*, February, 171–177.

Steinglass, P., Bennett, L. A., Wolin, S. J. & Reiss, D. (1987). *The alcoholic family*. New York: Basic Books.

Stern, D. N. (1985). *The interpersonal world of the infant*. New York: Basic Books.

Terkel, S. (1972). *Working*. New York: Pantheon Books.

Thase, M. E. & Howland, R. H. (1994). Refractory depression: Relevance of psychosocial factors and therapies. *Psychiatric Annals, 24:5*.

Tienari, P., Soori, A., Lahti, I., Naarala, M., Wahlberg, K., Ronkko, T., Pohjola, J., & Moring, J. (1985). The Finnish adoptive family study of schizophrenia., *The Yale Journal of Biology and Medicine, 58*, 227–237.

Towns, A. (1994). Asthma, power, and the therapeutic conversation. *Family Process, 33*, 161–174.

Truax, C. B. & Carkhuff, R. R. (1969). The experimental manipulation of therapeutic conditions. *Journal of Consulting Psychology, 29*, 119–134.

Vaillant, G. E. (1977). *Adaptation to life*. Boston: Little, Brown.

Vaillant, G. E. (1978). Natural history of male psychological health: VI. Correlates of successful marriage and fatherhood. *American Journal of Psychiatry, 135:6*, 653–659.

Vaillant, G. E. (1993). *The wisdom of the ego*. Cambridge, MA: Harvard University Press.

Waring, E. M. (1988). *Enhancing marital intimacy through facilitating cognitive self-disclosure*. New York: Brunner/Mazel.

Waring, E. M., Chamberlaine, C. H., Carver, C. M., Stalker, C. A., & Schaefer, B. (1995). A pilot study of marital therapy as a treatment for depression. *The American Journal of Family Therapy, 23(1)*, 3–10.

Warrick, P. (1993). That male-female chemistry. *The Dallas Morning News*, December 19.

Watzlawick, P. (1984). *The invented reality*. New York: W. W. Norton.

Weakland, F. H. (1974). Family somatics—A neglected edge. Presented at the Nathan F. Ackerman Memorial Conference.

Weems, R. (1994). The statistical marriage myth. *The Dallas Morning News*, July 7.

Weingarten, K. (1992). A consideration of intimate and non-intimate interactions in therapy. *Family Process, 31(3)*, 45–59.

Weiss, R. S. (1982). Attachment in adult life. In C. M. Parks & J. Stevenson-Hinde (Eds.), *The place of attachment in human behavior.* New York: Basic Books.

Weissman, M. M. (1987). Advances in psychiatric epidemiology: Rates and risks for major depression. *American Journal of Public Health, 77(4)*.

Wellings, K. (1994). Quoted by J. Darnton in The extent of monogamy in Britain. *The New York Times*, February 1, 1994.

Whitbeck, L. B., Hoyt, D. R., Simons, R. L., Conger, R. D., Elder, G. H., Jr., Lorenz, F. O. & Huck, S. (1992). Intergenerational continuity of parental rejection and depressed affect. *Journal of Personality and Social Psychology, 63(6)*, 1036–1045.

Wynne, L. C. & Wynne, A. R. (1986). The quest for intimacy. *Journal of Marital and Family Therapy, 12(4)*, 383–394.

Yalom, I. D. (1980). *Existential psychotherapy.* New York: Basic Books, Inc.

Zahn-Waxler, C., Robinson, J. L., & Emde, R. N. (1992). The development of empathy in twins. *Developmental Psychology, 28(6)*, 1038–1047.

Zinner, J. & Shapiro, R. (1972). Projective identification as a mode of perception and behavior in families of adolescents. *International Journal of Psychoanalysis, 53*, 523–530.

Name Index

Ackerman, D., 247
Agras, W. S., 43
Ainsworth, M. D. S., 104
Albee, E., 90
American Psychiatric Association (APA), 49
Amundson, J., 142
Anderson, C., 52n
Andreas, D., 107
Angier, N., 103
Anthony, E. J., 93
Auerbach, A., 33

Bacal, H. A., 30
Balfour, F. H. G., 30
Balint, M., 2, 3
Ball-Rokeach, S. J., 22, 125, 185
Barnett, P. A., 38
Barnhart, F. D., 18
Barry, W. A., 116
Bartholomew, K., 105
Beahrs, J. O., 4
Beavers, W. R., 15, 40, 72, 247–248
Belsky, J., 32
Bennett, A., 140n
Bennett, L. A., 166
Berman, E. M., 118
Bernier, H., 107
Berry, W., 142
Boutin, P., 107
Bowen, M., 190
Bowlby, J., 100, 104, 111
Braverman, S., 31
Brody, J. E., 43
Brothers, L., 103
Brown, G. W., 31, 33, 38
Bruner, J., 51
Burman, B., 44

Cacioppo, J. T., 43
Callenback, E., 25
Carkhuff, R. R., 221
Caron, C., 107
Carson, D. I., 18
Carver, C. M., 39
Caspi, A., 31
Cassidy, J., 32, 111
Casti, J. L., 50
Catherall, D. R., 206, 207, 210, 211
Chamberlaine, C. H., 39
Chee, M. A., 43
Chess, S., 101

Chessick, R. D., 50, 51
Cicchetti, D., 32
Cloninger, C. R., 101
Cohler, B. J., 93
Cohn, D. A., 32, 105
Conger, R. D., 39
Cote, R., 107
Cowan, C. P., 32, 105
Cowan, P. A., 32, 105
Cox, M. J., 15, 73
Crits-Christoph, P., 33

Dandeneau, M. L., 216
Davidson, R. J., 102
Dawson, G., 102
Dicks, H. V., 206
Doane, J. A., 65
Dyer, B., 22

Egeland, B., 21, 31, 32
Eisenberg, L., 185
Ekman, P., 102
Elder, G. H., Jr., 31, 81, 164
Emde, R. N., 103
Ewart, C. K., 43

Faucher, I., 103
Feeney, J. A., 105
Feigenbaum, H., 73
Feldman, L. B., 89, 116
Findelstein, F. O., 73
Fischmann-Havstad, L., 38
Fogarty, T. F., 116
Foucault, M., 142
Fox, N. A., 102
Fraenkel, P., 65
Freeman, S. J. J., 39
Freud, S., 18
Friesen, W. V., 102

George, M. S., 102
Gergen, K. J., 50, 51
Gibbons, J., 101
Glaser, R., 42, 43
Glenn, N. D., 22
Goering, P. N., 38, 39
Goldstein, M. J., 38, 65
Goldwyn, R., 32, 111
Goleman, D., 117
Gonzalez, S., 42, 62
Gossett, J. T., 15, 40, 72
Gotlib, I. H., 38
Gottman, J. M., 21, 44, 86, 89, 213, 214, 248

Greenberg, L. S., 116, 214, 215, 216, 250–251
Greenberg, M. T., 32
Griffith, J. L., 61
Griffith, M. E., 61
Gunnar, M., 107

Hadzi-Pavolvic, D., 30
Haley, J., 96, 141
Harris, T., 31, 33, 38
Havens, L. L., 248–249
Hazen, C., 105
Hendrix, H., 249–250
Herscovitch, P., 102
Hertel, R. K., 116
Higley, J. D., 103
Hill, D., 102
Hofer, M. A., 111
Hoffman, L., 51, 63, 142
Holmes, T. H., 6
Horowitz, L. M., 105
Horwitz, B., 102
Howard, B. L., 18
Howland, R. H., 38
Hoyt, D. R., 39
Huck, S., 39

Jackson, D., 17, 18
Jacobson, N. S., 143, 210
Jacobson, N. W., 116
Jacobvitz, D., 21, 31
Johnson, M. O., 101
Johnson, S. J., 116, 214, 215, 216, 250–251
Johnson, S. M., 216
Jones, J. E., 65
Justice, B., 43

Kagan, J., 101
Kantor, D., 116, 251
Kaplan, N., 32, 111
Katz, L. F., 21, 86, 213
Kaufman, J., 31
Kernberg, O. F., 34, 113
Kestenbaum, R., 107
Ketter, T. A., 102
Kidder, T., 110
Kiecolt-Glaser, J. K., 42, 43
King, L. L., 47, 48, 49
Kitsen, J., 73
Klein, M., 34
Kliger, A. S., 73
Klinger, L. G., 102
Kluckhohn, C., 125, 127
Kluckhohn, F. R., 127

269

Name Index

Kolata, G., 103
Kraemer, H. C., 43
Kramer, N. S., 42, 62
Kramer, P. D., 251
Krokoff, L. J., 44, 213

Lachmann, F. M., 111
Lahti, I., 73
Lancee, W. J., 39
Lang, S., 107
Lansky, M. R., 210, 211
Laplante, B., 107
Laub, J., 31
Lazarus, R. S., 102
Lehr, M., 116
Lehr, W., 251
Levenson, R. W., 213
Levinson, D. J., 157
Lewis, J. M., 4, 15, 18, 20, 23, 37, 40, 41, 65, 72, 73, 78, 80, 82, 86, 104, 111, 113, 119, 123, 124, 158, 186, 211, 213, 221
Liddle, C., 30, 36
Lieberman, A. F., 32
Lief, H. I., 118
Lilly, A. A., 103
Linnoila, M., 103
Looney, J. G., 72, 80, 119
Lorenz, F. O., 39
Luborsky, L., 33, 163
Lynch, J., 32

Main, M., 32, 111
Main, T. F., 206
Malan, D. H., 30
Malarkey, W. B., 43
Mangelsdorf, S., 107
Mao, H., 43
Margolin, G., 44, 116
Markman, H., 44, 213
Marris, P., 45
Marston, A. R., 38
Maziade, M., 107
McGlynn, F., 17
McLelland, A. T., 33
Mehlman, P. T., 103
Meissner, W. W., 41, 114, 206
Merette, C., 107
Miklowitz, D. J., 38
Milich, R. H., 111
Miller, A. H., 44
Miller, J. B., 216
Mintz, J., 33, 38
Minuchin, S., 14, 40, 41, 66, 141, 142

Naarala, M., 73
Nance, E. P., 18

Napier, A. Y., 116, 252
Newton, T., 43
Noller, P., 105
Notarius, C., 44, 213
Nuechterlein, K. H., 38

O'Brien, C. P., 33
Owen, M. T., 15, 73, 111

Panagiotides, H., 102
Parekh, P. I., 102
Paris, J., 31
Parker, G., 30
Paterson, R. J., 32
Pearl, D., 43
Pearson, J., 105
Pearson, J. L., 32
Pennebaker, S. W., 42
Pensky, E., 32
Phillips, V. A., 15, 40, 72
Pierce, R. M., 221
Pohjola, J., 73
Polster, S., 206
Post, R. M., 102
Przybeck, T. R., 101

Quinlan, D. M., 73
Quinton, D., 30, 36

Rahe, R. H., 6
Rapaport, D., 61
Rausch, H. L., 116
Reiss, D., 42, 62, 125, 166, 252–253
Reznick, J. S., 101
Robinson, J. L., 103
Rodnick, E. H., 65
Rogers, C. R., 33
Rokeach, M., 22, 125, 185
Ronkko, T., 73
Rose, P., 119, 143
Ross, E. D., 103
Roy, A., 31, 38
Rutter, M., 30, 32, 36, 113, 114

Sager, C. J., 253–254
Sampson, R., 31
Saron, C. D., 102
Schaefer, B., 39
Scharff, D. E., 254–255
Scharff, J. S., 254–255
Seagraves, R. T., 255
Searles, H. F., 114
Senulis, J. A., 102
Shapiro, R., 206
Shaver, P., 105
Silver, D. H., 32, 105
Silverman, L. H., 111
Simons, R. L., 39
Skynner, R., 206

Slovik, L. S., 61
Smith, T., 22
Snidman, N., 101
Snyder, K. S., 38
Soori, A., 73
Spicker, S., 102
Spiegel, J., 125, 127, 185
Sroufe, L. A., 21, 31
Stalker, C. A., 39
Steidl, J. H., 73
Stein, M., 44
Steinglass, P., 166, 256
Stern, D. N., 104
Stewart, K., 142
Strodtbeck, F. L., 127
Suomi, S. J., 103
Svrakic, D. M., 101
Swain, M. A., 116

Taub, D. M., 103
Taylor, C. B., 43
Terkel, S., 19
Thase, M. E., 38
Thivierge, J., 107
Thomas, A., 101
Tienari, P., 73
Tolstoy, L., 18
Towns, A., 142
Traux, C. B., 221
Trestman, R. L., 44

Vaillant, G. E., 18, 19, 34, 35, 37, 256–257
Valentine, L., 142
Vickers, J., 103

Wahlberg, K., 73
Waring, E. M., 39, 118, 257–258
Watzlawick, P., 51
Weakland, F. H., 41
Weaver, C. N., 22
Weems, R., 22
Weingarten, K., 190, 216
Weiss, R. S., 32
Weissman, M. M., 38
Wellings, K., 22
West, K. L., 65
Wexler, J. P., 73
Whitbeck, L. b., 39
Wolin, S. J., 166
Woody, G. E., 33
Wynne, A. R., 119
Wynne, L. C., 119, 206

Yalom, I. D., 44, 110, 258
Youngblade, L., 32

Zahn-Waxler, C., 103
Zigler, E., 31
Zinner, J., 206

Subject Index

Affect-focused processes, relationship skills, 237–238
Affects, communication of, marital systems theory, 116–117
Apathetic couples, marital therapy, 220
Assessment, first contacts, 128–147
  case example, 128–139
  concepts discussed, 139–147
Assessment approach, 148–183
  coalitions and triangles, 169–170
  current developmental state and external stress, 170–171
  developmental stages, 159–160
  dyadic formulation, 173–179
  family-of-origin history, 160–164
  impeding circumstances, 181–183
  individual interviews, 172–173
  interpersonal relationships, 164
  overview, 148–150
  problem definitions, 151–152
  relationship history, 152–159
    courtship, 154
    early years, 157
    first meeting, 153–154
    honeymoon, 156–157
    life dreams, 157–158
    marriage decision, 155
    parenthood, 158–159
    wedding, 155–156
  relationship variables, 164–166
  special areas, 166–169
    finances, 167–168
    religion, 167
    rituals, 166–167
    sexuality, 168–169
  special procedures, 171–172
  treatment planning, 179–181
Attachment research, 15–16
  marriage as self-healing, 32
  separateness-autonomy and connectedness-intimacy, 100–101, 105
Attraction to specific others, marital systems theory, 112–115

Biologic determinants, separateness-autonomy and connectedness-intimacy, 100–103

Central dyadic relationship, defined, 18. See also Marriage
Chaotic marriage, described, 93–94
Child abuse
  marriage as self-healing, 31
  prevalence of, 21

Childhood
  central relationship in, marital systems theory, 111–112
  family-of-origin history, assessment approach, 160–164
Children
  chaotic marriage, 93
  competent marriages, 77–78
  conflicted marriage, 90
  parental relationship structures, marital systems theory, 122–123
  symptomatic, marital therapy, 219
Closeness, defined, 118
Coalitions, assessment approach, 169–170
Cognitive set, marital therapy, 201–202
Commitment, defined, 118
Communication, of affects, marital systems theory, 116–117
Communication skills, marital therapy, 200
Competence. See Marital competence
Conflicted marriage, described, 88–91
Conflict intervention, marital therapy, stabilization/destabilization, 207–218
Conflict resolution task, assessment approach, 171–172
Connectedness-intimacy, defined, 98. See also Separateness-autonomy and connectedness-intimacy
Constructivism
  empiricism and, 47–52
  marital therapy and, 52–66
Countertransference, marital therapy, 185–186
Courtship, relationship history, 154

Death, of child, 6–7, 8–9, 12, 13
Defenses, immature, marriage as self-healing, 34–35
Delinquency, marriage as self-healing, 31
Depression
  marriage as harmful, 36, 37, 38–39
  marriage as self-healing, 31, 33
  retirement and, 1–2
Developmental determinants, separateness-autonomy and connectedness-intimacy, 104–105
Developmental stages, assessment approach, 159–160
Devitalized couples, marital therapy, 220
Diagnosis
  empiricism and constructivism, 49–52
  managed care, 4
  medical illness, 2–3
  negotiation in, 2–3
  psychopathology, 3–4

271

Diagnostic and Statistical Manual of Mental Disorders (DSM-IV), 49, 182
Distance
  regulation of, marital therapy, stabilization/destabilization, 204–207
  therapist's use of, 190
Divorce, prevalence of, 22
Domestic violence, prevalence of, 21
Dominant-submissive marriage
  constructivism and empiricism, 65–66
  described, 84–88
  marriage as harmful, 36–37
Dreams, family-of-origin history, assessment approach, 163
Dyadic formulation, assessment approach, 173–179
Dysfunctional marriage
  chaotic, 93–94
  psychotic, 92
  totally alienated, 91–92

Early memory, family-of-origin history, assessment approach, 163
Ego, marriage as self-healing, 34–35
Empiricism
  challenge to, 46
  constructivism and, 47–52
  human systems and, 62, 63–66
Ethnicity, marital competence, 80
Existentialism, marriage and meaning, 44–45

Family-of-origin history, assessment approach, 160–164
Family role, family-of-origin history, assessment approach, 162–163
Family structure, family-of-origin history, assessment approach, 162
Family systems
  empiricism, 46
  physical health and, 39–44
  psychopathology and, 17, 31
Family therapy. *See* Marital therapy
Fears, marital systems theory, 110–111
Finances, assessment approach, 167–168
First meeting, relationship history, 153–154

Grief, morbid, physical health and, 41

Hermeneutics, empiricism and constructivism, 50–51
History. *See* Relationship history
Holding function, marital therapy, 198–200
Homework assignments, relationship skills, 222–223
Honeymoon, relationship history, 156–157
Human systems
  characteristics of, 97
  therapist's view of, 186–187

Illness. *See* Medical illness; Physical health
Immature defenses, marriage as self-healing, 34–35
Immune response, social supports and, 43–44
Individual interviews, assessment approach, 172–173
Infidelity, prevalence of, 21, 22
Initial interview
  marital therapy, 1–14
  working alliance, 14–15
Institution-raised children, 30
Intervention, therapist's approach to, 188
Intimacy, defined, 118–119

Life dreams, relationship history, 157–158
Life satisfaction, marital satisfaction and, 22–23
Listening exercise, relationship skills, 236–237

Managed care, diagnosis, 4
Marital competence, 67–95
  case examples, 67–70, 79
  competent marriages, 73–79
    described, 73–79
  conflicted marriage, 88–91
  continuum of, 79–82, 94–95
  dominant-submissive marriage, 84–88
  dysfunctional marriage, 91–95
    chaotic, 93–94
    psychotic, 92
    totally alienated, 91–92
  observer subjectivity, 71–73
  pained but competent marriage, 82–84
Marital satisfaction
  life satisfaction and, 22–23
  research in, 18–20
Marital systems theory, 96–127
  affect and communication, 116–117
  attraction to specific others, 112–115
  childhood central relationship, 111–112
  healthy development, relational structures and, 121–122
  negotiations, 118–120
  overview, 96–98
  parental relationship structures, 122–123
  premises, summary table, 98–99
  psychological maturity or health, 109
  relationship definition, 115–116
  relationship structures, developmental course of, 123–124
  repetitive interactional patterns, 120–121
  separateness-autonomy and connectedness-intimacy, 100–109
    balance in, 108–109
    biologic determinants, 100–103
    described, 100
    developmental determinants, 104–105
    social determinants, 105–108
  underlying fears, 110–111
  value systems, 124–127

Subject Index

Marital therapy, 184–197, 198–220
    assessment, first contacts, 128–147
    cognitive set, 201–202
    communication skills, 200
    conflict free relationships, 219–220
    constructivism and, 52–66
    couple's view of therapist, 202–203
    goals, 190–191
    holding function, 198–200
    initial interview, 1–14
    mate selection, 17–18
    motivation for, 1–2
    outcomes, 241–243
    relationship skills, 221–243. *See also* Relationship skills
    sources of personal approach, 191–197
    stabilization/destabilization, 203–218
        conflict intervention, 207–218
        projection, projective identification, and distance regulation, 204–207
    therapist's central relationship, 186
    therapist's intervention approach, 188
    therapist's personal experience, 184–185
    therapist's power, 188–189
    therapist's use of distance, 190
    therapist's values, 185
    therapist's view of human systems, 186–187
    transference and countertransference, 185–186
Marriage
    decline in, 21
    harmful, 36–39
    meaning and, 44–45
    physical health and, 39–44
    as self-healing, 24–36
    strength of, 22–23
    variety in, 18
Marriage decision, relationship history, 155
Mate selection, marital therapy, 17–18
Meaning, marriage and, 44–45
Medical illness. *See also* Physical health
    diagnosis, 2–3
    marital competence, 81
Metaphorical distance, defined, 96
Money. *See* Finances
Morbid grief, physical health and, 41

Negotiations, marital systems theory, 118–120

Objectivity, empiricism and constructivism, 50–51
Object relations theory, marriage as self-healing, 34
Observer subjectivity, marital competence, 71–73
Outcomes, marital therapy, 241–243

Pained but competent marriage, described, 82–84
Parental relationship structures, marital systems theory, 122–123
Parenthood, relationship history, 158–159
Parents, family-of-origin history, assessment approach, 160–161
Physical health, marriage and, 39–44. *See also* Medical illness
Power
    assessment, first contacts, 140–141
    defined, 119
    therapist's position on, 188–189
Projection, marital therapy, stabilization/destabilization, 204–207
Projective identification, marital therapy, stabilization/destabilization, 204–207
Psychological maturity or health, marital systems theory, 109
Psychopathology
    diagnosis, 3–4
    empiricism and constructivism, 47–52
    family systems and, 17, 31
    marriage as harmful, 36–39
    marriage as self-healing, 31–32
Psychotherapy, healing element of, 33
Psychotherapy function task, assessment approach, 172
Psychotic marriage, described, 92

Reality, empiricism and constructivism, 50–51
Referral, assessment, first contacts, 128–129
Relationship definition, marital systems theory, 115–116
Relationship history, 152–159
    courtship, 154
    early years, 157
    first meeting, 153–154
    honeymoon, 156–157
    life dreams, 157–158
    marriage decision, 155
    parenthood, 158–159
    wedding, 155–156
Relationship skills, 221–243
    homework assignments, 222–223
    initial assignment, 226–235
    instructions, 223–226
    overview, 221
    results, 241–243
    subsequent assignments, 235–241
        affect-focused processes, 237–238
        listening exercise, 236–237
        topics for exploration, 238–241
Relationship structure
    developmental course of, marital systems theory, 123–124

Relationship structure (*continued*)
  development of, marital systems theory, 120–121
  healthy development and, marital systems theory, 121–122
  parental, marital systems theory, 122–123
Relationship variables, assessment approach, 164–166
Religion, assessment approach, 167
Repetitive interactional patterns, marital systems theory, 120–121
Retirement, marriage and, 1–2
Rituals, assessment approach, 166–167
Rokeach Value Survey, assessment approach, 171

Separateness, defined, 119
Separateness-autonomy, defined, 98
Separateness-autonomy and connectedness-intimacy, 100–109
  balance in, 108–109
  biologic determinants, 100–103
  described, 100
  developmental determinants, 104–105
  social determinants, 105–108
Sex-role stereotyping, marriage as harmful, 36–37
Sexuality
  assessment approach, 168–169
  competent marriages, 78

Siblings, family-of-origin history, assessment approach, 161–162
Social constructivism, empiricism and, 51
Social determinants, separateness-autonomy and connectedness-intimacy, 105–108
Social supports, physical health and, 43–44
Socioeconomic factors, marital competence, 80–81
Stabilization/destabilization, marital therapy, 203–218. *See also Marital* therapy
Subjectivity, of observer, marital competence, 71–73
Suicide, of child, 6–7, 8–9, 12, 13

Totally alienated marriage, described, 91–92
Transference, marital therapy, 185–186
Treatment planning, assessment approach, 179–181
Triangles, assessment approach, 169–170

Umpire metaphor, 52
Underlying fears, marital systems theory, 110–111

Values
  marital systems theory, 124–127
  of therapist, marital therapy, 185

Wedding, relationship history, 155–156
Working alliance, initial interview, 14–15